Unrest

Unrest

ART IN THE AFTERMATH OF THE 1992 LOS ANGELES RIOTS

Rose Salseda

The University of Chicago Press CHICAGO AND LONDON

The University of Chicago Press, Chicago 60637
The University of Chicago Press, Ltd., London

Published 2026
Printed in the United States of America

35 34 33 32 31 30 29 28 27 26   1 2 3 4 5

ISBN-13: 978-0-226-85080-1 (cloth)
ISBN-13: 978-0-226-85083-2 (paper)
ISBN-13: 978-0-226-85082-5 (ebook)
DOI: https://doi.org/10.7208/chicago/9780226850825.001.0001

Library of Congress Cataloging-in-Publication Data

Names: Salseda, Rose, author.
Title: Unrest : art in the aftermath of the 1992 Los Angeles riots / Rose Salseda.
Description: Chicago : The University of Chicago Press, 2026. | Includes bibliographical references and index.
Identifiers: LCCN 2026004896 | ISBN 9780226850801 (cloth) | ISBN 9780226850832 (paperback) | ISBN 9780226850825 (ebook)
Subjects: LCSH: Riots in art. | Rodney King Riots, Los Angeles, Calif., 1992. | Art and social conflict. | Art, American—20th century.
Classification: LCC N8237.8.R56 S35 2026
LC record available at https://lccn.loc.gov/2026004896

♾ This paper meets the requirements of ANSI/NISO Z39.48-1992 (Permanence of Paper).

Authorized Representative for EU General Product Safety Regulation (GPSR) queries: **Easy Access System Europe**—Mustamäe tee 50, 10621 Tallinn, Estonia, gpsr.requests@easproject.com
Any other queries: https://press.uchicago.edu/press/contact.html

The city burning is Los Angeles's deepest image of itself.

—JOAN DIDION, "Los Angeles Notebook," in *Slouching Towards Bethlehem* (1968)

Contents

List of Figures * ix
Prologue: Beyond the Frame of the First Los Angeles Riot * xiii

INTRODUCTION * 1
ONE. The Scarred Cityscape * 15
TWO. Post-Riot Looting * 55
THREE. Beyond Black and White * 89
FOUR. Vision in Ruins * 137
EPILOGUE. Recollecting the 1992 Los Angeles Riots Today * 175

Acknowledgments * 181
Notes * 185
Index * 223

Figures

1.1 Juan Capistrán, *Saturday, March 16, 1991 (Latasha)*, 2012 * 18
1.2 Juan Capistrán, *Rather than running the risk of injustice we preferred disorder . . .* , 2012 * 21
1.3 Juan Capistrán, *Wednesday, April 29, 1992 (Fidel)*, 2012 * 29
1.4 Juan Capistrán and Hazel Mandujano, *From a Whisper to a Scream* Exhibition Booklet, 2012 * 32
1.5 Juan Capistrán and Hazel Mandujano, *From a Whisper to a Scream* Exhibition Booklet (interior detail), 2012 * 33
1.6 Juan Capistrán and Hazel Mandujano, *Untitled*, 2012 * 34
1.7 Juan Capistrán, *Sunday, March 3, 1991 (Rodney)*, 2012 * 38
1.8 Andy Warhol, *Red Race Riot*, 1963 * 39
1.9 Jeff Beall, *Unsolved* (installation view), 2017 * 43
1.10 Jeff Beall, *Unsolved Site #4 (Wilson Alvarez)*, 2017 * 44
1.11 Kang Seung Lee, *Untitled (Korean Merchants on the Rooftop)*, 2017 * 45
1.12 Space Invaders 13 (Juan Capistrán and Mario Ybarra Jr.), *Sub/Lime*, 1998 * 49
1.13 Juan Capistrán, *Psychogeography of Rage (sending up searchlights in the form of flames), Broadway*, 2019 * 51
1.14 Juan Capistrán, *Psychogeography of Rage (sending up searchlights in the form of flames), Vermont Ave. 1992*, 2019 * 52
2.1 Seth Kaufman, Joseph E. Norman Sr., and Gary Matteson, *The Antiphony of Anarchy: Three Views After Curfew* (installation view), 1992 * 69
2.2 Seth Kaufman, *State of the Art*, 1992 * 70
2.3 Seth Kaufman, *That Was Then, This Is Then*, 1992 * 71

2.4 Ed Ruscha, *The Los Angeles County Museum on Fire*, 1965–68 * 72
2.5 Joel Nakamura, Frank Gutierrez, Seth Kaufman, Hyesook Park, and Phoebe Beasley, *Absolut Hope*, 1992 * 77
2.6 Seth Kaufman, *Absolut Triumph*, 1992 * 79
2.7 Bernie Casey, Young Joo Choi, Patti Heid, Marc Katano, and Gronk Nicandro, *Absolut Hope* (billboard and reception installation), 1993 * 81
2.8 Seth Kaufman, *Dwelling in Rebellion: A Year to the Day* (installation view), 1993 * 84
3.1 Adrian Piper, *Black Box/White Box* (installation view), 1992 * 90
3.2 Adrian Piper, *Black Box/White Box* (installation view), 1992 * 92
3.3 Adrian Piper, *Black Box/White Box* (interior detail), 1992 * 93
3.4 Adrian Piper, *Black Box/White Box* (interior detail), 1992 * 94
3.5 Lewis Baltz, *11777 Foothill Boulevard, Los Angeles, California*, 1991 * 99
3.6 David Hammons, *Black Star Line* (installation view), 1992 * 102
3.7 David Hammons, *Black Star Line* (installation view), 1992 * 104
3.8 Adrian Piper, *Vote/Emote* (installation view), 1990 * 117
3.9 Adrian Piper, *Four Intruders Plus Alarm Systems* (interior detail), 1980 * 120
3.10 Adrian Piper, *What It's Like, What It Is, #3* (installation view), 1991 * 123
3.11 Adrian Piper, *Imagine [Trayvon Martin]*, 2013 * 131
3.12 Juan Capistrán, *Still I Rise Above*, 2013 * 134
4.1 Latipa, *Civil Society*, 2008 * 138
4.2 Latipa, *Civil Society*, 2008 * 140
4.3 Latipa, *Civil Society*, 2008 * 145
4.4 Portia Cobb, *No Justice, No Peace: Young, Black, ImMEDIAte*, 1992 * 147
4.5 Portia Cobb, *No Justice, No Peace: Young, Black, ImMEDIAte*, 1992 * 147
4.6 Portia Cobb, *No Justice, No Peace: Young, Black, ImMEDIAte*, 1992 * 149

4.7 Portia Cobb, *No Justice, No Peace: Young, Black, ImMEDIAte,* 1992 * 150
4.8 Latipa, *Civil Society,* 2008 * 153
4.9 Latipa, *Civil Society,* 2008 * 154
4.10 Jean-Luc Godard, Jean-Pierre Gorin, and Anne-Marie Miéville, *Ici et ailleurs,* 1976 * 156
4.11 Jean-Luc Godard, Jean-Pierre Gorin, and Anne-Marie Miéville, *Ici et ailleurs,* 1976 * 157
4.12 Jean-Luc Godard, Jean-Pierre Gorin, and Anne-Marie Miéville, *Ici et ailleurs,* 1976 * 158
4.13 Tony Cokes, *Black Celebration (A Rebellion Against the Commodity),* 1988 * 161
4.14 Latipa, *Civil Society,* 2008 * 162
4.15 Latipa, *Civil Society,* 2008 * 163
4.16 Latipa, *Civil Society,* 2008 * 166
4.17 Latipa, *Civil Society,* 2008 * 169
4.18 Latipa, *Civil Society,* 2008 * 171

Prologue

BEYOND THE FRAME OF THE FIRST LOS ANGELES RIOT

I close my eyes as I hold a color photograph, slightly yellowed by the passing of time. I do not need to look at the image to describe it. I have seen it many times before. Besides, it is not what is in the frame that matters most.

The photo captures my father, George, and his best friend, Robert, taken decades earlier, in August 1965. Another friend, whose name I do not remember, snapped the small, square-format photo on the occasion of their dual seventeenth birthday at Yosemite National Park. Unexpectedly, this photo of the two birthday boys, taken during a celebratory road trip to one of California's "natural treasures," would mark their memories of the 1965 Watts Rebellion—first their unanticipated refuge at the protected nature park and then their frightening drive back home to South Los Angeles, the epicenter of the unrest. This photograph, including the recollections it incites, would become the vehicle by which I first became introduced, as a young girl, to the long history of violence and unrest in the so-called City of Angels. My own childhood recollections of the 1992 Los Angeles Riots, which occurred two weeks after my tenth birthday, would echo many of those my father shared.

While the photo of my father and his friend is now six decades old, it still clearly captures the youthful spirit of the two teenagers. The summer sun kisses their bronze-colored skin and casts dramatic shadows across their bodies, which emphasize their handsome features. Standing beside each other, Robert directly faces the camera, smiling with his eyes and flexing his arms to show off his large biceps. Perhaps teasingly, my father turns toward his brawny friend and strikes a superhero pose. With fists set at his hips, he turns his face to charm the camera with a broad smile. So intense was the sun that hot summer of 1965, it made Robert's crisp white T-shirt glow. Around the two boys, the grass seems to have been long dried out, and the parched patches of dirt have turned the boys' bare brown feet gray with dust. The clear waters of a creek can be seen flowing behind them, and, farther in the distance, a forest of dark green sequoias runs across the frame.

I am not sure why they chose Yosemite as the place to celebrate their birthdays. That was never a question I thought to ask my father before he died in 2022—and that was never the story he felt the need to tell. For him, the photo represented more than his and Robert's birthday and more than Yosemite National Park and the beauty of its valleys, trees, and bodies of water. It was what was off the frame, what the photo did not depict, that was most important in my father's recollection of the time. When violence, death, and fire leaves life in the balance, there are simply more vital things to remember. This is the principle that drives this book and the artworks I discuss in it.

My father and his friends learned about the unrest in Watts from the radio. Shortly after a white California Highway Patrol officer pulled over a young Black motorist, Marquette Frye, a scuffle broke out between them when Frye began resisting arrest. To understand life in Los Angeles is to understand the brutality of law enforcement, a long history that especially affects its poor and working-class communities of color. More police were called to the scene, and, after several arrests, including that of Frye's mother who had arrived at the scene after learning about the incident from her nearby home, law enforcement assaulted residents, and the residents fought back. The protests and initial fights then escalated to days of beatings, looting, and fires, culminating in what became known then as "the Los Angeles Riot."

They drove to the nearest phone and called their mothers. My grandmother Toni Jean insisted that my father and his friends stay at Yosemite as long as they could because, as she curtly explained, the distress still palpable in the memory of her voice, "The city is burning down!" My father and his friends obeyed, but soon their rising concerns forced their return.

On the drive back home, they traversed Los Angeles streets in awe. My father never described Yosemite with the same sort of wonder that the fire-ravaged buildings and debris sparked for him and his friends. Typically, especially in art history, we reserve the notion of the sublime for the vast and profound beauty a viewer registers in natural and painted landscapes. Yet the devastation caused by the 1965 Watts Rebellion swung the pendulum of the sublime to its lesser-known paradigm, that of an overwhelming fear and the reminder, not of the immensity or beauty of life, but of its limits and horror.

Never had they seen the city in ruins, and never had they encountered armed military forces on their streets. They were too young to have experienced World War II and still too young to be drafted into the growing war in Vietnam. But now they did not have to leave the country or even their hometown to witness the deployment of troops. The state sent thousands of National Guardsmen to Los Angeles. Not much older than my father and his friends, the guardsmen armed themselves with rifles and bayonets, created road blockages, and patrolled the streets. My father and his friends felt keenly aware of themselves and their surroundings. They were boys of Mexican and Japanese descent amid the inexperienced, trigger-happy, white troops. Deciphering destroyed landmarks and navigating closed streets and blockades, they marveled at their new burned and smoldering surroundings as they held on to the simple desire of returning home, safely.

While they eventually arrived back to their families, alive and unscathed, not everyone in South Los Angeles was as lucky. Tied to the photo of my father and his friend at Yosemite was the experience of a younger friend, Ronnie, who did not attend the birthday trip at all. As my father told it, after the National Guardsmen had been dispatched, Ronnie and his family struggled to find a street that was not blocked off in Watts. His uncle, driving the family car, wove in and out of the neighborhood. But as he approached another roadblock, guardsmen shot at the car, striking the uncle, who lost control and crashed. Accounts from my father and other family members vary, some saying that in the car with Ronnie and his uncle were other members of the family and, sometimes, even their pet dog. Despite whoever was or was not in the car that day, one thing was clear: The guardsmen killed his uncle. The tragedy underscored the senselessness and callous brutality of state violence.

Decades later, as I started to conduct research for this book, I visited the Southern California Library and Archives, founded in South Central Los Angeles shortly after the 1965 Watts Rebellion. While exploring the library's collections, I came across a list of all those who were killed during the unrest. The majority were civilian men, and a couple were law enforcement officers—shot by fellow officers. As I scanned the names of the dead, my body stiffened at the sight of number twelve on the list, and my eyes fixed on the last name: "Flores." Ronnie's uncle. Age forty at the time of his death, he was "shot by guard at roadblock." My heart dropped. Then, hit by the sudden realization, I thought, with eyes opened wide, "*I found proof!*" I immediately took a picture of the document with my phone and texted it to my father. I wrote, "I found Ronnie's uncle in the archive!" Shortly after sending the text, I realized that what I had sent was only data, and I felt ashamed. The list contained names of the dead, their ages, which ranged from seventeen to sixty-seven, and their causes of death. Perhaps unsurprisingly, most were killed by law enforcement bullets. My father did not need these statistics; he and his friends already knew, much more than what was listed in the document. In fact, their experiences and shared recollections did not need evidence because what they had lived was evidence enough for them—real and far too palpable to accurately be captured in a list. I have been trained to examine archives and use the materials and information found as resources to educate myself and others, as evidence to support arguments, or as inspiration to create new theoretical frameworks for understanding. But what I realized in that moment was how limited the archives can be, especially in contrast to what I had learned through family oral history and *testimonio*. The archive does not validate the existence, life, and death of Ronnie's uncle or of anyone else. I had proof from the narratives of those who remember and those who pass on the memories of others, their recollections validating life and death with love and care. They are the living proof, as am I, and now as you are too.

Art sometimes shares these goals, as with the artists and artworks I discuss in this book. They hold experiences and analyses deserving of our attention, expressing insights unlike other methods of historical documentation. Yet art is not mere documentation. Instead, art conveys the humanistic expressions of history, politics, ideas, and emotions, as well as the resonances of these experiences across time. Sometimes, like the story of the photo of my father and his friends, these artists recognize that what matters most is not always documented in official histories and images. So they make art to change perceptions of what we thought we knew and because sometimes it is only art that can capture what exists beyond the frame.

Introduction

On April 29, 1992, at 3:15 p.m., a jury acquitted the Los Angeles Police Department (LAPD) Officers Theodore Briseno, Laurence Powell, and Timothy Wind and Sergeant Stacey Koon of excessive force, assault with a deadly weapon, and falsifying a police report, among other charges. Almost a year before, on March 3, 1991, a bystander, George Holliday, videotaped the four policemen assaulting Rodney King, a motorist, on a residential street in the San Fernando Valley.[1] The video, arguably the first in history to go "viral," aired locally on KCAL-TV within a day of the attack; one day later, CNN broadcast it nationally.[2] Media outlets in the United States and abroad then screened the video and circulated stills from it repeatedly. The video and its widespread dissemination brought issues of excessive police force and racism to the forefront of public discourse like never before. The appearance of white policemen brutally assaulting an unarmed Black man also seemed to provide proof of the unjust hostility African Americans had long experienced in the United States. Due to the popular perception that police treated King with extrajudicial cruelty, the court ruling of acquittal dismayed many and drew immediate protests. As crowds swelled at the Simi Valley courthouse, Los Angeles Mayor Tom Bradley, the first African American to hold the office, then in his fifth term, declared, "The jury's verdict will never blind the world to what we saw on the videotape."[3] Demonstrations against the court ruling quickly spread to other parts of Southern California. Just a few hours later, at approximately 6:00 p.m., protests escalated to property damage, civilian-on-civilian assaults, looting, and arson throughout Los Angeles County. Most affected by the destruction were the Koreatown and South Los Angeles neighborhoods, with thousands of looted and burned stores.[4]

Within a five-day period, the 1992 Los Angeles Riots became the most economically devastating unrest in the history of the United States. There were nearly four thousand fires, and property damages totaled over $1 billion.[5] In addition, fourteen thousand people were arrested, two thousand were injured, and sixty-three people died.[6] It also became the most extensively documented unrest at the time, with photographs, video, live broadcasts, and other forms of news coverage transmitting the protests, violence, destruction, and fires across the nation and the world.

Many scholars have examined the video of King's beating and documentation of the unrest in attempts to understand why the events unfolded as they did and what their impact has been on popular culture, policing, and race relations, among other sociopolitical issues. Yet few have focused on the potential of visual art to speak to the history. While scholars have overlooked visual art in favor of the widely circulated images of King's beating and the looting, arson, and assaults that occurred during the unrest, several generations of artists have made work in response to these events. Many of the artists have connected the Los Angeles episodes of police brutality and racial violence to similar incidents in the city's past and even in other parts of the world. They have also explored the ongoing sociopolitical and visual legacies of these experiences. Though visual art is not a form of documentation in the same way that news footage and photography is typically understood, it is nonetheless valuable for our consideration of the reverberating effects of the 1992 Los Angeles Riots.

Unrest: Art in the Aftermath of the 1992 Los Angeles Riots examines artworks made by two generations of multimedia artists, including Juan Capistrán, Seth Kaufman, Adrian Piper, and Latipa (née Michelle Dizon). Their works chronicle the overlooked cross-racial, immigrant, and intergenerational experiences surrounding the unrest. Many of these works also capture, in different ways, the resounding loss that state-sanctioned violence, like police brutality, produced for Black and other marginalized communities. The artistic references to episodes of violence beyond the King beating reveal how it was not just the acquittal of his uniformed assailants that caused the unrest. It was the recurring experiences of state violence, oppression, xenophobia, and racism wielded against poor, working-class, and immigrant communities of color. Thus I argue that unrest is a riotous act of the bereaved that makes the unrelenting experiences of injustice visible in the landscape, physically manifesting its magnitude in ways that no one can ignore. At the same time, unrest is the driver of continued inquiry, both critical and creative, into society's penchant for violence and its ties to legacies of white supremacy and oppression. Unrest is what has driven artists to address the 1991 King beating, the 1992 Los Angeles Riots, and other episodes of racial violence for over thirty years. Indeed, unrest is the inability to rest in the face of ongoing injustice.

Art in the Aftermath of Unrest

This book is the first major art history of the 1992 Los Angeles Riots and the only art history that chronicles the unrest through work made by two generations of artists, but it is not a comprehensive account. In fact, it would be difficult to do this since such artworks exist across multiple generations of practitioners—including those born after the events. While a compendium would be worthwhile since it would recognize the many artists who have made work on the topic, not to mention the utter impact of this history on visual art, this is not what *Unrest* endeavors to accomplish. Instead, I have organized the book in four case studies, with each centered on one artist's work. I chose the specific work of Capistrán, Kaufman, Piper, and Latipa because they are understudied, yet complex, and at times difficult in their conceptual and formal makeup, relationality, and emotional registers. My close analyses of the smaller selection of art allows me to more thoroughly analyze how they work, create meaning, and relate to the history and experience of unrest. My recovery of the historical narrative through these artworks provides important insights into how we process extreme violence, especially through imagery; how the United States criminal justice system visualizes race and tolerates racial violence; and how Americans adapt and continue highly racialized modes of viewing. The visual art also provides an opportunity to understand the 1992 Los Angeles Riots anew by inciting deeper understandings of human experience through a lens that places value on visual analysis and viewer engagement. The artworks I examine in *Unrest* create space for the critical analyses of history, enabling viewers to see who is and is not recognized or valued, how violence and oppression become normalized, and how viewers might unwittingly contribute to these injustices. The art folds viewers into history and acknowledges the ways in which this history continues even after the events in question have passed.

I reveal how artists challenge the Black-white racial dichotomy that often frames and limits understandings of the racism and xenophobia surrounding the 1992 Los Angeles Riots and race relations in the United States. Through different and sometimes indirect means, Capistrán, Kaufman, Piper, and Latipa expand popular narratives of the 1992 Los Angeles Riots, which often favored polarizing media portrayals and exclusionary accounts, to help their viewers understand the relationship between racism, xenophobia, and unrest and to see how these conditions often bind us together. This connection unfolds to touch many communities and real lives deeply and traumatically affected by racism and xenophobia.

I also assert that the 1992 Los Angeles Riots were not politically or ideologically unified or limited to only one neighborhood or region. I broaden the framework of the 1992 Los Angeles Riots to bridge Los Angeles history to other locales across the United States and the world. As demonstrated by the artworks and their exhibition, the unrest occurred in multiple places across greater Los Angeles, including South Central Los Angeles, West Hollywood, and Culver City, and resonated in communities beyond the region, such as the Midwest, New Orleans, Mexico, and France. Indeed, the Black experience of racial violence is linked inextricably to that of others; and recognition of shared or intersecting histories resists narratives that aim to weaken cross-racial and transnational solidarity and coalition. This book establishes the relevance of visual art for understanding the historical legacy of white supremacy and oppression as it intersects with unrest—vital insights we need to move imagination on to the realization of a just and liberatory future.

As we move deeper into a discussion of the ways in which art reflects the experience and history of unrest, we must consider language. Many scholars prefer the terms "rebellion," "uprising," or "insurrection" to describe the 1992 Los Angeles Riots due to the historical negative connotations embedded in the word "riot" and the ways in which it often elides political motivations. I agree with these understandings; nevertheless, I find the alternatives problematic. None of them encompass the complexity of unrest, and they often attribute the motivation of those who participate in it to an assumed single and unified cause. In other words, these terms portray the events that occurred in April and May 1992 as utopic or romanticized, and they ignore how those who participated via protests, marches, looting, destruction, and assault did so for many different and complex reasons. To be clear, I do not believe that the 1992 Los Angeles Riots (or any episode of unrest for that matter) occurred without reason or are illustrative of irrational behavior. On the contrary, I believe unrest occurs with logic—sometimes throwing light on the illogical aspects of society and the law that repeatedly harm certain people and communities—an issue I discuss in this book. Furthermore, sometimes history has shown us that unrest can be a necessary tool to exercise agency and incite change when voices of dissent go unheard or other methods of protest have failed. Still, it is perhaps overoptimistic to believe that a word like "riot" can be fundamentally reimagined and redefined to encompass such complexities. So, for this book, I reserve use of those terms for the most common proper names, always capitalized—such as the 1992 Los Angeles Riots, the 1965 Watts Rebellion, or the Los Angeles Riots—or when quoting others.

I prefer the term "unrest." I am convinced, by oral histories, testimonials, research, documentation, and art on the 1992 Los Angeles Riots, that unrest is born from intergenerational experiences of loss caused by systemic racial and xenophobic violence. This repeating experience is why unrest is a suitable description and why I have theorized it as a physical manifestation of grief or bereavement that makes loss visible within a landscape. I do not mean to excuse the violence and destruction that often characterizes unrest or the injustices sometimes reenacted by the very communities protesting them. Instead, my understanding is an attempt to underscore and destigmatize the experience and multivalence of emotions and weaken the racist connotations tied to words like "riot" that aim to diminish or disregard the circumstances that lead to these events over and over. Unrest conveys disharmony and strife or the "state or fact of not being at peace."[7] For centuries, it also has been used to describe demonstrations and disorder.[8] Importantly, unrest, as I stated earlier, conveys the inability to rest in the face of injustice. With these meanings at hand, I aim to expand the understanding of unrest to include the refusal to abide by the logics of the state. The imperfection of unrest as a concept lies in the common understanding of the word's prefix as a binary; but by resisting the binary reflex, we also resist the authoritarian power that aims to use force to restore a status quo that is broken.[9] "Un-," when attached to a verb, "express[es] the reversal or cancellation of the specified action or process."[10] This notion of reversal suggests "rest" as the seemingly logical flipside of unrest, creating a binary understanding of the word that flattens lived experience. The binary also risks the casting of blame onto the individual shortcomings that do not allow one to "succeed" in rest. Artist and activist Tricia Hersey underscores in her writing how it is capitalism, "grind culture," and the scarcity mindset that blind people to the need for rest and their ability to enact it in their lives.[11] Thus it is dismaying to see "rest" co-opted by capitalists for the wellness industry and integrated as a sort of performativity of self-care against the very neoliberal structures that appropriate it and exploit bodies, minds, and labor, making efforts like Hersey's especially needed. To be clear, the way I conceive unrest does not abide by the logic of reversal, the logic of the lexicon, that its prefix implies. The intergenerational experience of those who have continued to struggle for what is right, what is deserved, and the imagination and implementation of liberatory futures is evidence that the logic of reversal is weak. But that is not to say that the fight for justice—that is, against state violence, oppression, or the violation of civil and human rights—is impossible or a fruitless endeavor. It is necessary and righteous. What I mean is that we must refuse the logic of reversal when it is a conditional and a threat that ultimately aims to reify and reinstate discriminatory conditions. Such a conditional is what contributes to the ignition of events like the 1992 Los Angeles Riots, and in visual art that addresses the sociopolitical conditions of so-called riots, we find unrest and an unrelenting drive for justice.

The first chapter discusses a series of artworks that Capistrán made for the twentieth anniversary of the 1992 Los Angeles Riots. I analyze his mixed-media paintings about three people and topics related to the unrest: Latasha Harlins, a childhood classmate whose unjust murder by a store clerk in South Central Los Angeles was captured on surveillance video the same month as King's police beating; Fidel Lopez, a Guatemalan immigrant who was brutally beaten on the first day of the unrest at the intersection of Florence and Normandie Avenues; and the South Central lots razed by arsonists during the unrest that remain undeveloped today. Capistrán's artworks expand the limits of the Black-white racial binary to recover the cross-racial experiences of Black, Latino, and Latin American immigrants during the unrest. I demonstrate how these experiences are interwoven and how the artist's work holds open space for cross-racial solidarity and coalition building, using the narrative frame of a neighborhood tour I conducted with Capistrán of the still-empty lots. Five years after the 1992 Los Angeles Riots, *Los Angeles Times* staff writer Hector Tobar described the empty lots as "ruins."[12] He explained that they had taken on "a certain permanence, much like the stretches of Watts that have remained undeveloped since the 1965 riots."[13] He followed with the cynical remark that in the community hit hardest by arsonists, South Central, each neighborhood seemed to have "its own local monument to the riots." At the time of his 1997 article, approximately one in three buildings destroyed or heavily damaged were not rebuilt. In 2016, when Capistrán and I toured South Central, many of these empty lots, or "ruins," still existed. Thus I explore the ongoing effects the 1992 Los Angeles Riots has had on residents. This is what first led me to argue that unrest is an act of the bereaved that makes racial injustice visible in the landscape *and* the driver of continued artistic inquiry into this history.

Like the assemblages made by Noah Purifoy and other artists in the aftermath of the 1965 Watts Rebellion, Kaufman made sculptures and found objects from the charred and melted remains of businesses burned down during the 1992 Los Angeles Riots. Kaufman excavated materials from lots near his home in West Hollywood immediately after the fires were extinguished. While Purifoy dubbed his artwork and that of his collaborators "junk art," Kaufman provocatively described his practice as "post-riot looting." In the second chapter, I explore the notion of post-riot looting and argue that Kaufman's practice encourages a reexamination of art-making in the aftermath of unrest with a critical look at race, class, and opportunism. Through interviews and research on his writing, I reconstruct the artist's firsthand experiences immediately after the 1992 Los Angeles Riots: his search for materials and artistic purpose, his direct and contentious encounters with immigrant small business owners whose property was burned down, and his commercial ventures to exhibit artwork with Absolut Vodka and at the 1992 annual art fair in Los Angeles. Kaufman's practice and words were at times admittedly distasteful and contradictory, and, for these reasons, his work stands apart from the other artists' works I examine in this book. Still, I assert that his artistic practice and art captures important experiences of loss and negotiation in the "post-riot" landscape that have been overlooked.

Stylistically and conceptually, artists like Capistrán draw from visual art legacies that Piper importantly contributed to and helped shaped. In chapter 3, I closely examine the artist-philosopher's multimedia installation *Black Box/White Box* (1992), which combined minimalism's pared down and sleek aesthetic with jarring visual and auditory devices to encourage viewers to critique the ways in which xenophobia and state violence framed the police beating of King. Through my close analysis of the installation, along with Piper's writing and references to music and literature, I argue that *Black Box/White Box* acts as a marked change in the artist's practice because of its specific combination of formally rigorous visual and sonic strategies and her use of the widely familiar King video. With the use of multimedia, I suggest the installation moved beyond philosophical contemplation to a deepened engagement with issues of race, xenophobia, and violence that also encouraged viewers to critically examine their relationship to these behaviors. Interestingly, Piper, who began planning the installation on the second day of the 1992 Los Angeles Riots, debuted *Black Box/White Box* in Columbus, Ohio, during the Columbus Quincentennial. Thus I place Piper's installation in a broader legacy of unrest and examine how this situation ties the events surrounding the 1992 Los Angeles Riots to a longer history of xenophobia and oppression. I also maintain that Piper's emphasis on black and white for her installation becomes a visual metaphor for the Black-white racial binary—one that drives national narratives and locates sites of conflict in the United States. Likewise, I assert her work is a critique that demonstrates the limits of the racial binary that simultaneously insists on an end to bigotry and an expansion of a shared humanity.

In chapter 4, I analyze *Civil Society*, Latipa's three-channel video installation. *Civil Society* explores the King video, its use during the trial of the police who beat him, and footage of unrest from the past and present. In line with the previous chapters' explorations of interwoven state violence, oppression, and everyday lives, Latipa connects the 1992 Los Angeles Riots with the 1965 Watts Rebellion, Hurricane Katrina, and the 2005 French unrest. She uses the King video and other footage to explore the dialectics of seeing, which she calls "a vision in ruins." By emphasizing what lies outside the frame, she makes visible the failures of technology to fully capture events and their injustices. Through video cuts, montages, conceptual soundscapes, and voice-over, the artist blends the seemingly disparate histories of unrest to highlight how the experiences of anti-Blackness, state-sanctioned violence, and xenophobic rhetoric threatens the citizenship and human rights of marginalized peoples. I argue that the technological failure of video and the "vision in ruins" that Latipa expresses in her work become metaphors for society's inability to recognize the injustices that marginalized peoples have experienced and continue to endure—and that this inability to see is tied to the faulty vision of white supremacy. I also maintain that Latipa's work urges viewers to recognize the sorrow caused by the enduring legacies of racial and xenophobic violence. Like Capistrán's work, Latipa's speaks to how unrest is an act of the bereaved that makes injustice visible in the landscape—an act not just contained in a US context, but marked by a larger, global legacy of white supremacy. Furthermore, through my analysis of *Civil Society*, including my own experience of the work, I argue that we—people of color and the marginalized—are the ruins of so-called civil society, the markers of white supremacy's faults and flaws, who must demand and see to its demise.

As in chapter 4, my voice and my experience are woven into the book, in the form of disclosing my interactions with some of the artists, my engagement and experience of their artwork, or my recollections of unrest. I come from several generations of Latinos who, on both sides of my family, were from the same two-mile radius across unincorporated South Los Angeles and Watts. I also grew up listening to and learning from family oral histories about the experience of unrest—an experience I quickly came to know firsthand with the 1992 Los Angeles Riots. This places me in a unique position: I am a former resident of an epicenter of unrest, I am shaped by the multigenerational experiences of this history, and I am a scholar trained in art history—a discipline in which someone like me, from my neighborhood, class position, race, and ethnicity, continues to be an exception.[14] The inclusion of my voice in this book seeks to add depth to the art history I write, acknowledging what is usually left unsaid in academic writing: how historiography is subjective, in that the narratives recorded are affected by the lived experiences, inclinations, and training of the scholar. On why the public recollection of experiences like mine matters, especially in the context of art history, I have stated elsewhere, "The stories of advocacy, activism, persistence, resistance, resilience, the sweat and tears, and the real life-and-death stakes . . . are the Latino experiences that mark our class, our politics, our culture, and our positions as people of color in the United States. They're also what connects us to other people of color, to other oppressed peoples in this land and in all colonized and occupied lands."[15] Therefore, I understand what might be (mis)construed as individual experience as one that resonates with those of others and why testimonio, the political and urgent remembering of lived history, not only counts, but bears significant weight. I borrow the understanding of testimonios from the Latina Feminist Group: "narratives lodged in memory, shared out loud and recorded"; that which speaks to the similar and complex experiences of a community; and that which seeks to "mediate power relations" and express lived experiences often kept from or ignored by the public.[16] Indeed, in Latino and Latin American studies, testimonio is recognized as an important methodology and tool for recovering little-known histories, especially those that counter the official histories of the state. As the Latina Feminist Group has explained, testimonio is "a crucial means of bearing witness and inscribing into history those realities that would otherwise succumb to the alchemy of erasure."[17] I resist erasing myself and those I carry with me.

Previous (Art) Histories of Unrest in Los Angeles

It is important to recognize the art histories that preexist this book. Only one major catalog archives a visual art exhibition on the 1992 Los Angeles Riots: *No Justice, No Peace? Resolutions . . .* (1992), a group show impressively organized by Lizzetta LeFalle-Collins for the California Afro-American Museum shortly after the unrest.[18] While many of the works by the nineteen artists were not related directly to the events surrounding the 1992 Los Angeles Riots, LeFalle-Collins explains that the artists' works speak to the "social issues that impact [the artists'] everyday lives" and the racism they encounter as Black people.[19] On the topic of the everyday, the collection edited by Roland Charles and Toyomi Igus, *Life in a Day of Black L.A.* (1992), features the work of ten photographers who aim to capture both quotidian life and the unrest as a counter to the negative racial representations perpetuated by the media and the film industry.[20] The photographs center the dignity and humanity of subjects with accompanying short descriptions.[21] Several decades after their publication, the two works continue to stand as the largest catalogs of visual art that address the legacy of the 1992 Los Angeles Riots, following in the footsteps of *Junk Art: 66 Signs of Neon* (1966) and its documentation of the traveling group exhibition curated by Noah Purifoy and Judson Powell.[22]

Likewise, only a few articles and book chapters provide close readings of individual artworks made in response to the King video and the 1992 unrest. The works of scholars Min Hyoung Song and Cherise Smith stand out for their explorations and analyses of race in this cultural legacy. In *Strange Future* (2005), Song considers the politics of the 1990s and the pessimism that overwhelms the literature and films inspired by the unrest.[23] Through close readings of text and images from sources like the film *Strange Days* (1995, dir. Kathryn Bigelow), Anna Deavere Smith's book based on her play *Twilight: Los Angeles, 1992* (1994), the documentary film *Sa-I-Gu: From Korean Women's Perspective* (1993, dir. Dai Sil Kim-Gibson), and Chang-Rae Lee's novel *Native Speaker* (1995), Song argues that the works overwhelmingly reflect a narrative of national decline through the portrayal of a weakening social fabric. Song discusses the visual resonance of the videotaped police beating of King in American culture and argues that the reenactment of the violent incident on film exemplified a familiar Black-white trope that "fix[ed] the coordinates of our hatred," yet expressed racial anxiety about national identity during a time of significant demographic and economic changes in Los Angeles.[24] These changes can be traced to new immigration policies such as the *Hart-Celler Immigration and Nationality Act* (1965); the migration of refugees from US-sponsored civil wars in Central America; and a recession that devastated Black and Latino residents at grossly unequal rates, especially in South Central Los Angeles.[25] Song explores the painful and difficult contact with others in his analysis of Smith's interview with the white truck driver Reginald Denny in *Twilight,* a collection of interviews on which the artist based her play and film adaptation of the same name. During the 1992 Los Angeles Riots, Black men targeted Denny, pulled him out of his truck, and severely beat him—an incident captured live in helicopter coverage.[26] Though the media filmed similar beatings involving those of other races, the Denny incident became the image many media outlets chose to emphasize. Song discusses the dichotomous Black-white nature of the politics of race when he invokes the Denny beating as a parallel for the beating of King.[27]

Although Song eschews an in-depth look at Smith's performative version of *Twilight,* Cherise Smith gives a detailed performance analysis of several scenes from the film adaptation in *Enacting Others* (2011).[28] In *Twilight,* filmed in 2000, Anna Deavere Smith recounts the experiences of twenty-five interviewees during the 1992 unrest. She performs as the people she interviews and adopts their gestures, mannerisms, dialects, and intonations. Cherise Smith's interest lies in the artist's performance as self and Other and the ways in which the method portrays a "liberal humanist utopian world without discrimination."[29] She argues that the artist's personal identity hinders the breach of identity boundaries and threatens to undermine the "utopia" of the performance.[30] Though the artist's method of acting often essentializes the identities of the interviewees, Smith suggests that the artist's performance creates an ambivalence that signals a then-burgeoning post-identity discourse. Post-identity, as explained by the art historian, refers to a "mythical present" where one's particular identity bears no weight on one's successes or failures in society.[31] While "post-identity" can mean an investment in redefining the complexities of race and identity, Smith also discusses an American political climate in the 1990s that increasingly became hostile to identity politics and was labeled "anti-integrationist, separatist, and isolationist," all while marginalized populations in the United States were stripped of programs created to ensure their equality and civil rights.[32] With the rise and fall of multiculturalism and disapproval of the seeming essentialism and exclusionary practices many believed all these ideas entailed, race and identity continued to be intrinsic to the history of the 1992 Los Angeles Riots and artists' responses to the events, as I show.[33]

There are many works that offer political, social, and economic analyses of the 1992 Los Angeles Riots, and several helped shape my understandings of the unrest beyond visual art. Paul Ong and Suzanne Hee collected and published data on the impact of the 1992 Los Angeles Riots in *Losses in Los Angeles Unrest* (1993), providing critical information on every building burned and damaged and statistics on how various communities, particularly Korean American property owners, were affected economically.[34] Ong and Hee's data continue to provide the most comprehensive listing of property losses during the unrest, and it became a vital resource for me regarding specific buildings and businesses that played prominent roles in the art history I write here. In "Transmitting Race" (1994), Erna Smith discusses how the media frequently portrayed the unrest as a Black and white issue—a frame also used to describe past episodes in American history, such as the 1965 Watts Rebellion.[35] Historian George J. Sánchez argues in "Reading Reginald Denny" (1995) and "Face the Nation" (1997) that this binary obscures how the unrest in 1992 involved multiple racial and ethnic groups, particularly Latino and Asian immigrants.[36] Nancy Abelmann and John Lie address a similar issue—one that emphasizes a Black-Korean binary—in *Blue Dreams* (1995). They find that this binary emphasized conflict, fueled antagonism, and dismissed acts of solidarity between the two communities.[37] Altogether, their work helps one understand the ways in which the racial binary eschews the complex causes for and circumstances of unrest in Los Angeles. This gives insight into the reasons many visual artists held the Black-white binary suspect after the 1992 Los Angeles Riots and instead often favored a cross-racial framework that emphasized shared experience and solidarity.[38]

With that said, before there were the 1992 Los Angeles Riots, there was the 1965 Watts Rebellion. Historian Gerald Horne's documentation and analyses of the latter event in *Fire This Time* were critical to my own understanding of the wider legacy of unrest.[39] Particularly influential were Horne's sociopolitical and demographic contextualization of Los Angeles and his exploration and analysis of "rainbow racism" or, in his words, "compounded racism."[40] Examining how discrimination between different racial and ethnic groups often moved within and beyond the Black-white binary, Horne underscores the particular social, economic, and political situations and practices in workplaces and neighborhoods across the city.[41]

For historiographies on the visual and wider cultural arts before the 1992 Los Angeles Riots and surrounding the period of the 1965 Watts Rebellion, two books immediately rise to the top: *South of Pico* (2017) by art historian Kellie Jones and *Black Arts West* (2010) by Daniel Widener.[42] Both scholars document artists' efforts to carve out space for Black creativity, activism, and organization in Los Angeles. Jones explores the frame of artists' migration to the city and the resulting "dislocations and cultural reinvention," "loss and possibility," and "reinscription of the new" in their practices and relationships to or development of museums, galleries, and other art organizations. Widener captures the broader cultural landscape of the arts, including visual art, literature, music, film, and arts organizations as a "modality of black politics" that became a regionally distinctive continuation of the Black Arts Movement.[43] Both authors' approaches delineate the numerous key figures and programs in the cultural landscape—an approach that we continue to need for the 1992 Los Angeles Riots.[44]

My focused, object-based inquiry does not capture the numerous subjects and organizations in the cultural landscape surrounding the unrest in 1992 and, as I have previously stated, the many artists whose work either addressed directly or was influenced by the events surrounding this history. These artists and their works include Sandow Birk and his many history paintings of Los Angeles, such as *The Apprehension of Rodney King* (1992) and *George Bush Visiting the Riots in L.A.* (1993); Mark Bradford's *Scorched Earth* series (2015); Chris Burden's *L.A.P.D. Uniform* (1993); Nick Cave's earliest soundsuit (ca. 1991/92); Sung Ho Choi's *Choi's Market* (1993); Robbie Conal and Patrick Crowley's *Taken Out and Shot* (1991);

Robbie Conal's *Disarm* (1993); Elsa Flores's *Stigmata over the City of Los Angeles* (1992); Pat Gomez's *Stay Tuned* (1992); Elmer Guevara's *Dried up on a Sunday* (2023); Salomón Huerta's *Three Horsemen* (1992); Shaun Leonardo's *Rodney King, Before BLM* (2017); Patrick Martinez's *Nine Deuce* (2016) and *Vintage Throwback Po-lice* (2016); Willie Middlebrook's *In His Own Image* (1992); Yong Soon Min's *Defining Moments* (1992); Michael Richards's *A Loss of Faith Brings Vertigo* (1994); Danny Tisdale's *Rodney King Police Beating* (1992); Mark Valen's *No Justice, No Peace* (1992); Carrie Mae Weems's *Commemorating* series (1992); and Gloria Westcott's *Adios Hollywood* (1992), to name just a few. In the four chapters of this book, I analyze work that captures the resounding nature of racism, xenophobia, and loss in the history of the 1992 Los Angeles Riots by closely analyzing the art of just a few of the many artists who have made work about this history. As a result of my close readings, I contend with efforts to create spaces for viewers to engage critically with images and histories of violence and oppression. My analyses also enable us to see how they are inextricably connected to this history and to each other, demonstrating the sociopolitical relevance of visual art within and beyond the legacy of the 1992 Los Angeles Riots and revealing the ways in which this art history continues to live, demanding continued study, new research, and additional narratives of unrest.

1

The Scarred Cityscape

On a sunny November afternoon in 2015, I waited for Juan Capistrán in front of Numero Uno Market #103, a grocery store catering to the Spanish-speaking community of South Central Los Angeles.[1] The brightly painted pink and green building was the first stop in a tour of sites that arsonists burned down during the 1992 Los Angeles Riots—sites also significant to the artist's practice, which includes numerous individual and collaborative projects on the destruction of the unrest and related episodes of racial violence. Yet the grocery store never burned down. In fact, it did not exist then.

Before the late 1990s, when the growing Numero Uno Market chain purchased and renovated the site for its third store, the location was home to Empire Liquor Market Deli. The year before the 1992 Los Angeles Riots and two weeks after four police officers brutalized Rodney King on videotape, a surveillance camera caught the tragic shooting death of Latasha Harlins, a fifteen-year-old African American girl, by Soon Ja Du, the Korean proprietor of Empire Liquor. The recorded shooting and resulting trial contributed to the 1992 Los Angeles Riots and surrounding episodes of racial violence. The unrest the death and trial caused scarred the South Central neighborhood and left an indelible mark on many of the residents for years and decades to come.

Rewind

Harlins entered Empire Liquor Market Deli on the morning of Saturday, March 16, 1991.[2] She walked to the refrigerated section of the convenience store and placed a bottle of orange juice in her backpack before the surveillance camera recorded her approaching Du at the checkout counter. Without sound, the camera captured the woman yelling at Harlins. Beyond the camera's frame and near the store's exit, two younger Black children witnessed Du accuse Harlins of stealing the juice and the girl denying it and showing the woman the money she had in her hand. The camera then captured Du as she reached across the counter and jerked the child's sweater. Suddenly, the two began to wrestle. Harlins hit Du in the face twice, breaking free from the woman's grip. Du then threw a stool at the girl, before retrieving a handgun from below the cash register. Off camera, the other two children ran out of the store. On camera, Du pointed the gun at Harlins as she bent down to retrieve the fallen beverage. She handed it to Du, who yanked it down to the counter. The girl slowly turned away from the woman and began walking toward the store's exit. But she took only a few steps before Du shot her. Harlins immediately collapsed to the floor, and Du's face contorted with inaudible wails. Later, investigators found the girl's hand still clutching two $1 bills—enough money to pay for the $1.79 bottle of orange juice.[3]

Both the King and Harlins videos seemed to evidence the horrifying reality of violence against Black people. Yet in the news and during the trial of King's uniformed assailants, pundits and lawyers debated over whether the Black motorist caused, and thus deserved, the police beating. During Du's murder trial, the defense tried to position Harlins as a party guilty in her own death. Du's attorneys described Harlins as the aggressor and emphasized she was larger and stronger than Du to argue that Du acted in self-defense, recalling the defense lawyers' description of King during the police trial. In response to Du having first grabbed the child, the defense argued that she had the right as a store owner to "detain" and "investigate" someone thought to be stealing.[4] Yet the surveillance camera captured the girl's death with clarity: She was leaving the store when the woman shot her in the back of the head.[5] Given the videotape evidence, Harlins's family and friends hoped for justice.[6]

In November 1991, a jury found Du guilty of voluntary manslaughter, which could have yielded a maximum prison sentence of sixteen years.[7] However, the presiding judge, Joyce Karlin, ordered that Du spend no time in prison. She began her sentencing decision with a series of rhetorical questions that she herself answered.

> Does society need Mrs. Du to be incarcerated in order to be protected? I think not. Is the defendant a danger to society? I think not. Is state prison needed in order to encourage the defendant to lead a law-abiding life or isolate her so that she cannot commit other crimes? I think not. Is state prison needed to punish Mrs. Du? Perhaps.[8]

Karlin reduced Du's sentence to a suspended ten-year prison term, five years of probation, and four hundred hours of community service and ordered her to pay the cost of Harlins's medical expenses and funeral. She also ordered Du to pay a $500 fine.[9] The Harlins family walked out of the courtroom devastated by the decision. Family and friends described it as an injustice and as Du "getting away with murder."[10]

Harlins's death, King's beating, and the resulting trials exacerbated cross-racial antagonism in Los Angeles. These events especially incensed tensions between the Black and Korean communities, inciting additional acts of assault and murder.[11] Five months after Du's light sentence was handed down and the same day a jury acquitted the LAPD officers who beat King, these cross-racial antagonisms sparked the arson, looting, and assaults that were called the 1992 Los Angeles Riots.

Fast Forward

To coincide with the twentieth anniversary of the 1992 Los Angeles Riots, Capistrán produced the multimedia art series, *From a Whisper to a Scream* (2012), which recognized the racial violence surrounding the unrest. For instance, the paintings *March 3, 1991* and *March 16, 1991* mark the dates of King's beating and Harlins's death (Figures 1.1 and 1.7). Capistrán's artistic commemoration indexed the significant role each event played in the history of the 1992 Los Angeles Riots.

Like freckled skin, a thin brown wash with small dark and textured fragments covers the centered sans serif vinyl characters that compose the date of *March 16, 1991* (Figure 1.1). These fragments, which break the surface's consistency, were an unexpected chemical reaction that occurred when the artist combined the wash's ingredients: tears, sweat, blood, and orange juice. Through the date painting, Capistrán remembers the significance of Harlins's death and Du's no-prison sentence in shaping the history of the 1992 Los Angeles Riots.[12] Until recently, historical narratives often overlooked these contributing factors of the unrest.[13] Yet, perhaps most significant to the artist, the painting also marks the loss of a childhood schoolmate. Before his transfer to a junior high school in Venice, California, Capistrán met Harlins at Bret Harte Preparatory Middle School in South Central.[14] Therefore, the painting is more than a mere addendum to major historical narratives. Using the aesthetic strategies of minimalism and conceptualism, Capistrán pared down his reference to Harlins, using only her death date and orange juice. He further abstracted reference to her body and his own with the bodily fluids comprising the painting's

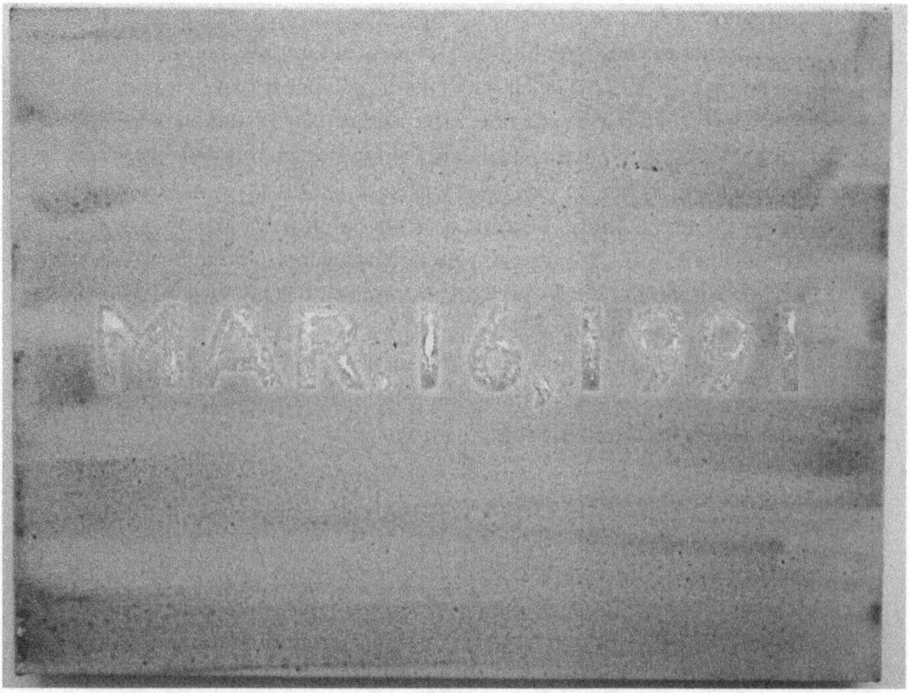

FIGURE 1.1 Juan Capistrán, *Saturday, March 16, 1991 (Latasha)*, 2012. Blood, sweat, tears, and orange juice on canvas, 18¼ × 24⅜ inches (46.3 × 61.9 cm). Courtesy the artist.

media. Made with blood, sweat, and tears, the painting is an expression of pain and a representation of the bodily excesses of sorrow. At the same time, the formal decision to abstract the body becomes a metaphor of the physical obliteration caused by violence and death. The artist's painting links the collective experience of the unrest with personal meaning, marking years of mourning in the neighborhood where Harlins died and the fires of the 1992 Los Angeles Riots first blazed.

Capistrán's visual strategies delve into the Black-white racial binary of violence. However, the Latino artist complicates this binary, including tropes about South Central Los Angeles, to cast light on the intertwined diversity of experiences surrounding the unrest. While he is far too young to be part of the generation of artists that developed minimalism and conceptualism in the 1960s, Capistrán is of the generation that inherited the visual art languages that had long become mainstream in art and largely depoliticized in establishment venues. Thus his work provides a corrective to historical narratives that have privileged palatable, one-dimensional understandings of race, violence, and art.

Undergirding Capistrán's revitalization of the visual art languages with racial politics is the lived experience of unrest. Although Capistrán was just a teenager during the 1992 Los Angeles Riots, they went on to drive and define much of his artistic development, career, and subject matter. Of particular relevance is Capistrán's long, ongoing commitment to demonstrating the interwoven experiences of Blacks, Latinos, and immigrants in South Central. This is not only exemplified in how a Black girl's death forever affected a Brown boy's life, which is certainly relevant here; it is also exemplified in the intersecting experiences and consequences of racism, xenophobia, and violence in a Black, Brown, and immigrant community.

In this chapter, I demonstrate how Capistrán visualizes cross-racial solidarity, represents the enduring pain of violence, and challenges reductive narratives that exacerbate racial antagonisms. Importantly, I frame this through my recollection of the neighborhood tour I conducted with Capistrán in 2015. I had asked the artist to share with me the specific arson sites that much of his artwork on the unrest references. The sites we visited, most of which were lots that stayed empty or derelict for two decades, made me realize how the city's scars paralleled the psychic wounds caused by the violence surrounding the 1992 Los Angeles Riots. These sites and Capistrán's art are like portals that allow one to travel back and forth in time and see how the past exists in and continues to affect the present. The collapse of time in Capistrán's art, what the lots we visited represent and how the body and mind respond to such memories, influenced the structure of this chapter. It moves back and forth in time. This disordered pulse of history parallels the experience of unrest, which Capistrán demonstrates in his drive to continually make art about the 1992 Los Angeles Riots. Ultimately, I argue that unrest is both a riotous act of bereavement that makes the experiences of injustice visible in the landscape and the drive that gives way to enduring artistic contemplation on these events.

The Landscape Is Forever Scarred

After moving to South Central from Mexico at the age of three, Capistrán lived in walking distance from Empire Liquor/Numero Uno in a home where his parents continue to reside. He has passed this location countless times, before and after the 1992 Los Angeles Riots. Yet, while we stood together in front of Numero Uno at the beginning of our tour, he did not say much to me about the store or why he chose to meet here as our first stop. And I refrained from asking too many questions. I knew already that Harlins had died here and that she and Capistrán had once been schoolmates. It was just three years earlier, at a studio visit with the artist to see the in-progress *From a Whisper to a Scream* series, when I encountered the date painting referencing Harlins's death. It was still drying when I asked Capistrán about the wash and he revealed that it included his blood and tears. I quickly realized then the vulnerability the painting represented. It traversed creative, professional, and personal terrain. So, on the first stop of our tour of South Central, I stood silently with the artist—not because of discomfort or not knowing what to say, but because I understood that the moment needed silence as we both remembered and reflected on the tragedy that happened here.

Capistrán remembers first learning about Harlins's death on the evening news. He recognized her name and then later, in another news segment, her school picture. He talked about it with his friends, but he remembers not feeling surprised. He explains, "It was a common thing to hear about people getting shot and killed [in South Central]. You become numb to it. You don't cry until years later."[15] As Capistrán grew up, he began to reflect on his childhood experiences with violence. The anniversary of Harlins's death and the 1992 Los Angeles Riots became especially painful facts in his life. He first began to reference the events in his work as an undergraduate student at Otis College of Art and Design. Then as a graduate student at the University of California, Irvine, and as recently as 2019 for a series of site-specific installations, he returned to the subjects. Regarding the consistent referencing over his entire artistic career, he told me, "I'm still trying to understand my personal experience of being around so much trauma and poverty. [When I was younger], it was too overwhelming. I wasn't capable of reflecting on it."[16] The experiences went on to drive and define his artistic development, career, and subject matter, and his artwork became a necessary space of contemplation.

We peered through the mint-colored iron gate that surrounded the grocery store's parking lot. While quietly watching Latino families enter the store and exit with plastic bags of groceries, I remembered a statement Capistrán made when I interviewed him earlier in the year—one that could have been an adage for our decades-late tour of "post-riot" South Central: "The landscape is forever scarred."[17] Though we could no longer see Empire Liquor as it once was, the memories of Harlins and her murder remain entangled with the location where Numero Uno now stands.[18] The scarring in the city is both physical and emotional, historical and ever present. Such wounds never fade, especially when there are those left behind to remember how they were made.

After Du killed Harlins in 1991, Empire Liquor shuttered. With Du on trial for manslaughter, residents picketed the store and spray-painted it with messages condemning her disregard for Black life.[19] The convenience store's otherwise plain off-white exterior and modest plastic and hand-painted signage then stood out among the neighborhood's other modest storefronts. However, Empire Liquor became much more than a canvas for tagging righteous grievances. When the 1992 Los Angeles Riots ignited in South Central, the same day a jury acquitted the police officers who beat King and just several months after Du walked free despite a manslaughter conviction, locals kept Empire Liquor safe from the arson consuming other neighborhood buildings. With water-filled buckets and garbage cans, residents put out four arson attempts. This was not a favor to the Du family. Instead, residents put out the flames to save their homes at Webb Motel, which shared a wall with the convenience store, and to ensure the Du family could not cash in on any potential insurance policy.[20] In the wake of Harlins's murder and Du's light sentence and in the midst of what would become the worst episode of unrest in the history of Los Angeles, South Central residents both lit the store on fire and put out the flames. By 1993, the Du family could no longer endure the financial burden of their shuttered business, triggering the foreclosure of their property by the California Korean Bank.[21]

Capistrán addresses the significance of Empire Liquor and Numero Uno in *Rather than running the risk of injustice we preferred disorder . . .* (2012) (Figure 1.2). The three-panel painting, also part of the series *From a Whisper to a Scream*, includes two black-and-white photographs: Empire Liquor on the left panel and Numero Uno on the right panel. For the center panel, the artist rendered the incendiary demand, "Burn This Mother Down!," which he observed among the several imperatives spray-painted on Empire Liquor shortly after Du killed Harlins.[22] The phrase recalls the repeated chorus of the Trammps' 1976 hit song, "Disco Inferno." Sung over a driving, funky bass line, electric keys, and several punctuating brass instruments, the chorus is a call and response between the Trammps' lead vocalist, Jimmy Ellis, and the band's backup singers:

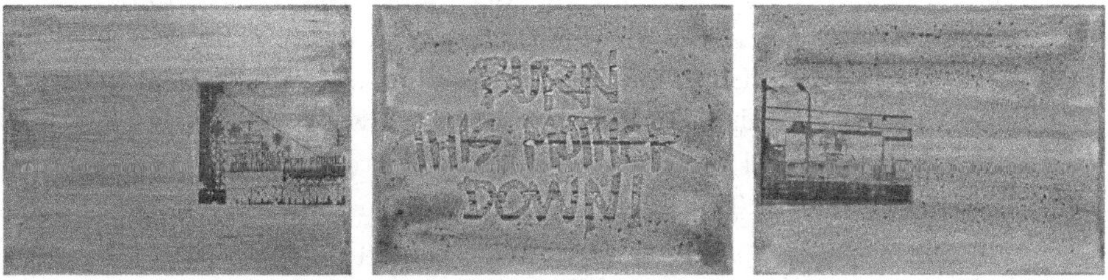

FIGURE 1.2 Juan Capistrán, *Rather than running the risk of injustice we preferred disorder . . .*, 2012. Blood, sweat, tears, and orange juice on canvas. Triptych, each canvas 18¼ × 24⅜ inches (46.3 × 61.9 cm). Courtesy the artist.

I hear somebody say
"Burn, baby, burn"
Disco inferno!
"Burn, baby, burn"
Burn that mother down[23]

In August 1991, five months after Harlins's death, someone answered the spray-painted demand, "Burn This Mother Down!," by attempting to raze the building with fire. Then three months later, the month of Du's sentencing, someone tried to set it ablaze again.[24]

While Empire Liquor suffered little damage, violent incidents between Black patrons and Korean convenience store owners in South Central increased after Harlins's death. For instance, on June 4, 1991, Tae Sam Park, a Korean owner of Chung Liquor on Western Avenue, killed Lee Arthur Mitchell, a Black patron who pointed at Park's wife what turned out to be a pretend gun. As a result, the business bore two arson attempts and Los Angeles Mayor Tom Bradley held a news conference about the increase in violence.[25] Yet the hostility continued throughout the year and exponentially intensified with the 1992 Los Angeles Riots. Korean and Korean American business owners bore the brunt of destruction, with over two thousand of their properties looted and burned.[26]

After the murder, trial, and unrest, Empire Liquor stood for several years as a de facto memorial to Harlins and a painful reminder of the injustices surrounding her death. The girl's family and the Latasha Harlins Justice Committee, founded by family friends and supporters, sought to turn the convenience store into a community center to honor Harlins's memory. However, they could not afford to purchase the property. In the late 1990s, after the California Korean Bank foreclosed on the property, developers purchased and renovated it for the construction of Numero Uno.[27]

In Capistrán's triptych, the viewer is unable to distinguish which site should be burned down. Does "Burn This Mother Down!" apply to Empire Liquor or Numero Uno? Since Empire Liquor was razed for redevelopment as Numero Uno, viewers might interpret it as meaning that the newer business should be torched in its place. However, this would be a simplistic, superficial interpretation of Capistrán's artwork.

In *Beloved* (1987), Toni Morrison develops a concept about the enduring nature of place, which might offer the best explanation for the idea behind Capistrán's three-panel painting. The protagonist, Sethe, says to her daughter Denver:

> It's so hard for me to believe in [time]. Some things go. Pass on. Some things just stay. I used to think it was my rememory. You know. Some things you forget. Other things you never do. But it's not. Places, places are still there. If a house burns down, it's gone, but the place—the picture of it—stays, and not just in my rememory, but out there, in the world. What I remember is a picture floating around out there outside my head. I mean, even if I don't think it, even if I die, the picture of what I did, or knew, or saw is still out there. Right in the place where it happened.[28]

Sethe, a formerly enslaved woman, understands history as tangible in the present. As the scholar Christina Sharpe explained, "[Sethe] wants to keep Denver from standing in the place where it was and is and will be; she wants to keep her from being overtaken by the past that is not past."[29] In her introduction to the concept of the wake, a multivalent framing to account for the ongoing legacy and impact of slavery and anti-Blackness, Sharpe explains that "in the wake, the past that is not past reappears, always to rupture the present."[30] The traumatic past in *Beloved* is inescapable and lingers, affecting more than the specific individual who directly experienced harm and scarring the place wherein this experience occurred.[31] To a certain extent, this concept resonates with Capistrán's triptych and with other paintings in the same series. As found in the painting that marks the date of Harlins' death, the past haunts the present. It suggests that the violent death of Harlins is tied to the place of Empire Liquor/Numero Uno. It also suggests that the grief caused by her death is permanent. Time does not heal past wounds because those wounds, as the artist explained, forever scar the landscape.[32]

We Preferred Disorder

The title of Capistrán's triptych painting, *Rather than running the risk of injustice we preferred disorder . . .*, makes a direct reference to Albert Camus's "Second Letter." Written by the French philosopher in 1943, the last year of the German military occupation of France during World War II, the letter is to an imagined German friend, about the occupation and the French Resistance.[33] In the letter, Camus recalls the experience of a sixteen-year-old boy who, along with ten Frenchmen, was taken by German soldiers from a prison to a nearby cemetery for execution.[34] Many of the prisoners were members of the Resistance; however, others, like the boy, had no involvement. Camus explains, "This hour is harder for them because they are dying by mistake or as victims of a kind of indifference."[35] He then retells the story of the boy's attempt to escape and how a German priest alerted soldiers, who caught him and returned him to his imminent death sentence. The priest's actions seem especially appalling to Camus; instead of siding with the teachings of God—with the love of his fellow man—the priest sided with his country and helped murder the boy. Camus writes, "It took only a dead child for us to add wrath to intelligence, and now we are two against one."[36] This unjust murder, as Camus argues, caused a rage that further united the French Resistance and fueled their fight against German occupation.

Capistrán's reference to Camus's "Second Letter" seems to suggest a parallel between the death of the French teenager and the shooting death of Harlins. Indeed, many South Central residents believe that the 1992 Los Angeles Riots were incited in part by the death of the fifteen-year-old girl and Du's light sentence for her murder. However, I suggest a deeper, edifying reading. In "Second Letter," Camus indirectly provides a description of a system of oppression that favors nationalism and turns people against one another, even when it goes against their self-interest, ethics, or belief system, such as the case of the priest who led the innocent boy to his unjust death. The essay thus becomes an opportunity for us to contemplate how we operate within and treat others under oppressive systems. To this end, Camus encourages us to consider the toxicity of white supremacy and oppression as well as its threat to citizenship and human rights. While Camus seems to wonder if we can truly emerge from under the power and influence of oppressive systems, he also forcefully indicates that we must undertake this struggle with all our might—adding wrath to intelligence.

Camus's "Second Letter" thus provides a critical framework for us to consider while analyzing Capistrán's art and the historical and political contexts of Los Angeles. White supremacy contributed to a system of power that often positioned the Black, Latino, and immigrant communities against each other while also obscuring the larger discriminatory forces that led to such conflict. In fact, Capistrán often reflects on two pivotal childhood experiences that relate to this phenomenon: the anti-Mexican racism he was subjected to by Black neighbors and the radical lessons he was taught on the history of Black struggle by an African American art teacher.[37] These simultaneous experiences helped him connect how he and his Black neighbors were both contending with similar systems of oppression and how cross-racial violence in a poor and working-class neighborhood like South Central was a way to divide and distract people from the greater exploitative forces controlling their lives.

Decades earlier, on April 14, 1967, Reverend Dr. Martin Luther King Jr. addressed the Stanford University community in a filmed speech known as "The Other America" in which he tied the experiences of oppression among the poor to the unrest that occurred in Watts and other cities across the nation. First, Dr. King explains the existence of two Americas, a lived experience—not just a mere rhetorical device—that underscores the stark socioeconomic disparities between the middle class and the poor. He emphasizes the racial and ethnic diversity of communities that fall into the "arena of blasted hopes and shattered dreams" in this other America by explaining how "some are Mexican Americans, some are Puerto Ricans, some are Indians, some happen to be from other groups. Millions of them are Appalachian whites." He continues, "But probably the largest group in this other America in proportion to its size in the population is the American Negro." After further describing the "triple ghetto" of race, poverty, and misery that Black Americans face, he ties the cross-racial disenfranchisement of the other America to the goals of the civil rights movement and describes it as a concerted effort to eliminate the disparities between the two Americas so the nation can be united as one. He later goes on to dispel the notion of "so-called white backlash" to the civil rights movement by revealing how this is merely a "new name for an old phenomenon" that is linked to discriminatory practices. Providing a recent example relevant to his Stanford audiences, he explains:

> The fact is that the state of California voted a fair housing bill out of existence before anybody shouted black power or before anybody rioted in Watts. It may well be that shouts of black power and riots in Watts and the Harlems and the other areas are the consequences of the white backlash, rather than the cause of them. What it is necessary to see is that there has never been a single, solid, monistic, determined commitment on the part of the vast majority of white Americans on the whole question of civil rights and on the whole question of racial equality. This is something that truth impels all men of goodwill to admit.[38]

Dr. King then describes the poor conditions found in the other America as the potential "powder kegs" that lead those in "moments" of anger and bitterness to rioting. While he asserts that he does not condone the violence of unrest, he simultaneously vows to continue condemning the ongoing conditions that cause them and invites America to do the same. He explains:

> A riot is the language of the unheard. And what is it that America has failed to hear? It has failed to hear that the plight of the Negro poor has worsened over the last few years. It has failed to hear that the promises of freedom

> and justice have not been met. And it has failed to hear that large segments of white society are more concerned about tranquility and the status quo than about justice, equality, and humanity. So, in a real sense, our nation's summer's riots are caused by our nation's winters of delay. And as long as America postpones justice, we stand in the position of having these recurrences of violence and riots over and over again. Social justice and progress are the absolute guarantors of riot prevention.[39]

The "winters of delay" of social justice and progress, as rightly recognized by Dr. King, led to an event like the 1992 Los Angeles Riots.

Returning to Camus's essay and as referenced in Capistrán's painting of Empire Liquor/Numero Uno, the only possible reaction to the injustice of the Harlins or King case was disorder. And how can one resist the influences and control of an existing system of oppression? Refuse to abide by its logic—a logic that allowed those who brutalized Black people on videotape to walk free. Thus disorder is unrest, and unrest is a riot. Unrest isn't easily predicted or controlled, making it a powerful tool of resistance and expression. It is a tool, too, whose abuse has the potential to replicate unjust violence.

Rewind: April 1992

On the afternoon of April 29, 1992, fifteen-year-old Capistrán was on his one-and-a-half-hour bus ride home to South Central from high school in Venice—a school his parents thought would create a safe distance between him and the violence in their neighborhood. Capistrán remembers hearing more whispering than what was typical of the usually quiet bus passengers. But he did not pay much attention, preferring to keep to himself during the long trek. However, as he got closer and closer to home, he recalls the passengers' conversations becoming louder, clearer, and more troubled: The jury acquitted the cops who beat King. After he got off the bus and approached his family's home, his mother met him outside, worried and screaming in Spanish, "Where were you? Don't you know what's happening?" The neighborhood was erupting, and news stations were already broadcasting live the protests-turned-looting and the assaults at Florence and Normandie Avenues just a couple of miles away. Indeed, the violence that happened at this intersection would make the neighborhood infamous and forever marked as a site of so-called revenge.

During our tour of empty lots over twenty years later, we jumped into Capistrán's blue pickup and drove less than two and a half miles from Numero Uno to the intersection. I could still visualize the protests, fires, and devastation, especially the righteous anger caused by the acquittal of the police officers who brutalized King and the spectacular re-creation of this brutality in the damage inflicted on non-Black bodies. There were no visible signs of the unrest left around the bustling intersection of cars, buses, pedestrians, and mom-and-pop stores. Even some of the decades-old, blighted lots were being rebuilt with fresh wooden framing for new constructions. Still, the intersection holds onto the history of unrest, not only in its still-empty lots, but in those who witnessed and survived the destruction.

On the first day of unrest in 1992, helicopter reporter Bob Tur and cameraperson Marika Gerrard, who together constituted the Los Angeles News Service, captured the events as they unfolded in real time at the intersection of Florence and Normandie. Tur piloted the helicopter and narrated the disturbing attacks that Gerrard recorded, and news stations across the world picked up the live feed and replayed recordings of the shocking and gruesome scenes over and over for their audiences.[40]

Early in the recording, Tur expressed shock that there were no police at the scene Gerrard was capturing—a scene where people were looting a convenience store and pedestrians were attempting to stop drivers in the street. He interrupted his narration to make distress calls to authorities but learned that police officers were given a tactical alert to stay out of the area. Gerrard then scanned the surrounding neighborhood with her camera, confirming that there were no police within range. In fact, emergency responders would never arrive.

Several times, Tur and Gerrard sounded sirens and lowered their helicopter in an attempt to frighten attackers away from victims. Their efforts were ineffective, and instead their helicopter became a target.[41] Tur's expressions of helplessness at the inability to thwart attacks accented the horrific images Gerrard captured on the live broadcast.

One of the assaults Tur and Gerrard captured was that of Reginald Denny, a white truck driver who was attacked by six Black men. Tur would describe this incident as "the bookend" to the beating Rodney King had endured the year before.[42] Sánchez describes Denny's physical assault as a "counterimage of the inhumane beating" of King.[43] Yet such attempts to liken the beatings to each other wholly overlook the profound differences between them. King was a civilian who was assaulted by policemen public servants and representatives of the law—while other law enforcement officers watched and none of them intervened. A better comparison to the police beating of King would be the numerous other unjust assaults Black civilians have endured at the hands of the law since the early days of the country. It is easier and more convenient to ignore how our country's long history of state-sanctioned racial violence played a role in the King beating than to acknowledge just how rare it is for Black civilians to violently assault a white one. The careless attempts to compare the King and Denny beatings push to the periphery the fact that Black civilians were those who also came to Denny's rescue—not police. If anything, the two beatings make clear that law enforcement cannot be trusted to serve and protect civilians.

Tur's footage of Denny's beating seared an indelible image into the nation's collective memory of the unrest. News outlets played the film and reproduced stills of it again and again as they had aired King's videotaped assault over and over in the year leading to the acquittal of the police officers. With a bird's-eye view, Gerrard captured the Denny beating in broad daylight, and television viewers saw the disturbing assault with unprecedented clarity. From the expressions of the men as they hit and kicked Denny to the blood that seeped from his head and face, Denny's attack was vivid and gruesome. Perhaps the graphic imagery explains, in part, the seemingly endless mass consumption of the footage. Yet Denny's was not the only attack caught on tape. In fact, over thirty other people were assaulted.[44] While Denny was one of two white people, both men, attacked at the intersection, the rest of the victims were men, women, and in one case a child of Asian and Latino ethnicities.[45]

In "Reading Reginald Denny," Sánchez notes, "The dramatic image of the fallen Denny, a white victim of black rage, signified for many the mayhem of the worst modern race riot in U.S. history."[46] He then warns, "[Denny's] representation as a victim promises to continue to obscure racial privilege and to condone racial fears."[47] Anna Deveare Smith observes in *Twilight: Los Angeles, 1992* (1994), "We tend to think of race as us and them—us or them being black or white depending on one's own color."[48] The Denny beating seems to have reinforced the familiar history of white and Black racial violence in the United States—a racial narrative that arguably defines the nation. It also allowed Americans to conveniently simplify the complexity of the unrest that took place at the intersection of Florence and Normandie Avenues, obscuring the multiethnic and cross-racial nature of the assaults in our national collective memory.

The Latino Experience of Unrest

In addition to the date paintings dedicated to Harlins and King, Capistrán painted *Wednesday, April 29, 1992 (Fidel)* (2012) to reference both the first day of the unrest and Fidel Lopez, a Guatemalan immigrant beaten at the intersection of Florence and Normandie (Figure 1.3).[49] After Denny

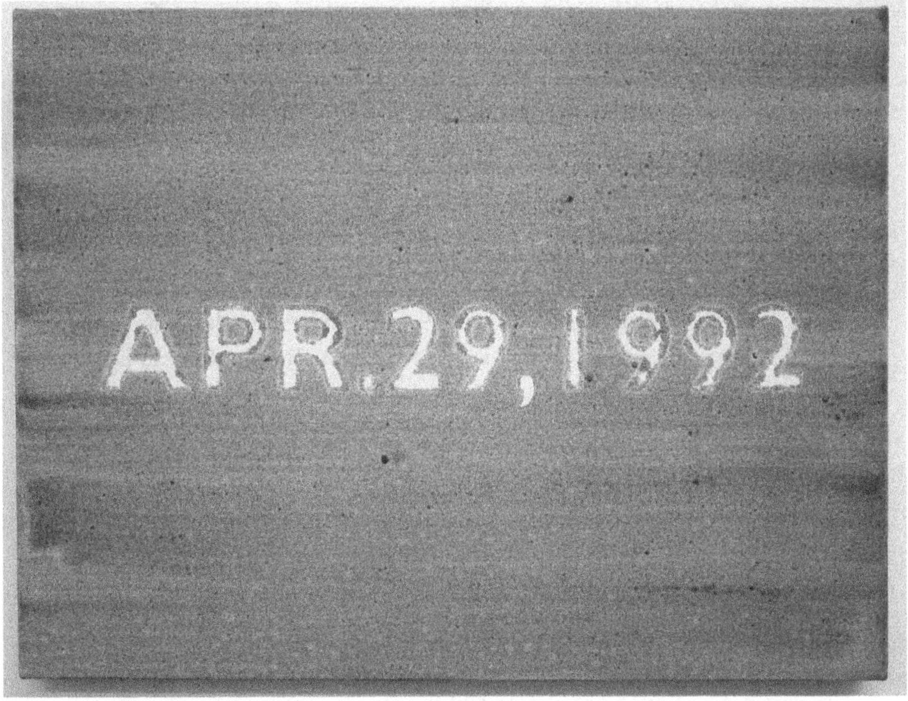

FIGURE 1.3 Juan Capistrán, *Wednesday, April 29, 1992 (Fidel)*, 2012. Blood, sweat, tears, orange juice, and ash on canvas, 18¼ × 24⅜ inches (46.3 × 61.9 cm). Courtesy the artist.

escaped with the help of two bystanders, some of his assailants began pulling other drivers out of their vehicles. One of these victims was Lopez, and although he experienced a harrowing beating like Denny's, his attack was given far less news coverage.[50] Unlike Denny's assault, the attack on Lopez did not neatly fall into the white-Black framing of racial violence and did not make sense as retribution for the white-on-Black violence that occurred with the police beating of King or even the Korean-on-Black violence that happened when Du killed Harlins. Did his attackers view him as white? Then what of the diverse Asian residents whom they also beat? How do we make sense of the ethnic and racial diversity of these victims?

As a survivor of a horrific videotaped assault, Lopez experienced a secondary form of violence. Thousands of television viewers had witnessed the pain he endured during the unrest, yet the Denny beating overshadowed it. Most historical and scholarly accounts of the unrest also ignore Lopez's experience.[51] His value as a person and his presence in history have been, for the most part, disappeared. This also holds true for the twenty-eight other Latinos, Latin Americans, and Asian Americans attacked at the intersection of Florence and Normandie Avenues. Their ethnicities complicated the popular Black-white racial binary that media and scholars preferred in their efforts to make sense of the event and its disorder. As a result, the racially and ethnically complex experiences of the unrest fell out of popular memory.

Like his date painting of Harlins, Capistrán rendered the remembrance of Lopez and his assault with white sans serif text and a wash composed of blood, sweat, and tears. The wash for the painting also contained orange juice—a reference to Harlins's death and an implication that it and Du's sentencing were key factors that led to the unrest. The painting for Lopez included an extra ingredient: ashes. Capistrán collected what he describes as "ashes" from empty lots near the intersection of Vermont Avenue and Manchester Boulevard in South Central—empty because during the unrest arsonists had burned down the buildings that stood on them. The dirt he gathered from these properties is symbolic. It represents the ashes that rained down on Los Angeles after the first fires were set. It also symbolizes the ashes of those who died, like Harlins and others killed by acts of racial violence. At the same time, they refer to the bereaved—those left behind to mourn the dead and carry on their memories.[52] Even those who survived, like Lopez or witnesses of the events, carry with them the experience and memory of the senseless brutality. In fact, Capistrán's memory of Lopez's beating, which he first saw on TV, was concretized through the recollection of the beating by Lopez's nephew, whom the artist met in college.[53]

To be sure, it is imperative for us to consider the Latino experience of the 1992 Los Angeles Riots explicitly. Their role wasn't inconsequential or even secondary to that played by Blacks, Koreans, or whites. The fact is that Latinos were both the victims of violence and the victimizers.[54]

Capistrán reflected on the history of the Latino experience even in his choice to debut *From a Whisper to a Scream* at Zona Maco, a contemporary art fair in Mexico City, instead of in Los Angeles or elsewhere in the United States.[55] Capistrán recalls how viewers at the fair connected the violence he references in his art to that of Mexican police and cartels in the country's ongoing drug wars. Yet the unrest in Los Angeles affected Mexicans directly. Between April 29 and May 5, 1992, Latinos, including Mexican nationals and people of Mexican descent, owned between 30 and 40 percent of the stores that were destroyed during the unrest. These Latinos made up the second largest ethnic group, after Asians, to lose property.[56] And Latinos were the single largest ethnic group arrested by law enforcement, comprising 51 percent of those arrested for civil disturbances within the jurisdiction of Los Angeles.[57] This number includes Latin American immigrants, both legal residents and undocumented workers, mostly from Mexico.

On July 6, 1992, the Los Angeles Office of the District Director of the Immigration and Naturalization Service (INS) reported statistics regarding "riot aliens" who were arrested and interviewed for removal. Of the 1,234 Latin American immigrants listed as being interviewed by the INS, 994 were Mexican. Of these Mexicans, INS officials processed 908—over 91 percent—for deportation.[58]

After the unrest, when independent investigators interviewed Police Chief Daryl Gates about the overwhelming number of Latino arrests by the LAPD, he responded, "This was essentially a black riot, right from the beginning. A lot of Hispanics got caught up in it."[59] His answer was at best unsatisfactory. At worst, it was tied so strongly and blindly to orthodox racial views of unrest that he was completely dismissive of the significant Latino experiences as both participants in the unrest and police targets for arrest. Together, despite the cross-racial and multiethnic participation in looting and the city's relative population rates according to race and ethnicity, Latinos and African Americans made up 87 percent of those who were arrested during the 1992 Los Angeles Riots.[60]

Capistrán continued to explore Black and Brown connections in a limited-edition booklet for the Zona Maco exhibition of *From a Whisper to a Scream*, which he made in collaboration with his wife, graphic designer and book artist Hazel Mandujano (Figure 1.4).[61] On its surface, the booklet is understated, with black font against a white background. The simple design also mutes the incendiary implication of the text on the back of the booklet. Unfolded, the booklet reveals a short exhibition essay by writer Margaret Zuckerman. On the other side, it contains floating images from a work Capistrán made with two $1 bills that slowly fold into an origami gun (Figure 1.5). The folded dollar bills simultaneously reference Harlins, who was shot dead while clutching $2, the childhood activity of creating toy weapons out of paper, and the normalization of violence in our culture.

Inside the booklet is a separate print. The offset poster consists of an untitled full-bleed image that Capistrán took from an amateur video recording of Lopez's beating (Figure 1.6).[62] The still is dark in tone, slightly blurred, and looks reminiscent of those that Tur and Gerrard captured via helicopter of assault victims. However, the bystander who filmed Lopez's beating captured it close-up and at street level. It shows Lopez in the foreground, on his hands and knees. Directly behind him stands a Black man with his arms raised above his head. He wasn't one of the men who attacked Lopez. Instead, he was the person who saved Lopez's life.

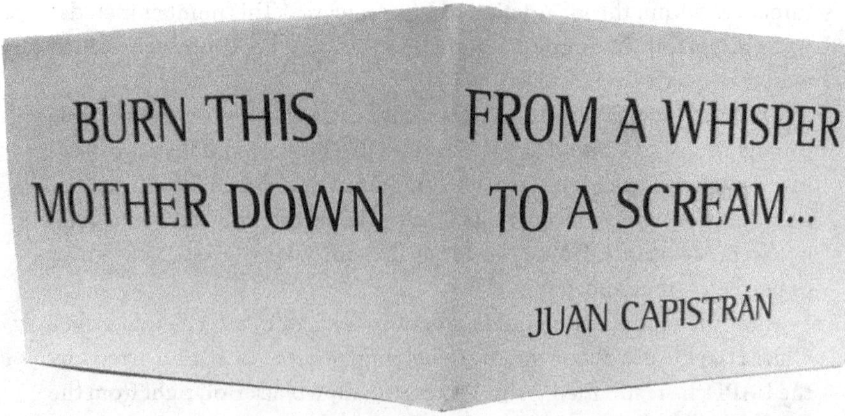

FIGURE 1.4 Juan Capistrán and Hazel Mandujano, *From a Whisper to a Scream* Exhibition Booklet, 2012. Courtesy the artists.

Not long before this moment was captured on videotape, South Central resident Reverend Bennie Newton watched live coverage of the Denny beating. Fearing the truck driver would die without intervention, Reverend Newton ran to the scene.[63] Denny escaped with the help of other television viewers who came out to the street to rescue him, but the mob continued to assault other passersby before encountering and pulling Lopez out of his truck. They repeatedly punched and kicked him, smashing a heavy object into his head.[64] In the amateur video, as he lay on the street writhing in pain, blood seeped from his wounds, staining his light-colored shirt a deep crimson.[65]

Sánchez suggests, "The Los Angeles riots demonstrated that injustice can provoke African-American rage, not only against white authority, but also against 'racialized others,' most notably Asians and Latinos living among blacks in newly 'reintegrated' communities."[66] This "reintegration" of South Central was defined by the deindustrialization of the neighborhood and the loss of manufacturing jobs. While the economy struggled to recover, Asian and especially Latin American immigration increased in the 1980s—partly as a result of US economic policies that affected Mexico and US political intervention and aid to paramilitary groups in Central America. From 1979 to 1989, 40 percent of all jobs created in Los Angeles paid less than $15,000 a year, and many businesses hired recent immigrants for these low-wage positions.[67] Still, in the three years leading to the unrest, South Central lost 150,000 manufacturing jobs.[68] These circumstances left African Americans with few employment opportunities.[69]

By 1992, Latinos were the majority population in South Central and

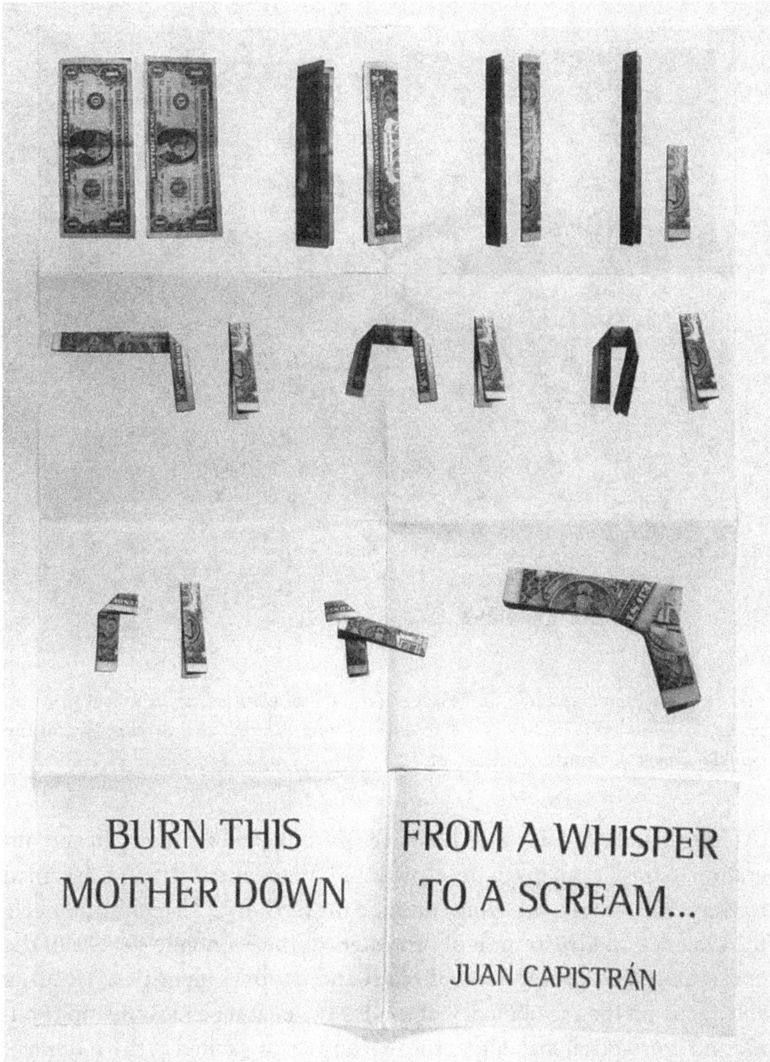

FIGURE 1.5 Juan Capistrán and Hazel Mandujano, *From a Whisper to a Scream* Exhibition Booklet (interior detail), 2012. Courtesy the artists.

made up 45 percent of the Koreatown population—another neighborhood of Los Angeles ravaged by looting and arson during the unrest.[70] Sánchez argues that at the intersection of Florence and Normandie Avenues, the violent assaults were "not about who was white, but who was not black."[71] The scholar then asserted that from the onset, the 1992 Los Angeles Riots were "fundamentally an anti-immigrant spectacle."[72] Despite

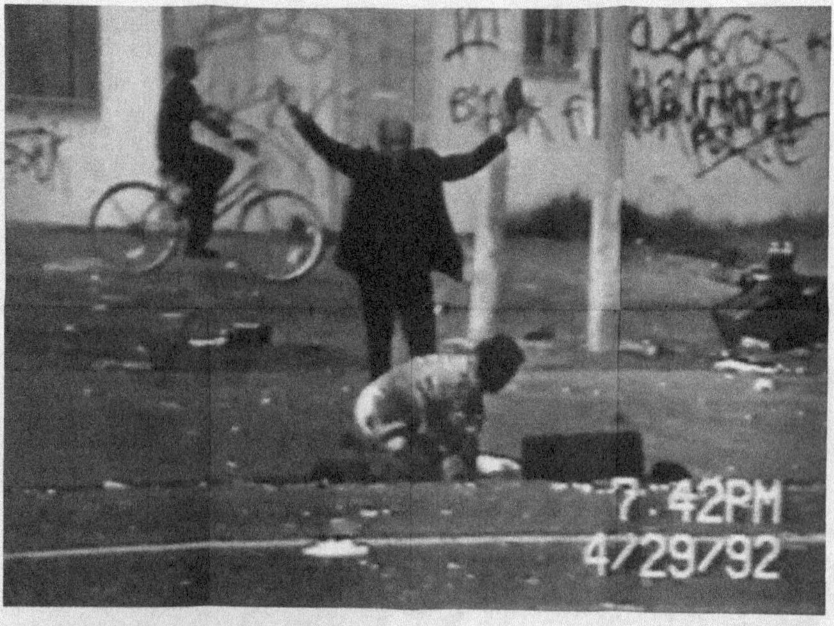

FIGURE 1.6 Juan Capistrán and Hazel Mandujano, *Untitled*, 2012. Offset print on paper, 19 11/16 × 27 9/16 inches (50 × 70 cm). *From a Whisper to a Scream* Exhibition Booklet (insert). Courtesy the artist.

the long history of Latino and Asian citizenship and residency in and migration to the city, many in the crowd at Florence and Normandie seemed to view these groups as having "invaded the territory."[73] Sánchez connects the violence and frustration of protesters to the economic demise of the community and perceptions of racial and national identities.[74] Thus, a sole focus on the racial binary of the Denny beating elides the multiethnic and cross-racial makeup of those who were assaulted at the Florence-Normandie intersection in South Central. It also obscures the complex socioeconomic histories at play that had devastated the neighborhood's economy and employment opportunities, which in turn led to heightened resentment of immigrants among working Americans of color.[75]

The irony of a sentiment such as Latinos or Asians "invading territory" in Los Angeles or California more broadly goes unquestioned, to harmful effect. While African-descended people were among the first group of Spanish colonizers to the land that would become Los Angeles in 1781, the population of African descendants remained very low through the nineteenth and early twentieth centuries, especially compared to the non-Black Latino and Asian populations. In 1910, there were only 7,599 African American Los Angeles residents. The Second Great Migration brought a wave of Black people to California, raising the number of African American residents in Los Angeles to 55,114 in 1940 and then to 118,888 in 1944.[76] Then, by 1960, the Black population in the city nearly quadrupled, to 461,546.[77] Yet, apart from Indigenous peoples and their descendants, all other racial and ethnic groups in California have been immigrants. The dominance of the Black-white racial binary skews this reality and obscures our understandings of who belongs. Furthermore, such obfuscation reinforces the misconception that white and Black residents have always resided in Los Angeles, whereas Latino and Asians residents are somehow always newcomers. These views, grounded in white supremacy and xenophobia, often pit marginalized peoples of color against each other in the fight for resources like "territory."

The emphasis on a Black-white racial binary weakens cross-racial solidarity. In her 1993 *Time* article on immigration titled "On the Back of Blacks," Toni Morrison argues that immigrants to the United States have economic and social opportunities at the expense of African American progress. She writes, "In race talk, the move into mainstream America always means buying into the notion of American blacks as the real aliens. Whatever the ethnicity or nationality of the immigrant, his nemesis is understood to be African American."[78] Sánchez, describing Asian Americans and Latinos as "lightning rods for discussions of race, equality, and the meaning of citizenship in contemporary America," argues that Morrison ignores the long history of racial discrimination in the United States that was aimed at these two groups. He states, "It is clear that all Americans can get caught in the white-black paradigm of race relations, a model that relies on opposites, opposites which too often substitute for the complexity and diversity of social and ethnic relations in the late twentieth century United States."[79]

What Morrison and Sánchez make clear is that the emphasis on racialized dichotomous thinking overshadows the ways marginalized populations experience similar forms of bigotry and discrimination. This not only creates dependence on the approval of white authority but also impedes cross-racial coalition building against economic, social, and political oppression.[80] Thankfully, for Lopez and several other victims who endured assaults at the intersection of Florence and Normandie, the anti-immigrant behaviors and racial/ethnic targeting that Sánchez observed did not thwart the rescue efforts of Reverend Newton and other Black residents.

In the amateur footage of Lopez's beating, the cameraperson captures him up close as he drifts in and out of consciousness and a Black man attempts to slice off his ear. Then another Black man douses Lopez with gasoline, and still another spray-paints Lopez's torso and genitals the color black. Once Reverend Newton approaches the scene, he covers Lopez's body with his own and screams to the assailants, "Kill him, and you have to kill me too!"[81] The reverend risked his own life to protect Lopez's, bravely enacting his love for a neighbor he did not know.[82]

The live televised beating of Denny and other victims at the intersection of Florence and Normandie Avenues emboldened Black residents like Newton who lived nearby to risk their own safety to save others. Among those who ran from their living rooms to the scene of the assaults were James Henry, who saved Belizean immigrant Raul Aguilar, who was beaten into a coma and run over by a car; Donald Jones, who protected Sai-Choi Choi after Choi had been beaten and robbed; and Gregory Alan-Williams, who rescued Takao Hirata from an assault by the crowd.[83]

I return now to the moment depicted in the appropriated video still of Capistrán's untitled print poster, which he included in the exhibition booklet for *From a Whisper to a Scream* (Figure 1.6). Eventually, when Lopez's attackers stepped back, Reverend Newton stood up, clutching a Bible. As Lopez roused and began lifting himself from the ground, Newton raised his arms in prayer. The image Capistrán mobilizes for the print depicts a man in the background who rides past the scene on a bicycle, seemingly unaware of or perhaps indifferent to the hostility. The artist could have reproduced an image of the scene without the bicyclist in the frame, but the apparent apathy of the bike rider seems to be a metaphor for our failure as a nation to recognize Lopez and remember the vicious attack he endured on the first day of the unrest.

On the back of the print, Capistrán includes a quote by Camus, from *The Rebel: An Essay on Man in Revolt* (1951), that reads, "We all carry within us our places of exile, our crimes, our ravages. Our task is not to unleash them on the world; it is to fight them in ourselves and in others."[84] Camus urges readers to resist oppression with regard for the fundamental value of human life because rebellion violently enacted against innocent others re-creates injustice and tyranny. The horrific violence that occurred at the intersection of Florence and Normandie Avenues and the secondary violence Lopez and other victims experienced when they were forgotten reinstated the forms of discrimination that many sought to protest during the unrest. Capistrán's print and the history it captures encourages viewers to resist both hatred and indifference. Indeed, our lives are too intertwined to be unscathed by the profound intergenerational loss such actions create, and we must not lose the opportunity to build lasting coalition and solidarity for justice. Still, when one considers the poster as part of the larger exhibition booklet Capistrán and Mandujano made, which includes the serial images of how to turn $2 bills into an origami gun, we are reminded of how easy and normal it is to enact violence against others. The most difficult thing to do is resist this logic of racial violence.

Art History Reimagined and Browned

Capistrán further explored notions of detachment and neutrality in the form, composition, and art-making techniques he used in his date paintings, which he borrowed from major artworks by On Kawara and Andy Warhol. More than mere copying, the younger artist's appropriation is an aesthetic and conceptual strategy to imbue a genealogy with the undeniable racial and class politics he deemed lacking in certain classic works.[85] Capistrán's revisions of Kawara and Warhol serve as sociopolitical critiques of art history, in addition to remembrances of unrest, which deepens the political efficacy of the aesthetic and broadens the scope of America's Black-white racial binary.

Compositionally, Capistrán's date paintings reference Kawara's *Today* series (1966–2014) (see Figure 1.7). Each of Kawara's paintings mark a particular hand-lettered date, centered horizontally across a solid monochromatic field of acrylic paint, which he usually rendered in shades of blacks, blues, or reds. The dates, which Kawara typically painted white, adhere to the language and style of abbreviation specific to the city or country in which he made the work. Each painting documents the date the artist began and completed it. The artist also kept newspaper clippings for each painting he completed, which he stored in handmade boxes not meant for display. When Kawara failed to complete a painting in one day, he destroyed it.[86] Thus, the *Today* series is at once a record of the incommensurable and ordinary nature of passing time and a testament to the many destroyed paintings that did not meet the artist's parameters. Made over a course of almost five decades, until his death in 2014, Kawara's repetitive and ritualistic art-making practice informed the method Capistrán adopted.[87]

Unlike Kawara's unruffled surfaces, Capistrán's application of paint for each of his canvases is done with a large brush to purposely leave visible brushstrokes and uneven concentrations of color, echoing that of Andy Warhol in *Red Race Riot* (1963) (Figure 1.8). Warhol applied a thin and uneven wash of magenta paint over multiple prints of three black-and-white photographs taken by Charles Moore. Sourced from a 1963 issue of *Life* magazine, Moore's photographs capture three perspectives of two

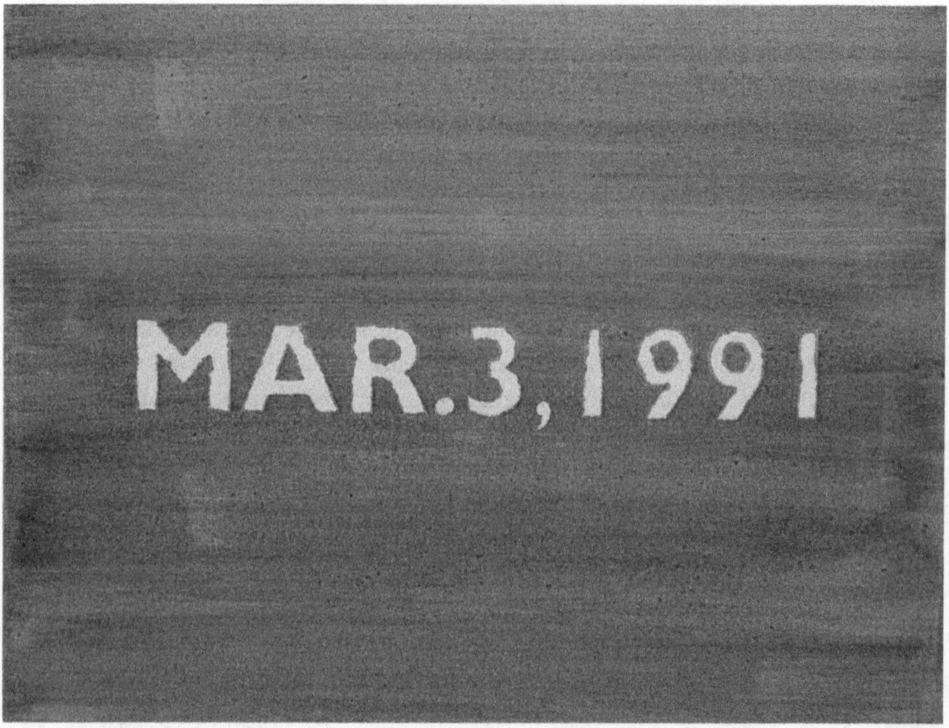

FIGURE 1.7 Juan Capistrán, *Sunday, March 3, 1991 (Rodney)*, 2012. Blood, sweat, and tears on canvas, 18¼ × 24⅜ inches (46.3 × 61.9 cm). Courtesy the artist.

police dogs attacking a Black man—not during a "riot" as the title of the painting suggests, but during a civil rights demonstration in Birmingham, Alabama. Warhol made *Red Race Riot* for a 1964 exhibition of new paintings, which would become known as the *Death and Disaster* series for its focus on media-documented tragedies, such as plane and car crashes, suicides, and funerals. Warhol also reused the Moore photographs for several other variations of "race riot" paintings. For these other iterations, the artist combined Moore's photographs in different arrangements, including the use of a single photo, and painted the canvases with different colored washes or none at all.[88]

Capistrán's art historical citations encourage a reconsideration of the emotional efficacy and politics of the avant-garde tradition he references.[89] Warhol understood the consequence of repeated images as one that alienates the viewer. He explained, "When you see a gruesome picture over and over again, it doesn't really have any effect."[90] Yet Warhol's *Red Race Riot* arguably reveals the opposite. His repeated use of Moore's photographs

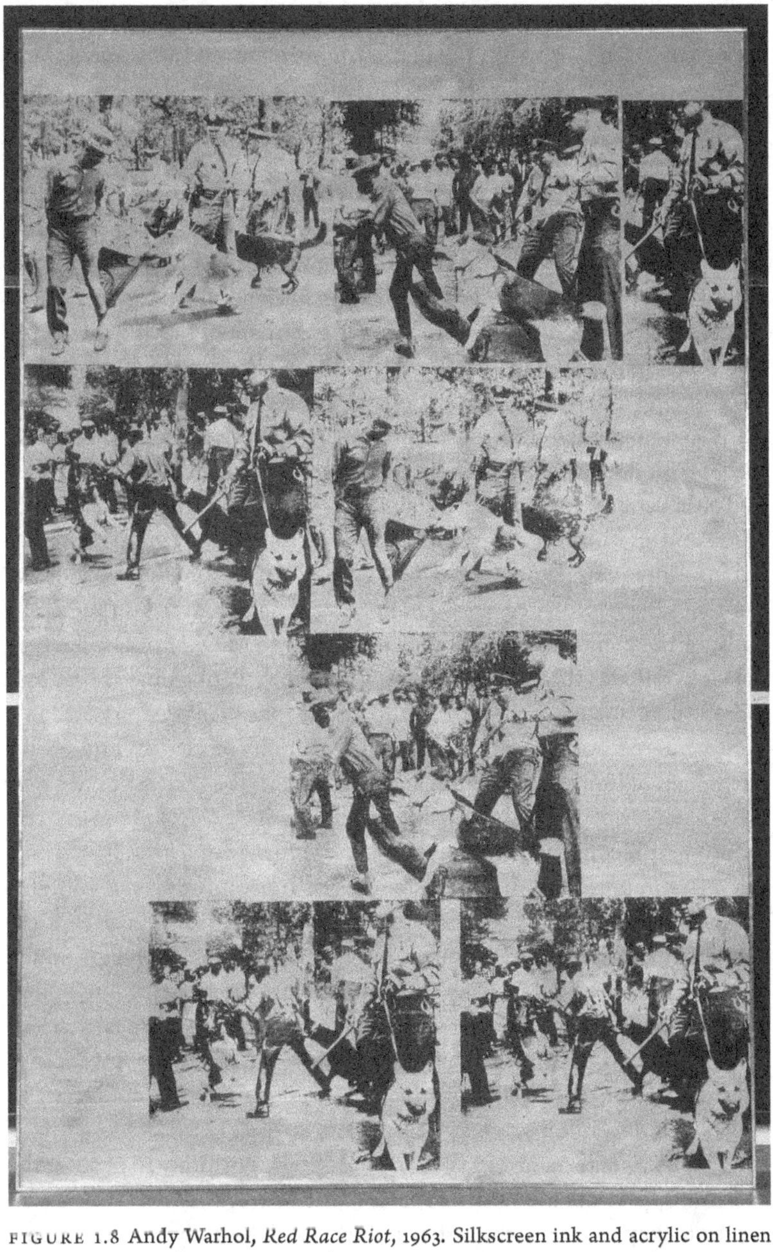

FIGURE 1.8 Andy Warhol, *Red Race Riot*, 1963. Silkscreen ink and acrylic on linen 128¼ × 83 inches (325.8 × 210.8 cm). Andy Warhol, Image and Artwork © 2025 The Andy Warhol Foundation for the Visual Arts, Inc. / Licensed by Artists Rights Society (ARS), New York.

along with the painting's overwhelming, larger-than-life scale and jarring neon-pink color emphasize the disassociation captured at the civil rights demonstration: The white police seem to watch, devoid of feeling, as their dogs maul a Black man and tear off his clothing with their teeth. The artistic emphasis on the violent image with the large dimensions, color, and repetitious use of images increases our awareness of the police's inhumane treatment.[91] This is not to say that the photographer's original publication of the images didn't have any effect. Quite the contrary, Moore's photographs of the Alabama civil rights demonstration moved readers of *Life* and encouraged critiques of the police mistreatment of Black civilians. We can instead understand Warhol's statement on the consequences of repetition as one that recognizes the potential of inciting indifference, particularly in a media-determined environment and consumer-driven system that exploit the pain of others for consumption and entertainment.

To this end, Capistrán's paintings align with those of Warhol in technique and method, even as the younger artist refuses figural representations. This strategy denies the perverse pleasures some viewers derive from looking at violence, particularly violent acts inflicted on the Black body, or the racial stereotypes they may bring to the artwork. Indeed, in the United States there exists a long legacy of circulating images that capture the pain, torture, and murder of Black people. While Capistrán could have rendered nonviolent figural representations of Harlins and others referenced in his date paintings, such a choice in the context of the 1992 Los Angeles Riots still carried risks. So-called riots in the United States often arouse preconceived notions of race, criminality, and criticism, which can result in profound misunderstandings of unrest (or even civil rights demonstrations, in the case of Warhol's "race riot" series). As artist Kang Seung Lee observes about his own series of inscrutable drawings on the 1992 Los Angeles Riots, "Even though there are no recognizable bodies in the works, people still see race."[92] Historically, media representations and mainstream political talking points about "riots" often paint them as episodes of senseless Black criminality—fantasies that also often paint whites as innocent targets.

Capistrán's date paintings allow viewers the opportunity to observe the date and appreciate the formal aspects of the artwork. Then, on closer inspection, they recognize the artist's references to the body, with the blood, sweat, and tears that the wash is made of and his use of first names in the subtitles. Knowledge of the bodily fluids as a medium in the paintings is intended to prompt an affective response in viewers and to signal the subject matters' deeper meaning inasmuch as the paintings capture more than mere dates or the passing of time, as in Kawara's series. In this way, Capistrán indirectly asks viewers to consider the stakes that led to tears, blood, and sweat and then the use of them to paint over the dates.

Of course, it is possible that viewers would not recognize the references to the body without the information of a wall label or other informative text. Indeed, Capistrán realizes that many viewers might only understand a portion of any given work or might never read his art as he intends. This is not unique to Capistrán. It is a quandary that is nearly universal, especially for conceptual, minimal, and abstract art.[93] For instance, Byron Kim, in his popular ongoing series *Synecdoche* (1991–present), matches his paint to the specific skin colors of sitters; yet viewers may not register the resulting solid-colored paintings of various brown hues as representations of real people's skin colors. Both Capistrán's and Kim's gestures nonetheless inscribe modern and contemporary visual art languages with notions of race and speak to art history's obsession with a formalism whose intentions never seem to be questioned if the artist is white.

I assert that the two artists highlight the way that the concept of race itself is a type of modern visual language—a historical convention used to classify people based on physical appearance.[94] Moreover, Capistrán, like Kim, blurs racial difference in his artworks by eliminating figurative representations and markers of physiognomy, race, and ethnicity. The artist thus forces us as viewers to contend with the variations of hue in his allusions to race, encouraging us to make sense of what we see and find relationships between the date paintings. In doing so, we begin to recognize patterns of similarities between paintings that represent those who might otherwise be seen as vastly different because of processes of racialization. The brownness of paintings like Capistrán's and Kim's thus highlight our collective Brownness as humans. In *The Sense of Brown*, José Esteban Muñoz articulates a collective Brownness, which he calls the "Brown commons" and describes as those whose existence in the world has been defined, in part, by vulnerability to the violence of capital, racism, and xenophobia. Furthermore, this collective Brownness, he asserts, is "coexistent, affiliates, and intermeshes with blackness, Asianness, indigenousness, and other terms that manifest descriptive force" without erasing or devaluing the particular identities subjects may find useful and critical for their being in the world.[95] Similarly, the surfaces for Capistrán's date paintings are like a brown skin (Figures 1.1–1.3). The real human subjects each painting represents are bound by the experience of racial violence. While each individual painting comprises a specific date and slightly different mixtures of media, together they are unified through style, composition, and application of materials. They are more alike than they are different. The artist's critical use of formalism highlights how racialization relies heavily on arbitrary markers of difference, and at the same time it reveals how racialization is a method of formalism that is faulty for its overreliance on difference. This reliance on difference instead of our collective Brownness or shared humanity can be instrumentalized to pull us apart. It dehumanizes and creates a false and dangerous us-versus-them binary—the currency of white supremacy and xenophobia.

Unrest and the Refusal of Representation

Capistrán's adoption of Kawara's simple gesture of painting a date creates work that is at once stripped of and loaded with content. When asked why he decided to revisit the memory of Harlins for *From a Whisper to a Scream*, Capistrán replied that he reexamines the event with every annual anniversary of the 1992 Los Angeles Riots.[96] His response suggests that he does not have a choice to ignore his memories or experiences of unrest. For Capistrán, the date of Harlins's death and the anniversary of the unrest mark a collapse of time—a collapse of the past with the present. Whereas Kawara's date paintings may suggest the banality of time, Capistrán's date painting suggests that history haunts the present and that the experience of loss and the sorrow it incites endures the passage of time.

Recently, the twenty-fifth anniversary of the 1992 Los Angeles Riots yielded work by other artists who have adopted similar practices to obscure or abstract the human figure. For instance, Jeff Beall used the visual language of abstraction to reference the twenty-three still-unsolved homicides that occurred during the unrest in the two-part series, *Unsolved* (2017) (Figure 1.9).[97] The first part consists of black oil stick rubbings of the approximate locations in South Central, Koreatown, Compton, Watts, and Hollywood, among other places, where the homicides took place. The second part consists of photographs that capture the completed rubbings in the settings Beall made them. He placed the vellum-like paper for the rubbings directly on asphalt and pulled the black oil stick back and forth to capture the highly textured ground (Figure 1.10). He considers the drawings similar to gravestone rubbings, which capture "the memories of these 23 people."[98] In this vein, we can also understand Capistrán's painting of Harlins's death date as a type of death marker.

Beall's rubbings, when seen without his photographs, offer little information beyond their materiality. They create what art critic Carolina A. Miranda described as a "chapel of abstract reflection."[99] Indeed, Beall's influence for the rubbings came from Richard Serra's *Out-of-Round* series (1998–99) of black oil stick drawings, which were not only drawn on Serra's studio floor, but whose concern with materials, texture, and

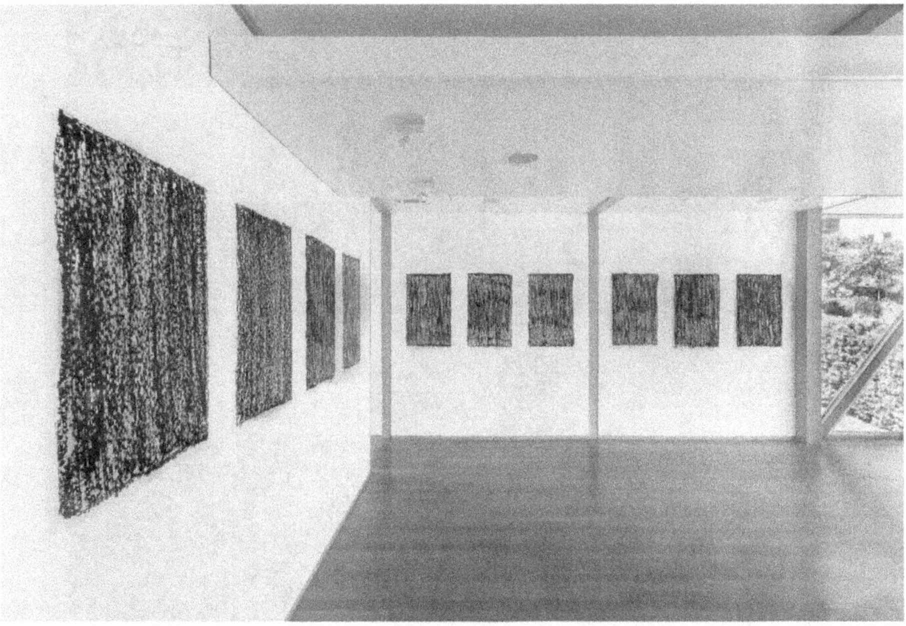

FIGURE 1.9 Jeff Beall, Installation view of the exhibition *Unsolved: 1992 LA Uprising @ 25 Years*, April 29–May 4, 2017, Gallery 169, Santa Monica, CA. Oil stick on polypropylene sheets, each 23 × 35 inches (58.4 × 88.9 cm). Photograph courtesy the artist.

pressure also created meditative images. However, like Capistrán's bootleg of Kawara's date paintings, Beall further reimagines Serra's process with metaphors of violence, murder, and remembrance. Beall's in situ photographs of the rubbings also tie these ideas to public sites and the everyday city streetscapes of greater Los Angeles. During an interview, as the artist and Miranda stood together in South Central where a victim was killed, Beall notes, "Santa Monica is only a 20-minute drive away from here. We are much closer than anyone seems to feel. Yet it's so easy to be in the Silver Lake hipster bubble or the Westside bubble or the Hollywood bubble, and you forget how close we really all are."[100] The artist's formal and material consistency across all twenty-three drawings ties them together even as the settings in the photographs change. That is, the photographed drawings link the seemingly disparate streetscapes together for the viewer.[101] Furthermore, like Capistrán's rendering of Harlins's death date and minimalistic painting with bodily fluids, the texture that Beall's drawings capture represent the human form symbolically and abstracted beyond visual recognition. Likewise, Capistrán's persistent making of artworks about the unrest and Beall's commitment to making rubbings and photographing

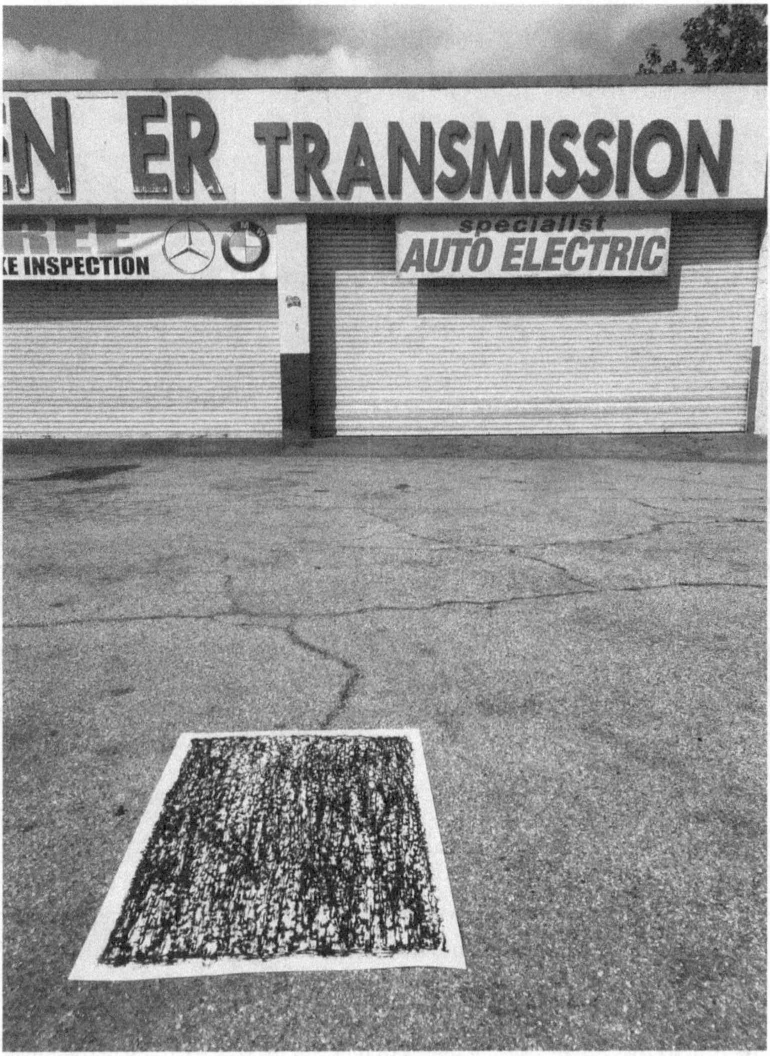

FIGURE 1.10 Jeff Beall, *Unsolved Site #4 (Wilson Alvarez)*, 2017. Inkjet print on paper, 8½ × 11 inches (21.5 × 27.9 cm). Courtesy the artist.

the place of death for all victims are a type of ritualistic, process art that Kawara exemplified in the *Today* series.

Also marking the twenty-fifth anniversary of the 1992 Los Angeles Riots was Kang Seung Lee's series *Leave of Absence* and *Untitled (la revolución es la solución)* (2017), which included drawings referencing Latasha Harlins and her death alongside photojournalistic portrayals of scenes from the looting, violence, and protests of 1992.[102] Like Capistrán and Beall,

Lee removed the human body from his works (Figure 1.11). He did so by digitally erasing or blurring the human figure in photographs, which were originally published in newspaper and magazine articles. The artist then rerendered the doctored images in graphite.[103] Lee explains his process of obscuring the human figure as a visual metaphor for "all the lives and memories lost and injured during the riots and other social unrest."[104] Conceptually, this idea is similar to what motivates Capistrán's and Beall's work. Like Capistrán, too, Lee's process of obscuring the body beckons viewers to consider who is and is not depicted in popular images of so-called riots. This notion especially resonates with Lee's use of sensational *Los Angeles Times* photographs portraying Korean and Korean American armed vigilantism and African American looting. Yet Capistrán's and Beall's reinterpretation of abstraction and minimalism does more than obscure the body. It speaks to how bodies were eradicated by physical assault and murder. As Capistrán once said to me about the need for ongoing conversations about complex histories of violence, "They can't be resolved with a pretty picture."[105] Representation fails. As does any attempt to contain the disorder caused by tragedy and loss. This disorder, like the

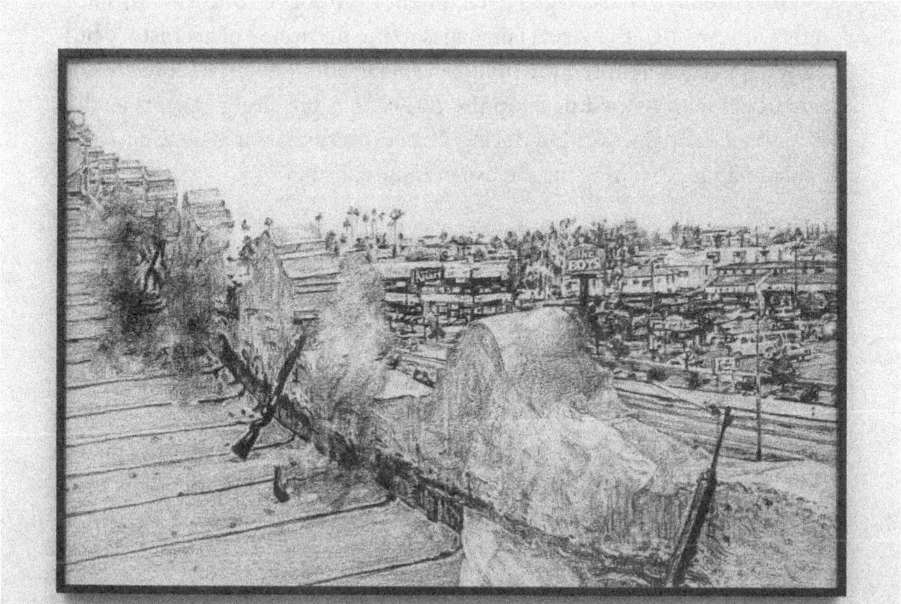

FIGURE 1.11 Kang Seung Lee, *Untitled (Korean Merchants on the Rooftop)*, 2017. Inkjet print (framed), 32¾ × 48¾ inches (83.1 × 123.8 cm). Photo: Ruben Diaz. Courtesy the artist.

disorder Camus speaks of, is related to unrest. Unrest creates disorder in the cityscape, making the so-called riot unknowable. No commission, politician, news pundit, activist, or scholar can easily define it. Because there is no neat definition that can truly capture it, the words "riot," "insurrection," "revolt," or "uprising" fail. Unrest requires an image that cannot be read easily. The aesthetic decisions made by Capistrán, or Beall and Lee, visually represent our failure to see the unrest racial violence causes just as it conveys the loss injustice creates. The refusal to represent the figure is a visual strategy that refutes immediate and facile consumption.

During the 1992 Los Angeles Riots, there was no single agenda or motivation among those who protested, looted, burned, beat, and killed. Instead, what I have recognized through the analysis of art, as Capistrán and others in this book capture, is the undercurrent of unrest—the bereavement, sorrow, grief, anger, and mourning—that resulted not only from the failure of the justice system to punish King's attackers or Harlins's murderer, but from the continual, intergenerational injustices that poor, working-class, Black, Brown, and immigrant peoples have experienced.

Capistrán's particular use of abstraction and minimalism deepens the social and emotional efficacy of the visual languages, which otherwise found currency via its alleged detachment from social concerns. This not only whitewashed the visual languages in the discipline of art history but often negated or ignored the political, social, and identarian concerns of the artists who helped develop them too.[106] After citing Harlins as the subject of his date painting during a 2012 interview with me, Capistrán explained his reasoning for the use of minimalism.

> There are always these personal narratives or threads [in my art]. I make work about the things that I know, the things that I love, and the things I experience. When you look at what I do, I want you to know that it's sincere. The work is very personal. Maybe that's why I end up choosing a very minimal aesthetic—because I want to detach it from me in a way.[107]

The artist's desire to create work that is visibly steeped in personal stakes, yet detached at the same time, is contradictory. This contradiction is a result of Capistrán's self-described "indoctrination" in the Western canon of art history and the visual languages of modernism and postmodernism in art school.[108] Indeed, through his process of referencing and appropriating other artworks, the artist demonstrates a certain respect for dominant visual languages and popular works in the Western canon even as he challenges their primacy or supposed indifference to politics and race.[109] Yet Capistrán's referencing also attests to his commitment to unravel the knotted threads that these dominant visual languages have sewn in him through his ongoing effort to further, reimagine, and create new understandings that express the importance of race and the resounding nature and impact of loss and injustice.

Post-Riot Tour: Memorialization and the Sublime

Back in Capistrán's truck, we headed one and a half miles southeast from the Normandie-Florence intersection to the intersection of Vermont and Manchester Avenues, which was less than a mile from where we started our tour at Numero Uno. We parked on Vermont across the street from the historic Pan Andreas West Theatre and the former Western Regional Headquarters of the Nation of Islam (NOI).[110] On this block stood a few empty lots whose cracked cement was surrounded by old chain-link fencing. However, one stood out for its wooden outline for a new building. This specific lot, finally slated to be rebuilt decades after its original building was razed by the fires of 1992, is significant to Capistrán's years of art-making.

In the late 1990s, as an undergraduate student at Otis, Capistrán began to delve into the legacies of the burned properties within a one-mile radius of Empire Liquor/Numero Uno. For one project, the artist proposed an anti-monument to the unrest located at the very lot we stood in front of on Vermont Avenue. The untraditional commemorative structure was to be placed at this location, across the street from the NOI headquarters.[111] The young artist's idea included a storage container that visitors could enter. Once inside, they would encounter a network of underground corridors that led to other properties across the community that had also burned down during the unrest.[112] The long trajectory of Capistrán's artistic inquiry into the 1992 Los Angeles Riots demonstrates his commitment to the history and recognition of the ongoing experience of unrest. His project also points to the importance of memorialization, especially amid this history's lingering effects on both the personal and community levels.[113]

In 1995, the City of Los Angeles awarded Chicana artist Judith F. Baca a grant for a multisite monument proposal to commemorate the 1992 Los Angeles Riots.[114] *Cultural Explainers: Portals, Bridges and Gateways* was to involve three structures that would incorporate reliefs, panels, or tiles with images of Korean, Latino, and Black Americans—those racial groups most affected by the unrest. The monuments were to include a large-scale *pyong poong*, or Korean folding screen, located in Koreatown at Ardmore Park; a shrine-like Mayan-style structure in Pico-Union at Alvarado Park; and interactive poles similar to the "ancestral poles" in West African Yoruba culture, which were to be erected in Leimert Park Village in South Central.[115] However, the project was never completed.[116] In contrast to Baca's multicultural and multisite monuments, Capistrán's anti-monument embraced its unattainability, the impossibility of linking privately owned empty lots with an underground tunnel system. To this day, no public monument or memorial exists for the 1992 Los Angeles Riots.[117]

Shortly after the anti-monument proposal, in 1998, Capistrán formed Space Invaders 13 with artist Mario Ybarra Jr.[118] The collective became interested in the ways South Central residents used the chain-link fences that surrounded the razed lots. After the unrest, locals converted the fences into makeshift community bulletin boards covered in homemade advertisements for goods and services.[119] Appropriating this practice, the artists hand-painted six signs with visual and textual puns on found plywood (Figure 1.12). They then tied the signs to the chain-link fences of empty lots near the intersections of Manchester Avenue and South Broadway, Manchester and Western Avenues, and Florence and Normandie Avenues.[120]

The series of signs comprised "sublime" paintings, which consisted of the word "sub" above the image of a green lime. These paintings invoked contemporary music references, such as the ska-punk band Sublime from nearby Long Beach whose song "April 29, 1992 (Miami)" (1996) includes the singer's first-person recollection of looting stores during the 1992 Los Angeles Riots. The lyrics also analyzed the causes for the unrest via a working-class, poor, and anti-police point of view.[121] For instance, after singer Bradley Nowell recalled how he witnessed a mother and her children looting a store for diapers, he clarified for listeners over the band's steady drumming and offbeat guitar rhythm:

> They said it was for the black man
> They said it was for the Mexican, and not for the white man
> But if you look at the street, it wasn't about Rodney King
> And this fucked up situation, and these fucked up police
> It's about coming up and staying on top
> And screaming, "1-8-7" on a motherfuckin' cop
> It's not in the paper, it's on the wall
> National Guard!
> Smoke from all around![122]

That the lyrics open an analysis to include cross-racial and class-based experiences with poverty and policing is significant, especially for Capistrán, who strove to recover experiences of the unrest beyond racial binaries.[123]

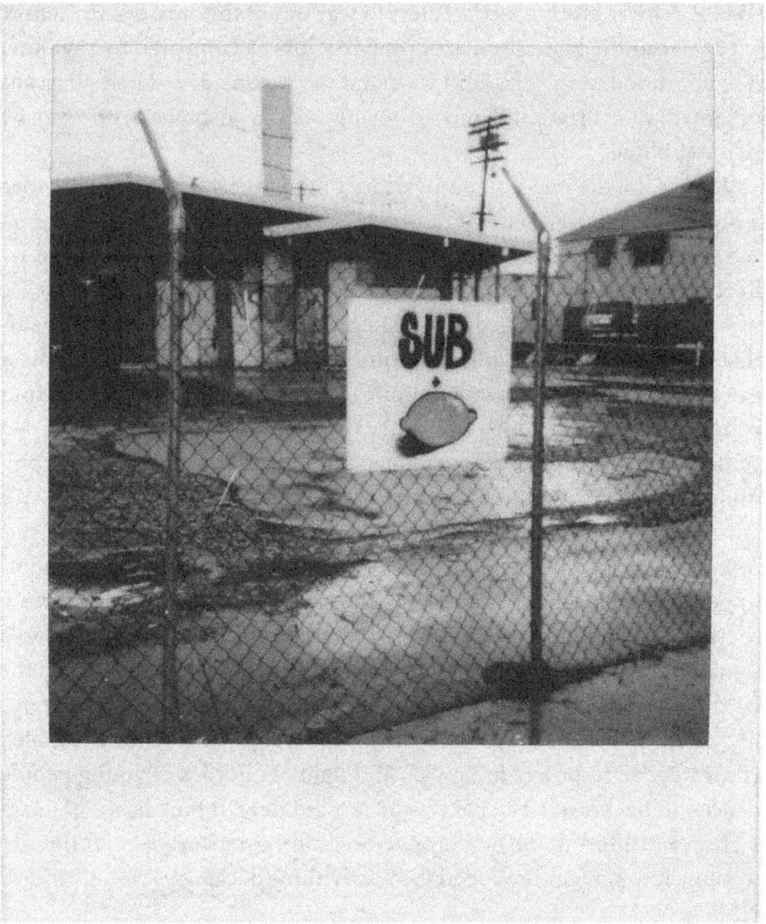

FIGURE 1.12 Space Invaders 13 (Juan Capistrán and Mario Ybarra Jr.), *Sub/Lime*, 1998. Photographic documentation of public installation of painting. Courtesy the artists.

In addition, the "sublime" paintings also marked the empty lots with the art historical reference of the "sublime," a term used to describe the aesthetic grandeur that inspires awe and wonder in viewers. Capistrán and Ybarra hung their signs near intersections in South Central that endured some of the highest rates of destruction and arson during the 1992 Los Angeles Riots. As previously mentioned, the intersection of Florence and Normandie Avenues was the notorious epicenter of the unrest and the location where looting, arson, and multiple televised beatings occurred, including those of Denny and Lopez. The intersection was also where television viewers learned from the helicopter reporters Tur and Gerrard that the LAPD was given a tactical alert to stay out of the area. South Central experienced the highest rates of property loss as compared to any other neighborhood in the city, and we can describe this devastated cityscape of looted, vandalized, and burned businesses as a postapocalyptic version of the sublime.[124]

In 1993, on the one-year anniversary of the unrest, Capistrán attended a rave in an exposed basement of a burned-down building near the intersection of Broadway and Manchester.[125] Years later, he began to reflect on the temporal, subcultural repurposing of the ruined property. He described the rave as a cathartic experience after the devastating events that led to and occurred during the unrest.[126] Many of his works on these events are attempts to create a similar purgative space. During our tour in 2015, the site of the 1993 rave still existed as an exposed basement—a testament to the long-term consequences the unrest has had for the community and perhaps the only type of monument we will ever see. We got out of the truck and walked the perimeter of the lot, which was surrounded by a chain-link fence, like so many of the others in the neighborhood. While the fences often seemed to signal only the notion of private property—even those emptied of all physical assets—this one served a functional purpose. The basement was a deep, hollowed-out gouge in the earth with nothing but planks of wood reinforcing its dirt perimeter. I imagined the mobile deejay setup, the generator, and the miles of jumbled cords needed to power the music and lights as hordes of young people danced in the bowels of what was once a building. It took heaps of imagination and effort to throw a rave here—and extreme neglect for the city to allow it to stay undeveloped for nearly three decades.

Sending Up Searchlights

Several years after our tour of South Central, Capistrán returned to the burned-out lots and the subject of the 1992 Los Angeles Riots. The series, *Psychogeography of Rage* (2019), comprised eight multimedia artworks set in South Central lots near Century Boulevard, Broadway, Vermont Avenue, and Martin Luther King Boulevard. Most were installations of giant, 4 × 1 × 2 foot, faux-brick sculptures made of fiberboard, wood, and paint that the artist leaned precariously against each other, photographed, and left unattended (Figure 1.13). Another was a digitally manipulated photo that documented the trajectory of an oversize "brick" the artist tried to throw across a lot (it did not travel far). To be sure, these "bricks" were absurd. Not only were they extremely large for an object with typical dimensions of just 8 × 2 × 3 inches, but they were extremely lightweight and

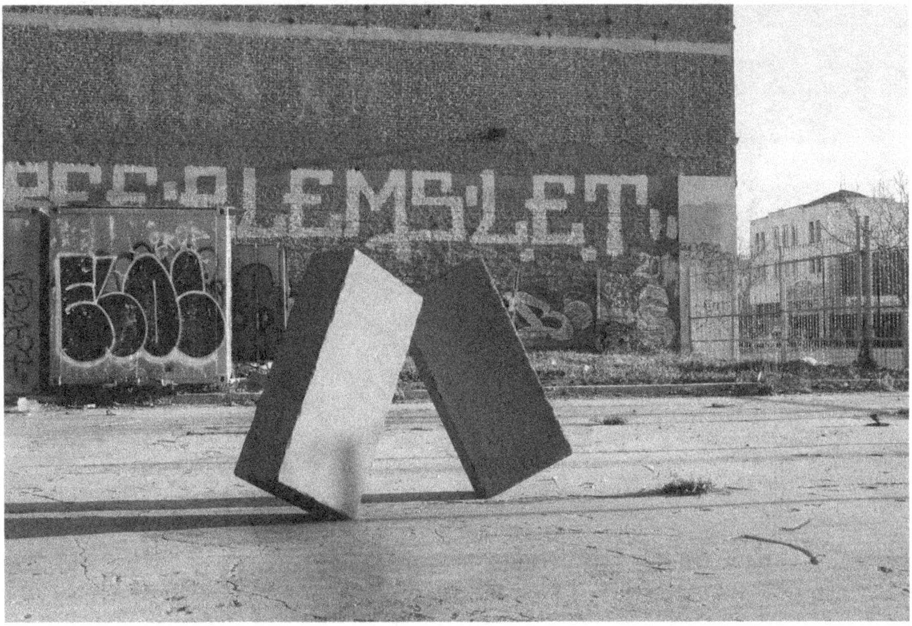

FIGURE 1.13 Juan Capistrán, *Psychogeography of Rage (sending up searchlights in the form of flames), Broadway*, 2019. Light jet print, 20 × 30 inches (50.8 × 76.2 cm). Courtesy the artist.

delicate for objects that builders typically use in construction for their strength and durability. Because of their flimsy material, the "bricks" were subject to falling over. At least one passerby crushed a "brick" and took another.[127]

The last work in the series is a video of an installation with balloons and real bricks in a concrete and grass lot, which the artist titled *Psychogeography of Rage (sending up searchlights in the form of flames), Vermont Ave. 1992* (2019) (Figure 1.14). A camera records three piles of typical-size bricks that hold down the yellow ribbons of black mylar balloons shaped as the numbers 1-9-9-2. The balloons waver in the breeze as a soundtrack of busy city noises plays. Quickly, the sound changes to glass shattering and falling onto concrete before being crushed under the feet of people whose voices we hear speaking and shouting to each other. In the mostly inaudible dialogue, Spanish and English phrases like "pasame," "dale," and "come on!" are heard as the balloons double into a superimposed and slightly delayed image of themselves. The camera begins to shake as it is adjusted by someone behind the lens, before the artist, followed by his echo, walks into the frame to release the bound "1992" from the bricks. The

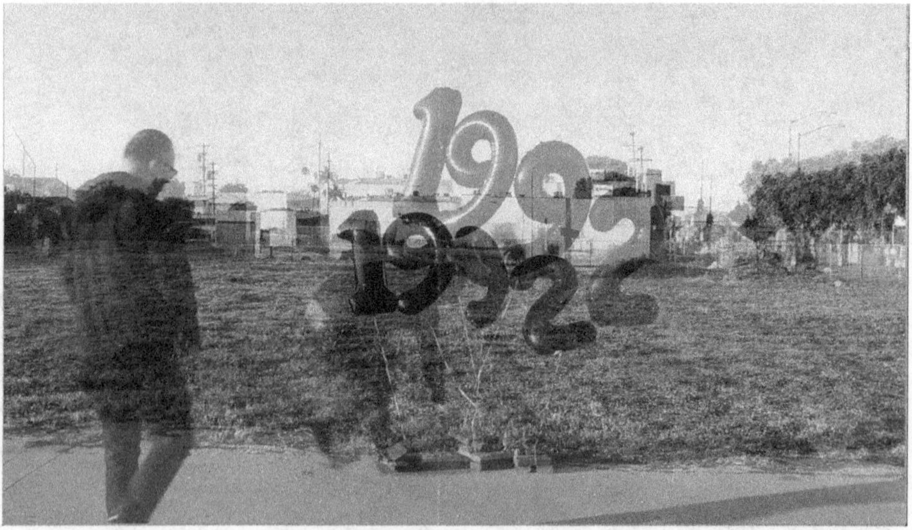

FIGURE 1.14 Juan Capistrán, *Psychogeography of Rage (sending up searchlights in the form of flames), Vermont Ave. 1992*, 2019. Video, duration 6 minutes. Courtesy the artist.

camera follows the number-shaped balloons into the cloudless sky as the doubled image synchronizes and becomes one again. Eventually, alarms begin to sound as the balloons turn into tiny, abstracted specks against a solid-blue background. One might interpret the release of the black balloons as a release of the "rage" cited in the video's title. But the fact that they, along with the sound, never completely fade away is noteworthy.

Regarding the installations of "bricks," Capistrán stated that they were purposefully ephemeral.[128] A *Los Angeles Times* article by Makeda Easter quoted the artist about the brick motif.

> Bricks are ambiguous, Capistrán said. They are the building blocks for constructing something new, but he also referenced Damian "Football" Williams, who was part of the mob that attacked Reginald Denny in the early hours of the 1992 riots, smashing the trucker in the head with a brick. A brick, which "could easily be an object of revolution," Capistrán said, also "could quickly be turned to an object of destruction."[129]

Minus the documentation, the installations were temporary and fleeting. While seemingly benign due to the lightweight materials of the faux-bricks and the use of the real bricks as mere weights for balloons, the symbolism and history they carry, as cited by the artist, range from the transformative to the hostile. They also signal how the transformative often yields hostile behavior and how easily one can use transformation as an excuse to wield unjust violence. At once, Capistrán's faux-bricks transform a revolutionary's tool and worker's building material into a benign, humorous, and useless object. Then, in the video, the real bricks are neither thrown nor used for construction. Instead, they temporarily restrain delicate ribboned balloons that become the objects that hold transformative potential.

The origins of the soundtrack and titular references of the video add to the symbolic weight of meaning behind the larger series. The artist took audio samples from decades-old video recordings of the unrest that users uploaded to YouTube.[130] *Psychogeography of Rage* is a play on the title of a book and arts terminology: *Geography of Rage: Remembering the Los Angeles Riots of 1992*, a 2002 anthology of essays edited by Jervey Tervalon that I shared with Capistrán when he was looking for resources years ago; and the term "psychogeography," which is an idea developed by Guy Debord of the Situationist International (SI) to describe how geographic environment or location affects the emotion and behavior of individuals.[131] *Sending up searchlights in the form of flames* references a line about the arson fires of the 1965 Watts Rebellion that Lynell George wrote for the *LA Weekly* in her report of the 1992 unrest.[132]

The play on Tervalon's book title and Debord's concept creates a complex of meaning in which Capistrán links the geography of Los Angeles and memories of the unrest with the psychological effects it has on emotions and behaviors. George's poetic line about the Watts Rebellion adds further conceptual layers that tie the first "Los Angeles Riot" in 1965 to the city's second in 1992, underscoring their similarities and relationship as well as the ongoing, intergenerational struggles the community of South Los Angeles has experienced across decades. Capistrán's 2019 series suggests that these struggles continue today. It also signals how some have willfully blinded themselves to recognizing the experiences even when buildings are set on fire—the building ablaze being the ultimate dazzling "searchlight" of unrest—or when razed lots leave enormous, decades-long gaps in the cityscape. About the series, Capistrán shared with me, "Sometimes, I'd like to make other things. But I can't help make things like this. It's like a love letter."[133]

These "love letters," in the form of artistic recognition of those who experienced injustice and remembrances of how the city became scarred, reveal insights into the ongoing effects the 1992 Los Angeles Riots and its history continue to have on the community. Capistrán's series reminds viewers that research on the unrest and its visual legacy necessarily involves the recovery and witness of multiple ethnic and racial histories. While popular accounts of the unrest often ignore the Latino and Latin

American experience, Capistrán's series asserts that the Brown experience is imperative to understanding the history and shared experiences of violence and loss across racial groups.[134] Despite the overwhelmingly high rates of arrests, destroyed businesses, and widespread deportations, few news outlets, writers, and historians have seriously contended with Brown experiences. Instead, the Black-white racial narratives of the 1992 Los Angeles Riots have formed the foundation for how we understand the most economically devastating episode of unrest in the history of the United States. Yet, as I continue to reveal in this book, unrest is much more than a Black and white problem. Unrest is an act of bereavement that makes injustice visible in a landscape; it is disorder against the logics of white supremacy, xenophobia, and state-sanctioned violence; and it is what drives artists, again and again, to make work about these experiences from a place of deep care and love. Through numerous artistic references and dedications, especially to Harlins and Lopez, Capistrán blurs the racial differences often used to pit groups against each other and reveals how the Brown experience of the unrest was and still is inextricably linked to that of Black people. Remembering this expands narratives and offers much-needed space for coalition, solidarity, and change.

✷ 2 ✷

Post-Riot Looting

Over the span of a year, between 1992 and 1993, Seth Kaufman made approximately fifty-five found objects and assemblages with items he procured from properties that burned down near his home in West Hollywood during the 1992 Los Angeles Riots.[1] Titled *L.A. Rebellion*, the series included singed paper items, like magazine pages, posters, religious icon cards, scorched wood, melted glass, and fire-damaged metal pieces, such as screws, cameras, film canisters, and office and kitchen supplies. He curated some of the artworks he made as part of the 1992 group exhibition *Antiphony of Anarchy: Three Views After Curfew* for ART/LA92, an annual art fair held at the Los Angeles Convention Center; successfully pitched his work as part of a two-part billboard campaign for Absolut Vodka, the liquor company; and, in the spring of 1993, showcased his series of works in the solo exhibition *Dwelling in Rebellion: A Year to the Day* at the Zero One Art Gallery.[2] As a new visual artist with no formal training and limited art world connections, his hustle to show his work paid off with extraordinary opportunities. While his art-making practice and group exhibitions evoked previous art histories of Los Angeles unrest, particularly those of assemblage artists during the 1965 Watts Rebellion, Kaufman's work stands apart for its contentious relationality. From the start, his search for purpose and materials in the immediate aftermath of unrest brought him to the ruins of others' livelihoods. While he sought a way to express his feelings and experience of the 1992 Los Angeles Riots, he struggled in his efforts to make art, market his work, and address the realities the community faced.

The Jewish American artist's found objects and assemblages recall those made by the African American artist Noah Purifoy and his collaborators in the aftermath of the 1965 Watts Rebellion. The first director of the Watts Towers Arts Center, Purifoy organized with musician Judson Powell *66 Signs of Neon*, a group exhibition that comprised assemblages made from detritus that the two obtained from the remains of businesses that residents had set on fire in Watts. On August 11, 1965, Lee Minikus, a white California Highway Patrol officer, placed Marquette Frye, an African American motorist, under arrest for driving while intoxicated. The incident escalated to altercations between the officer, the arrestee's mother, and other residents, which then ignited unrest for six days in Watts and surrounding Los Angeles neighborhoods.[3] Purifoy explained that he and Powell "watched aghast the rioting, looting and burning during the August happening. And while the debris was still smoldering, we ventured into the rubble like other junkers of the community, digging and searching, but unlike others, obsessed without knowing why."[4] Purifoy went on to dub the artworks he and the other artists made "junk art," evoking the Black working-class cultural practice of "junking" or refurbishing used appliances and other objects.[5] Like these two artists, Kaufman would eventually come to an epiphany about his practice and art-making. However, Kaufman's conception of his practice and art was distinctive from that of Purifoy and others. He described his work as "post-riot looting," provocatively associating his practice with those who seized goods from businesses during the unrest.[6]

In this chapter, I reframe Kaufman's notion of post-riot looting as a method of critical inquiry to understand the aftermath of the unrest with a closer look at issues of race, class, and politics. Kaufman struggled to situate himself as a visual artist in the political context of the 1992 Los Angeles Riots, wrestling with issues of artistic accountability and exploitation. Through extensive interviews, I reconstruct the artist's firsthand experience of the 1992 Los Angeles Riots, his search for materials and artistic motivation, and his repurposing of the burned wood and other items he sourced from destroyed properties. I also explore Kaufman's direct encounters with business owners whose properties were burned and his commercial ventures for exhibiting art about the unrest at the 1992 Los Angeles art fair and with Absolut Vodka. The examination of these histories allows me to consider the roles of the art market and capitalistic and liberal opportunism surrounding the unrest. To be sure, Kaufman's interactions with shopkeepers and his work with Absolut Vodka and the art fair provide compelling experiences of the unrest even while they may be objectionable to some readers. If the "post-riot" landscape conjured images of political, racial, or social justice reckoning, this history reveals them as limited or inconsistent. Still, Kaufman's efforts led to an important archive, which contains assemblages, found objects, writings, and photographs that communicate key experiences of the unrest and its art history.

The First Days of Post-Riot Looting

In an interview I conducted with Kaufman in 2015, he recalled being on the phone with a friend as the 1992 Los Angeles Riots began to unfold on live television.[7] They quickly registered the connection of the events to the acquittal of the police officers who beat Rodney King and stayed on the phone as they watched the developing news coverage. Kaufman recalls the experience as defined not by what news anchors or helicopter reporters may have narrated about the events but by the voice-over his friend, who was African American, provided about the events over the phone. Hours seemed to pass before Kaufman finally turned his attention away from his television and toward his window, catching the first plumes of smoke as they began to rise from the city into the sky. His friend suggested they meet nearby, in the Hollywood Hills. Separately they drove to a lookout point, and with the sun setting, they watched the city burn.[8] Kaufman, in his early thirties at the time, had recently begun to shift his creative practice from acting to art-making.[9] He did not know then that the subject of the unrest and the materials of their aftermath would quickly transform his artistic trajectory in the days and months to come.

By Monday, May 4, 1992, the citywide unrest finally began to wane.[10] The five days of destruction included the incineration of entire city blocks, transforming the landscape across Los Angeles and in neighboring cities across the county. Buildings turned to rubble. Landmarks disappeared. With the cessation of disturbances, Kaufman decided to tour his West Hollywood neighborhood to see what was once familiar now made strange.[11]

Driving down Beverly Boulevard, the destruction of one intersection especially fascinated him. He circled the block several times before parking his car in front of the burned-out property.[12] Peering through his car windows, he wondered what had been there before the unrest. He had driven down this street countless times, but he could not remember what kind of businesses had occupied the space just days before. Kaufman felt compelled to explore the remains and exited his car. Ignoring the police barricades and warning signage, he stepped into the ruins of the property.[13]

Kaufman carefully traversed what was left of the structure and delicately explored the scorched debris, admitting later in interviews that he was less concerned with the disintegration of the fragile material or his own safety than the possibility that his sneakers, clothes, and skin might become blackened from the charred remains.[14] Even so, the artist uncovered a singed album of photographs, melted metal, and, ironically, a blackened pair of shoes.[15] He still could not make out what kind of business had occupied the space, but his curiosity was fleeting. The impulse to look through the rubble eclipsed the thought, as well as any plan to survey the detritus.

Just several days earlier, he had struggled to understand how he felt about the unrest and what he should do as an artist. Reflecting on this moment in a 1993 artist's statement, Kaufman wrote that he had asked himself, "How do I feel? What do I think? What should I say?"[16] He could not arrive at a conclusion. This was not due to indifference, he insisted, but instead was a result of being in a state of shock after witnessing the chaos and violence unfold across the city. He explained, "All attempts at expressing my feelings seemed arbitrary and trite compared to the enormity of what I was experiencing."[17] In a 1993 interview for the art magazine *Picturebook*, Kaufman elaborated:

> When the riots hit, I had a lot of feelings come up, not necessarily in relation to the riots, but mostly in relation to my feelings of security, my feelings of control, my feelings of safety, and it really rocked me. I was looking for an expression, I started writing poetry because there was no visual expression that I felt could compete with the television.[18]

After the live footage of demonstrations, looting, beatings, and fire, there came the replays. Thus Kaufman's exploration of the remnants of the structure became a search for visual expression beyond that which had been already heavily mediated by television.

The late springtime sun began to burn Kaufman's exposed skin, and he considered abandoning the site. As he rubbed his sunburned neck with his hand, he looked down and noticed a cluster of wood screws at his feet.[19] During the two years leading up to the unrest, Kaufman had been making pointillist-inspired sculptures for which he drilled screws into various materials. He altered the depths and concentrations of the metal objects to create patterns and emulate an assortment of textures and figures.[20] So, unlike the other fire- and water-damaged debris he came across at the site, the screws were a primary material in his art practice.

As Kaufman reached down to retrieve the familiar screws, he realized he was standing on top of hundreds if not thousands of them.[21] Having found his central medium in copious quantities, Kaufman felt he had found a sign for how to address the unrest with his artwork.[22] Without restraint, he kneeled down and dug through the charred debris with his bare hands, uncovering a trove of boxes containing the sharp three-inch spikes.[23] With stained hands and clothes, he scooped up as much of the supplies as he could and ran to his car searching for bags or anything else that could help him carry the supplies home.[24] He then decided to gather and take the other objects he had found earlier.[25] He drove away from the burned property feeling fortunate to have finally found inspiration.[26]

The next day, Kaufman returned to the same property in search of more art supplies. He dug through and sorted debris.[27] Completely absorbed with the process of unearthing materials, he did not realize that another man had entered the site and he was no longer alone. That is, not until he heard screams. The emotion and volume shocked Kaufman, immediately shifting his focus to his surroundings. Quickly, he realized that the man was screaming at him. Kaufman recalled the man screaming first in Spanish and then in English, "We've been violated enough! We've been violated enough!"[28] The bewildered artist, with his heart pounding wildly, instinctively stood up and began walking backward, away from the man, to create distance between them.[29]

Kaufman quickly processed the situation—the ruined location, his digging, the man's anguish and words. *He must be the owner.* Until that moment, the artist later admitted during our interview, it did not occur to him that anyone owned the torched wood and melted metal that was left of most of the structure or that he was trespassing on private property.[30] Had the sheer devastating effects of the fires exhausted what seemed to be of any value for a business? As an attempt to explain why he was there taking the fire-ravaged items, he shouted, "I'm an artist! I'm collecting materials to make art!"[31] His anemic explanation failed to quell the owner, and Kaufman recalled he continued yelling. In that moment, he realized that, to the owner, he was no different from those responsible for destroying his store. Anxiously surveying the intense situation, it struck Kaufman that the day before he had found what the owner might recognize as a meaningful item that survived the fire. He cut through the barrage of screams with the confession, "I have your photos!"[32] Kaufman recalled the owner appearing disoriented by the information. "He was like waving in the breeze after a storm," the artist described.[33] The owner then pulled out a business card from his pocket and handed it to Kaufman.[34] With this, he learned that the site they stood on was Rod Martin's Custom Furniture Shop.[35] The artist promised to return the singed collection of black-and-white photographs to Mr. Martin, and he promptly left his property.[36]

The Politics of Post-Riot Looting

Years later during our interview, Kaufman admitted that he initially did not want to forfeit the album.[37] He recalled that he thought about incorporating its contents, which were filled with pictures of a young couple at a dance, into one of his newly imagined assemblages. He also shared that when expressing his excitement about the artistic potential of the album to a friend at the time, the friend was aghast that he considered making art out of such a personal item, one not his own. Kaufman accounted for his insensitivity in a 1993 interview: "I was so consumed with being able to exercise my feelings about the riots, and make a statement about the riots, that it never occurred to me that I was a post-riot looter. And I was really wrestling with that, I wanted this material, I wanted to say something with it."[38] Though he initially was torn about returning the album, Kaufman called the phone number on the business card and left a message with his contact information on the voice machine.[39]

The artist received a return phone call from Mr. Martin's wife, Elsa, who co-owned the furniture store.[40] When Kaufman described the contents of the photo album to her, Mrs. Martin began to sob. She explained that the photographs portrayed a cotillion that she and her husband attended when they were teenagers. The album was also one of the few possessions they took with them as they fled to the United States from the Castro regime in Cuba.[41] At that moment, Kaufman's selfishness struck him hard. Consumed by his desire to visually express himself about the events, he did not fathom how the same events complexly affected his neighbors or that he was taking important vestiges from their personal lives. Thus what he saw as an artistic free-for-all in the remnants of the burned-out building was instead a willful blindness to loss.[42]

While Kaufman initially sought to make sense of the unrest and his feelings about it, his experience with the Martins made him realize that he was not simply salvaging art materials. Instead, he was looting property. The realization that he was, in his words, a "post-riot looter" forced him to reconsider his artistic trajectory. When interviewed for *Print* magazine about his projects on the 1992 Los Angeles Riots, he recalled his conversation with Mrs. Martin and claimed, "From that point on, I worked with a sense of reverence and accountability."[43] In an October 2015 conversation with me, Kaufman elaborated the experience with the Martins.

> You know, I think that was a real blessing for me because I think that it gave me a deep appreciation for other people's experience. It rooted me in [the owner's] experience, rooted me in the broader economic, political trauma of my culture, of my people. And, I'm very fortunate because it is with that reverence that I then intruded—it made my intrusions less self-serving. Even though what I was serving was honest, it was still to some extent without a sense of consequence for other people's trauma. Right on

the heels of discovering my entrance, I was immediately thrust into a very conscious, you know, impact.[44]

This early exchange with the Martins was perhaps Kaufman's most formative experience as an artist. It moved his practice from one that was engrossed by formal inquiry to one that began to consider art's emotive registers and sociopolitical role. The unrest coupled with the experience he had with the Martins also made him extremely aware of his subjectivity as a Jewish American. He began to recognize parallels between experiences surrounding the 1992 Los Angeles Riots and the Jewish American experience. As he would later explain to me, it encouraged him to consider how his people—that is, fellow Angelenos and Jews in the United States—have experienced racism, xenophobic violence, and oppression.[45] Originally from a middle-class family in New Jersey, Kaufman explained that he grew up intimately aware of the atrocities Jewish people experienced historically and the antisemitism that continued to affect the community. Though he is not a religious adult, to underscore the realities of such violence, Kaufman curtly explained, "Being Jewish meant knowing that my synagogue could be bombed."[46]

His growing consciousness did not mean that Kaufman stopped visiting the sites of burned properties, though. Instead, he went on to develop a daily ritual of scavenging materials.[47] He obtained permission from the Martins to use the screws and other objects he had already recovered from the remains of their business. He also obtained permission to temporarily enter the property and acquire damaged camera and film equipment from the namesake co-owner of Samy's Camera, Samy Kamienowicz, which had been looted and set on fire a few blocks from the Martins' furniture store.[48] Most of the time, however, Kaufman was unable to locate the owners of destroyed businesses. So instead he negotiated permission to explore properties with security guards and watchful neighbors.[49]

Yet the permissive exploration of ruins was, at times, spurious. In a 2017 interview, Kaufman admitted to posing as a construction worker to gain access to sites and take materials.[50] A 1993 artist's statement seems to corroborate such actions. He wrote, in an arrogant tone:

> I risk my life and my freedom every time I cross a Police Barricade and step into the charred remains of buildings that were destroyed in the Los Angeles rebellion of 1992. I am a post-riot looter; A guerilla-Artist; an archaeologist of anarchy. I wander through the wounded streets of Los Angeles steeling [*sic*] burnt and melted artifacts.[51]

He followed this statement with an explanation that attempts to temper the bravado.

> It is not my intention to offend or shock. I want to build with what has been destroyed; to highlight what has been hidden. I make no value judgement; I take no moral stance. The assemblages I create are trophies of fear and monuments to love.[52]

Years later, Kaufman explained his self-described braggadocio as vestiges of his previous foray into hip-hop and the culture of self-promotion.[53] Still, his description of himself as a "post-riot looter" suited the contradictions inherent in his emerging practice and artist statements.

Kaufman found currency in being a "post-riot looter" after the 1992 Los Angeles Riots. Though he was working with items often destroyed by fire and water, the term recognized his practice as being connected to and complicit with looters. Indeed, at times he took items from businesses without permission. Yet Kaufman's term is not an easy equivalent or parallel to the act of looting.

Looting is an act that is inherently anticapitalistic. While the looter does not have to be politically aware to disrupt the system of capitalism, looting nonetheless rejects the logic of the market and the laws and social norms that police commerce and protect the monetary and material interests of merchants and property owners. As critic Vicky Osterweil deftly explains:

> Looting rejects the legitimacy of ownership rights and property, the moral injunction to work for a living, and the "justice" of law and order. Looting reveals all these for what they are: not natural facts, but social constructs benefiting a few at the expense of the many, upheld by ideology, economy, and state violence. [. . .] Looting is also an act of property destruction. When something is looted, that thing's nature as a commodity is destroyed by its being taken for free, out of the cycle of exchange and profit.[54]

Guy Debord, in his essay influenced by the events of the first "Los Angeles Riot," the 1965 Watts Rebellion, explained that looting, "through theft and gift," unveils the market and production of the commodity "to be arbitrary and unnecessary" and that its destruction reveals the "human superiority over commodities."[55] Debord further states, "Looting is a natural response to the unnatural and inhuman society of commodity abundance. It instantly undermines the commodity as such, and it also exposes what the commodity ultimately implies: the army, the police and the other specialized detachments of the state's monopoly of armed violence."[56] Debord ties looting to a person's demand to not merely "survive, but to live," and states that ultimately the unrest, even given its limited nature, "is a human protest against a dehumanized life, a protest of real individuals against their separation from a community" that had long neglected their fellow neighbors and each other's welfare and humanity in favor of the "spectacle-commodity economy"—that is, capitalism and the reign of consumerism.[57]

On the one hand, Kaufman's conception of the post-riot looter recognizes that as an artist he took materials without permission. It also signals empathy for those who looted or participated in other ways in the unrest.[58] In a 1993 interview, Kaufman used an analogy, explaining that when an individual injures himself it hurts; however, when an entire community has been wounded, it "translates into hundreds and thousands of times more pain." He then stressed, "What does that look like? It looks like thousands and thousands of buildings burned."[59] Unlike Kaufman, others tie morality to the act of looting, which frames the looter's character and worth as a person, differentiating between "good" and "bad" people and people who are "helping" or "hurting" a cause, community, or all of society—in other words, polarizing understandings of what it means to be human and neglect of the socioeconomic conditions that lead to unrest. Debord and Osterweil both addressed the contradictions in such stances, including the critiques of looting by the politically radical and left. As Osterweil bluntly states, "These so-called revolutionaries, who support the looting of bread, but not of liquor, reveal that they are only willing to support poor people in struggles for bare survival: in other words, in struggles that keep them poor."[60] In 2019, Kaufman reflected further on those who looted during the 1992 Los Angeles Riots: "A person is pushed to the edge. No one strolls to that edge. We are taken there."[61] Kaufman explained, "We look at the looters as perpetrators rather than the victims of great oppression."[62] Thus, the artist recognized the 1992 Los Angeles Riots as a collective expression of grievance and a response to systemic conditions that caused harm.

On the other hand, while the looter took goods out of capitalistic economic circulation, whether to use for themselves, or give to others, or sell illicitly, Kaufman's act of post-riot looting involved taking damaged materials, including personal items not meant for sale, to make art, not only for the sake of visual expression as he initially sought, but also with the intent of returning them anew to the market—a market that he sought entry into as an emerging artist. To be sure, Kaufman understood the art world as a structure of power—one he described to me during an interview as dominated by male white Christians, which made him feel vulnerable and excluded.[63] As an artist without university or other formal training in art-making who was entering an art world of the highly educated, one might understand this vulnerability as manifold. Still, as a secular white male from a middle-class background, it would be deceiving to blanket Kaufman's subjectivity as an underrepresented minority in the art world even as someone who still had a steep hill to climb. Moreover, Kaufman's conception of the post-riot looter hinged on a long history and recent experience of looting that often characterized poor and working-class African Americans and Latinos as immoral criminals and irrational destroyers of their own communities. Though Kaufman obviously expressed empathy and recognized the larger system that disadvantaged such communities and led to looting, he used the mainstream conception of looting as scandalous, immoral, and criminal to boost his image and credibility as an artist. Thus Kaufman's use of the term "post-riot looter" also became a marketing strategy that hinged on the sensationalism of looting, as well as the artist's relative safety from being charged with a crime, to bring attention and value to his art. While looting describes an inherent anticapitalistic act, disrupting the market and logics of capitalism, even when it is only a temporary disruption, Kaufman's term "post-riot looter" signals an indelible tie between art and commerce and race and class.[64]

Post-Riot Looting and Junk Art

Kaufman's self-imaging and practice as a "post-riot looter" brought him some attention and opportunities but did not translate into wealth.[65] However, the experiences of the 1992 Los Angeles Riots that led him to the term—Mr. Martin's confrontation at the ruins of his business and Mrs. Martin's revelation of the family history documented in the photo album—significantly changed his conception of his art practice. Scholars have noted a major shift in the art practice of Purifoy and his conception of junk art after the 1965 Watts Rebellion. While Kaufman was unaware of Purifoy, that is, until the major retrospective *Noah Purifoy: Junk Dada* opened at the Los Angeles County Museum of Art in 2015, Kaufman's practice calls on his work.[66] To be clear, Kaufman's unfamiliarity with Purifoy and the other artists of *66 Signs of Neon* in the early 1990s is not surprising, especially since he was a newer self-taught visual artist. Moreover, while Purifoy's work might be considered art historical canon today, especially in the fields of African American and Los Angeles art, it would be years before significant scholarship on his work would be published and widely read. In addition, after an eleven-year hiatus, Purifoy had only recently resumed his art practice in 1986, and a few years later he left the city for Joshua Tree.[67] As artists who made work from the detritus collected from properties burned down during episodes of unrest in Los Angeles, how were the practices and frames of "post-riot looting" and "junk art" similar or different?

Curator Yael Lipschutz provides an interesting view of Purifoy's art practice by first understanding the socioeconomic implications of the 1965 Watts Rebellion. Highlighting how the business district on 103rd Street in Watts was "struck en masse . . . on the third day of the uprising," Lipschutz asserted that residents substantiated Debord's argument that the 1965 unrest was a "rebellion against the commodity" with testimonials on how business owners unfairly up-charged residents for goods that were sold for considerably less in white neighborhoods and in downtown Los Angeles.[68] Lipschutz explained, "In Marxist terms, these statements indicate that part of what the community found so unacceptable was the complete disconnect in Watts between the commodity's exchange-value and its use-value, and the arbitrariness of its established price on 103rd Street."[69] By making clear the logic behind the residents' looting and destruction of Watts, she provided a path for understanding how Purifoy and Powell reimbued the ruined commodities they salvaged as "object[s] with use-value, with social-value, with communicative-value," and how Purifoy's art shifted from a process of loss to a rejection of capitalistic culture.[70] She aligned Purifoy's "sifting through the wasted remains of Watts" as "correspond[ing] with what Freud refers to as 'the work of *mourning*,'" suggesting that for Purifoy this loss comprised

> an ideal: the ideal of the commodity-as-life-fulfilling-wish-image; the lifestyle this ideal implied (bourgeois); the idea that obtaining such a lifestyle would somehow allow one to move past the racial/class barriers that structured African American life. The rebellion had stripped this idea bare—exposing capitalistic culture as the transitory, fragile, and vapid way-of-life.[71]

Lipschutz then tied together Purifoy's formal art education and his former work as an interior designer and furniture maker as signs of a "bourgeois way of life" that the unrest had "rendered . . . hollow, dead," which led him "into the rubble to begin the process of mourning" and to break "his ties to them."[72] While Lipschutz's tone is perhaps overly romantic, she connects this break to Purifoy's "self-inflicted state of poverty" and his statement that he "wanted to avoid these associations with the elite."[73] Relatedly, historian Daniel Widener described the wider political context in his examination of Black arts and culture as "follow[ing] a period in which black politics shifted from a cross-class alliance against racism to a sharp divergence along socioeconomic lines."[74] Purifoy seems to have been sensitive to this division within the Black community. Indeed, historian Richard Cándida Smith linked Purifoy's later skepticism about the effectiveness of helping the community as a professional artist to his understanding that the art world was exclusionary and elitist—and that this world was distinct from the creative process, which was "inherent to the human condition."[75] While Purifoy grew up poor and working class, he went on to earn bachelor's degrees in social science and art and a master's degree in social work.[76] The artist understood his experience in higher education and in the art world as one that granted him privileges that could potentially alienate him from the community he cared for, so he sought to undo the ways in which elitism proscribed creativity to the few.[77]

Other scholars cite Purifoy's deep interests in psychology, phenomenology, and existentialism to understand his thinking about the creative process as well as perception and the mind-body connection.[78] On the latter, scholar Kellie Jones cited Purifoy's understanding that art and culture was a "therapeutic force" that could be an aid in mental health and Black trauma by "reintegrating the mind and body."[79] Furthermore, she tied Purifoy's interests in such philosophies to his "concept of art-as-change," which she connected to the Beat Generation, the civil rights movement, and especially to the Harlem Renaissance and the New Negro Movement that understood "black cultural accomplishment as the key to ending prejudice."[80] Jones went on to explain, "In a coded way, art-as-change addressed racism and the so-called 'Negro problem' by being a catalyst to transform and eradicate the thoughts and behaviors that accompanied them."[81] In a similar vein, Jones explained Purifoy's interest in assemblage as tied not only to the "accessibility and availability of materials, because it was made from discarded things," but also to its "democratic" and nondiscriminatory character, which harbored the potential for Black people to create something that reflected their experiences and changed their perception of what was around them.[82] In relating *66 Signs of Neon* to the original maker of the famous Watts Towers, which Rodia also made from found materials, Purifoy explained, "I thought if we could emulate Simon [Rodia]'s concept of taking junk and making it into something else, it could serve as an example to people here. It can make people there realize that their junk, their lives, can be shaped into something worthwhile."[83] To this point, leading up to the unrest in August 1965, Purifoy organized "junk hunts" as part of the art-making process with children who attended classes at the Watts Towers Arts Center, which underscores his mission to change perceptions of the self and place.[84] This is furthered by the fact that Purifoy and Powell invited artists Debby Brewer, Max Neufeldt, Ruth

Saturensky, Leon Saulter, Arthur Secunda, and Gordon Wagner to make junk art with them, which they then debuted as *66 Signs of Neon* at the Simon Rodia Commemorative Watts Renaissance of the Arts Festival in 1966 before traveling it nationally.[85] While the multiethnic artists did not necessarily live in Watts, Purifoy anchored the practice, art-making, and exhibition in the neighborhood and among and with community.

Purifoy and Kaufman experienced major shifts in their understandings of their art practices in the aftermath of unrest, and both recognized the potential of destroyed objects—their nonmonetary and communicative means of value—yet they fundamentally diverged in their associations with capitalistic culture and community. Purifoy rejected capitalistic culture and elitism, was keenly aware of issues of class and race, and sought to integrate junk art as a philosophy and social tool, which he centered in community and in the neighborhood. Kaufman seemed to form a sort of reification of, borrowing Lipschutz's phrase, "the commodity-as-life-fulfilling-wish-image" with post-riot looting serving as a means to create and market his art.[86] Perhaps more than anything, though, unlike Purifoy, Kaufman exhibited a level of cluelessness that was endemic in the art world. In a 1966 essay for the *66 Signs of Neon* catalog, Purifoy explained the significance of the compositions he and the other artists made, stating that if their works and the works' exhibition "enable us only to see and love the many simple things which previously escaped the eye, then we miss the point. For we here experience mere sensation, leaving us in time precisely where we were, being but not becoming." He continued, "We wish to establish that there must be more to art than the creative act, more than the sensation of beauty, ugliness, color, form, light, sound, darkness, intrigue, wonderment, uncanniness, bitter, sweet, black, white, life and death. There must be therein a ME and a YOU, who is affected permanently."[87] Kaufman came to this understanding after his encounter with Mr. Martin, but he only arrived halfway. In practice, his adherence to sociopolitical consciousness wavered and seemed self-serving. However, over the course of the year, he encountered opportunities to showcase his work and that of other artists, for which he attempted to develop dialogue that spoke beyond the "creative act." Thus, he sought to effect change, even if those changes were uneven and transitory.

Post-Riot Art at the Fair

In the weeks after the unrest, Kaufman's stockpile of lifted materials grew and, so armed, he began making a series of assemblages and found objects that he was eager to share with audiences. Realizing that ART/LA92, the seventh international Los Angeles art fair, would open in the fall, he cold called the event's organizers to find out whether they intended to address the unrest.[88] Fair organizers had plans to coordinate with the City's Cultural Affairs Department's Arts Recovery Program, which distributed funding to artists and coordinated arts programming within the community as part of the city's post-riot rebuilding plan. They also considered organizing tours to local community art centers and planned to invite the administrators of "socially conscious arts programs" from other cities to speak at the fair.[89] However, there seemed to be no attempts to include an exhibition or booth dedicated to addressing the recent unrest.[90] Seeing a window of opportunity, Kaufman pitched an exhibition of his work. Fair organizers accepted but asked him to curate a group exhibition instead. In turn, he proposed a three-person showcase.[91]

In general, only galleries and other related enterprises showed work at the art fair, and the exhibition spaces were expensive. Although ART/LA 92 organizers gave early registrants a 25 percent discount for a booth, the "basic cost" of a 600-square-foot space dropped from $16,800 to $12,600.[92] This still would have been beyond the means of many artists, especially those without the backing of a gallery or patron. In addition, with no guarantee of selling work and only the mere prospect of "exposure," even an artist with financial security would second-guess the monetary risk. Luckily for Kaufman, he was able to acquire the exhibition space free of charge from the organizers.[93]

While this partly speaks to Kaufman's negotiating skills, ART/LA92 struggled to attract well-known galleries that year.[94] Before the unrest, the recession had taken its toll on the Los Angeles art scene with gallery closures and a weakened art market. In fact, the average number of exhibitors and attendees had been steadily dwindling since 1987.[95] With pressure to fill the fair's grounds, along with possible anxieties about the political climate, emerging artists, businesses, and organizations were able to secure spaces at ART/LA92 for an exceptionally low rate or, in a couple of cases, like Kaufman's, at no cost at all.[96]

Through his personal network, Kaufman located artists addressing issues surrounding the unrest and contacted several of them for studio visits. For the group exhibition, he settled on the photographs of Joseph E. Norman Sr. and the paintings of Gary Matteson. Together, the three presented *The Antiphony of Anarchy: Three Views After Curfew* at ART/LA 92, which was held at the Los Angeles Convention Center from December 3 to December 6, 1992 (Figure 2.1).

In the press release for the exhibition, which seemed to be penned by Kaufman, the stated purpose of the three-man show was not to address

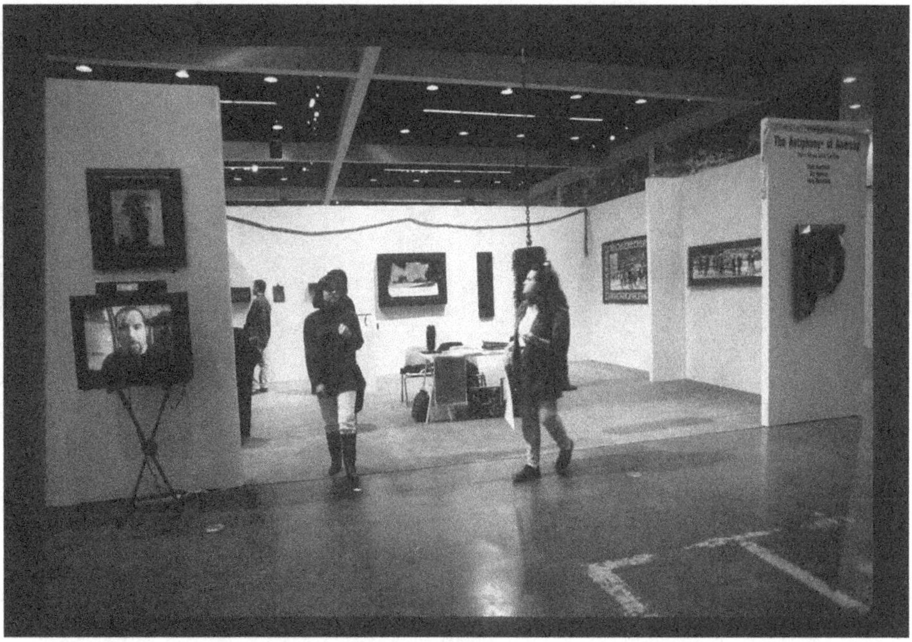

FIGURE 2.1 Seth Kaufman, Joseph E. Norman Sr., and Gary Matteson, Installation view of the exhibition *The Antiphony of Anarchy: Three Views After Curfew*, December 3–6, 1992, The 7th International Los Angeles Art Fair, Los Angeles Convention Center, Los Angeles, CA. Artworks by Seth Kaufman, front and center, and Gary Matteson, far right. Photo: Seth Kaufman. Courtesy Seth Kaufman.

the social or political circumstances surrounding the unrest. Instead, it was only supposed to convey how the unrest had affected the artists' lives and work.[97] Despite the inward framing, the artists' contributions nevertheless expressed the sociopolitical issues that informed the recent unrest, and this includes works by Kaufman. *State of the Art* (1992) (Figure 2.2) and *That Was Then, This Is Then* (1992) (Figure 2.3) are standout works among the series for the marrying of form and composition with political symbolism.

State of the Art comprises a fire-seared poster of architect Arata Isozaki's 1986 design for the Museum of Contemporary Art in Los Angeles, which Kaufman set atop a bed of ashes and framed with burned wood he recovered from the city's ruins. While the downtown museum survived the unrest, the assemblage recalled the numerous burned buildings and symbolically gestured to the demise of modernity.[98] Furthermore, the combination of its scorched materials with the title suggests, not the innovative design or development of the building, but a political critique

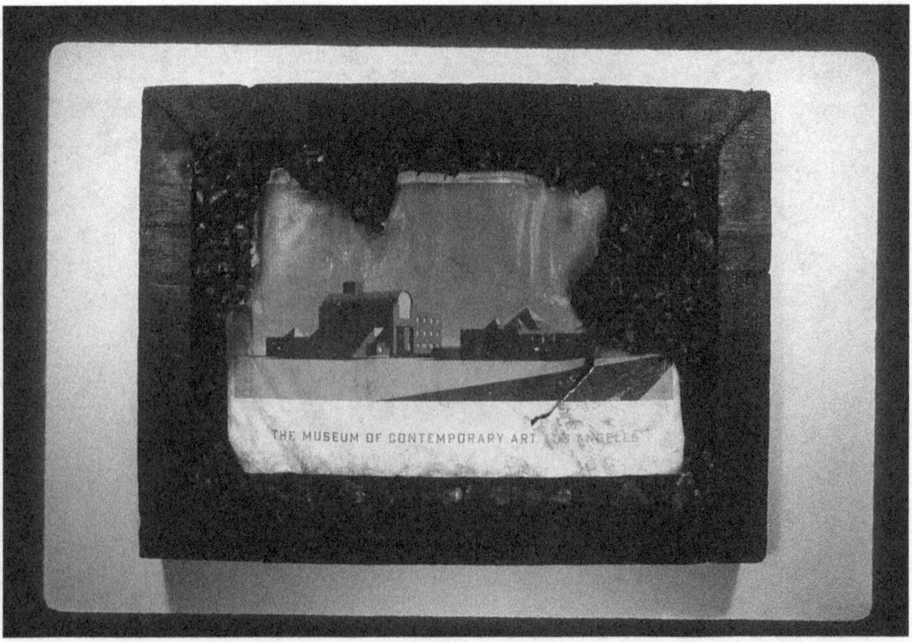

FIGURE 2.2 Seth Kaufman, *State of the Art*, 1992. Poster, embers, nails, corner guards and wood, 37¾ × 51¼ × 5¼ inches (37.7 × 130.1 × 13.3 cm). Courtesy the artist.

of art institutions or the art world at large. The work evoked Ed Ruscha's iconic painting, *The Los Angeles County Museum on Fire* (1965–68) (Figure 2.4), made at the same time the museum opened to the public. Ruscha carefully rendered the Brutalist-style building, its grand promenade, and reflecting pool moat with tight, nearly undetectable brushstrokes. The blaze and billowing smoke rising almost horizontally from the rear and top of the main building, along with the strangeness of a yellow-green atmosphere, suggests a meaning that is more than a mere showcase of architect William Pereira's design. When asked about the intention behind the work decades later, Ruscha stated, "If you want to see that as a political painting, you can—a revolt against an authority figure." In this case, the authority figure was the art world. He later elaborated:

> About this time that I was painting this picture, I had some oh, maybe, personal gripes about the art world in general. And I felt like the museums were not really doing their jobs as far as opening their doors to contemporary art. . . . I didn't have a hatred for museums, but maybe, like, I had a healthy distrust for museums. And so I guess part of this painting grew out of that.[99]

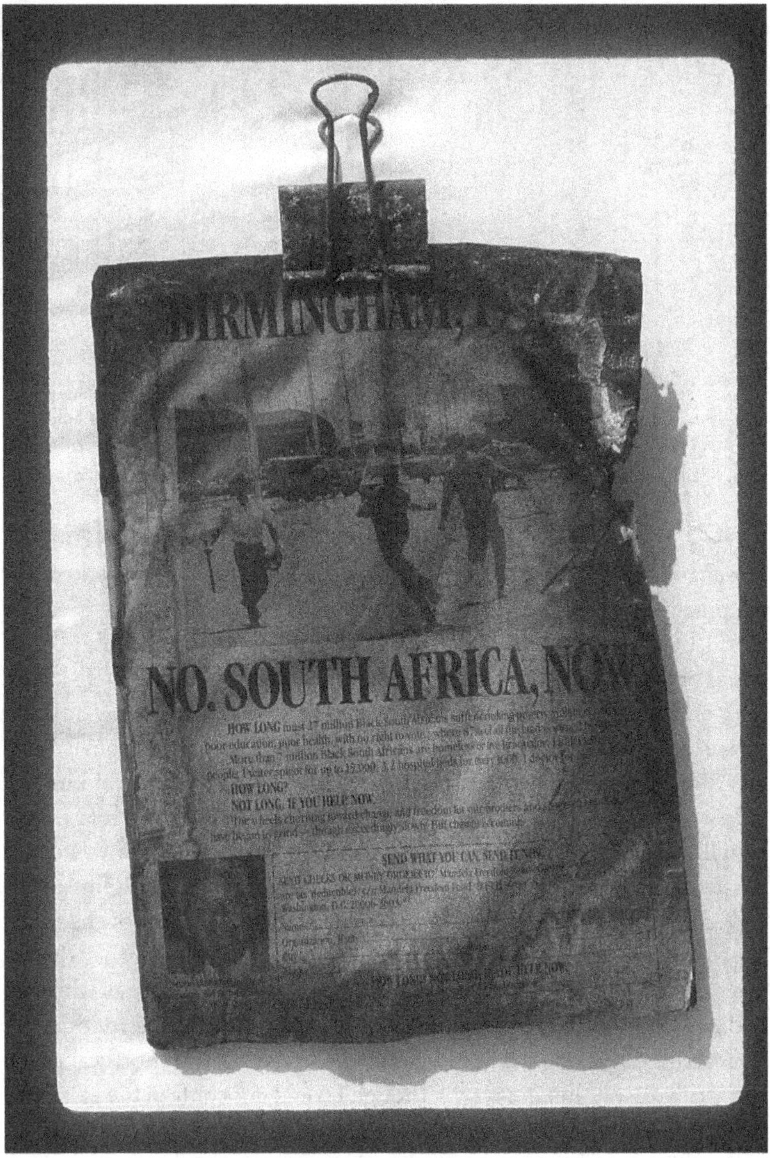

FIGURE 2.3 Seth Kaufman, *That Was Then, This Is Then*, 1992. Burned magazine, binder clip, screw, 12½ × 7¾ × 2¼ inches (31.7 × 19.6 × 5.7 cm). Courtesy the artist.

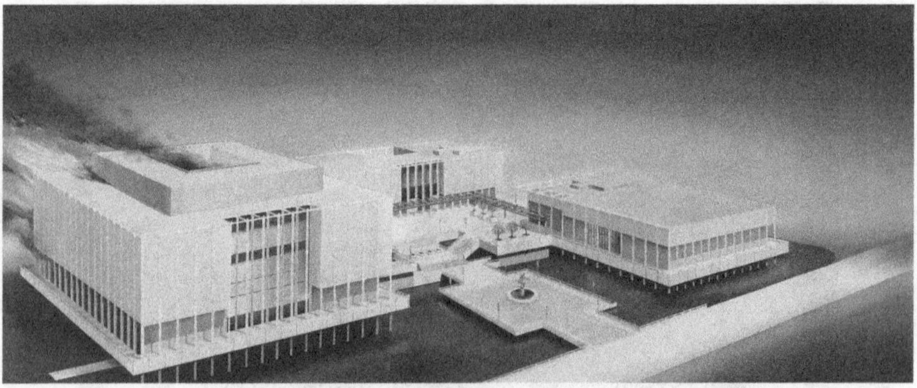

FIGURE 2.4 Ed Ruscha, *The Los Angeles County Museum on Fire*, 1965–68. Oil on canvas, 53½ × 133½ inches (135.9 × 339.1 cm). Hirshhorn Museum and Sculpture Garden, Smithsonian Institution, Washington, DC, Gift of Joseph H. Hirshhorn, 1972.

Ruscha's explanation for his painting spoke to the slow acceptance of new art practices, especially that of American art, not just by the general art world, but the art market, which swayed the collections and exhibitions of major art institutions. With that said, can museums and by extension an art world driven by capital ever be trusted to be inclusive of new or innovative and thus financially risky art? While Ruscha's painting envisioned an art museum in flames, Kaufman's underscored the real threat Los Angeles's art institutions experienced when societal issues, such as police brutality and racism, breeched their terrain, questioning their relevancy, destroying commerce and capital, and overwhelming the systems of enforcement that sustain them.[100] Kaufman later recollected how he made the frame for *State of the Art* from shipping crates that were burned during the unrest, which he claimed had belonged to Jewish refugees who had fled antisemitism in the Soviet Union during perestroika, an economic restructuring of the country led by Mikhail Gorbachev, and shortly after the country's dissolution in 1991.[101] Though I could not confirm the existence or burning of the crates, the situation would certainly underscore a potential reading that further connects the misuse of power and xenophobia—a generative line of research that could help unfold the Jewish experience of the 1992 Los Angeles Riots.

While *State of the Art* may elicit readings of institutional critique, the image and text of *That Was Then, This Is Then* encourages viewers to consider that of the nation. *That Was Then, This Is Then* comprises a found object culled from a burned property, with very little manipulation by the artist. The object is a fire- and water-damaged advertisement page, held by a burned and rusted metal binder clip, that shows a photograph of a Black man being chased by two white men (see Figure 2.3). One of the white men, in uniform, holds a billy club in his fist. The photographer captured the other, in plainclothes, as he dropped his baton and leaned slightly toward the unarmed Black man, who dramatically tries to distance himself from him. Several vehicles, some of which appear to be paddy wagons with large emblems on the doors, are parked haphazardly in the street behind them.[102] Surrounding the image is large bold text that reads, "Birmingham, 1956? No. South Africa, Now." Below, in small type, is a list of the inequalities that Black South Africans have experienced and, with a portrait of Nelson Mandela, tells readers how to donate money to the advocacy organization responsible for the ad.[103] While the image captured an episode of racial strife in South Africa and indirectly referenced the fight against apartheid, Kaufman's reuse of it for *That Was Then, This Is Then* speaks to the episodes of racial violence encapsulated in the 1991 police beating of King and the 1992 Los Angeles Riots. Furthermore, the found object conjures the ongoing legacies of racism and state violence and the devastating effects they have had on Black communities across the world. In a 1993 interview, Kaufman stated, "I know that great change is capable of taking place and I think that that's what the last riots did. People took apart a structure."[104] He continued, "It seems like we smashed it, but in the course of history, it would seem like a drop in the bucket. Look at what people go through. We live in a city with people who suffer a great deal, they survive and they move on."[105] Events like the 1992 Los Angeles Riots create watershed moments of racial reckoning that can potentially affect and change institutions, but ensuring that the changes are more than just momentary is the dilemma Kaufman identifies in his statement and recognizes in the water-damaged magazine page he found. Such impermanence can be used as an excuse to not seek transformation at all. If one is to look only for "great change," the risk is overlooking the changes that occur on smaller scales or in the everyday lives of those most often oppressed by discriminatory systems.

Joseph E. Norman Sr.'s contribution to the ART/LA92 exhibition accounted for the city's physical changes after the unrest. In the months leading to the fair, Kaufman invited Norman to his apartment, and he arrived with a duffle bag over each shoulder and one in each hand. All four were filled with photographs.[106] Norman felt that his pre–art school experience as a combat photographer for the military was the best way to document the aftermath of the unrest.[107] So, using a point-and-shoot camera, the artist captured the devastated cityscape and recorded the dramatic physical changes that resulted.[108] The photos included documentation of businesses that had been destroyed by looting and buildings that had been burned. Each place he photographed was systematically photographed again and again, depicting the changing facades after debris had been hauled away and buildings were either demolished or rebuilt. Over the seven-month period between the end of the last fires in May and the December exhibition at ART/LA92, the artist claimed to have documented post-riot Los Angeles with thousands of photographs.[109] For the exhibition, he decided to simply tape his 4 × 6 inch photographs to two sections of the booth's walls. The images completely covered each section, from top to bottom and side to side. The installation provided viewers with an overwhelming yet systematic look at the city in a process of transformation. By presenting the physical alterations caused by the unrest and clean-up efforts in numerous small photographs, Norman required viewers to get close and pay attention in order to trace the changes. In this way, the artist transformed the great change the city underwent during and after the unrest into small, everyday changes only realized through consistent focus.

An American flag, suspended between the two sections of Norman's photographs, suggested that the destruction and rebuilding prompted by unrest was a uniquely US tradition. Indeed, Norman's artist statement for the exhibition, which noted the socioeconomic and racial issues that contributed to the 1992 Los Angeles Riots, recognized the events' similarities to the city's previous histories of unrest: "I had long seen the writing on the wall, with the homelessness, unemployment, the racial tensions, the emptiness in people's eyes, I knew that something had to give. When the riots first started, I was overwhelmed though. I couldn't believe that it was happening again."[110] Norman is referring to the 1965 Watts Rebellion, the last major episode of unrest in Los Angeles before 1992. Like the 1992 unrest, the Watts Rebellion had been filmed, photographed, televised, and written about in newspapers and magazines, capturing the attention of people across the United States. After the 1992 unrest, many people compared the 1965 and 1992 incidents and understood them as a continuum of police brutality and social and economic injustice in Los Angeles.

Like Norman, Gary Matteson used a camera to document the unrest. On the first day of the 1992 Los Angeles Riots, Matteson happened to be driving through the city with his camera. While he normally took snapshots of props as part of his job as a set decorator's assistant, he used his camera instead to document the progression of looting and destruction of businesses as he drove the Los Angeles streets.[111] Later, Matteson used the photographs as references for paintings that he made between January and June 1993.[112] However, for the exhibition at ART/LA92, he showed paintings from a previous series of city scenes that included depictions of police, pedestrians, and even a palm tree on fire.[113] Although these particular paintings did not represent the 1992 unrest specifically, the artist understood these "streetscapes" as relevant to the event because, as he explained, "causes of riots are just under the surface."[114] Matteson believed that a seemingly ordinary or banal day contains the makings for what could easily transform into unrest.

Instead of using canvas, Matteson painted on throw rugs for both his 1992 and 1993 series.[115] To Kaufman, the rugs Matteson used resembled the kind sold by street merchants who displayed their wares on chain-link fences in working-class neighborhoods around the city.[116] In actuality, Matteson acquired them from thrift shops and stores that sold cheap knock-off Persian rugs. The work of the French symbolist painter Jean-Édouard Vuillard inspired Matteson's project. Known for his paintings on folding screens and other decorative elements for the home, Vuillard believed that the painted interior was a reflection of the interior self. Thus, Matteson hoped to bring the urban outdoor setting and its psychological underpinnings into intimate interior spaces via seemingly innocuous household items like the decorative rug.[117]

The artist's use of throw rugs as canvas also alluded to issues of consumer culture and capitalism. In Matteson's artist statement for the ART/LA92 exhibition, he offered an interpretation of the unrest that recognized the economic disparities at play: "As I drove I took photos of cops, Firemen, Looters, Smoke, Debry, and I couldn't help feeling that some kind of celebration was taking place. People were smiling, it was like the biggest clearance sale these consumers had ever seen, everything was discounted 100%. The shoppers' rebellion of 1992."[118] He summed up his personal statement with an assessment of the power structures and oppression at play that led to the unrest.

> This wasn't just a matter of destroying property and looting[,] it was an expression of desperation and disgust. People were smiling and running amuck in the streets because they felt like they deserved it, after being suppressed for so long. We all know that the alliance between government and business only listens to the people when it starts costing them money. All I wonder seven months later is, have they heard and are we finished speaking? Time will tell.[119]

In a 2016 interview I conducted with Matteson, he recalled the interest that fair attendees had in the group exhibition, which made him realize the market potential for "riot-related" artworks.[120] After the exhibition closed, the artist went on to paint a couple of the street scenes he had photographed during the unrest; however, he quickly became uncomfortable with the series. He explained that he began to feel that continuing the series or selling the paintings would be opportunistic and even exploitative.[121] Matteson, who still possesses the paintings to this day, "didn't want to go there" and ended his project.[122] The other two artists also sold very few to no works themselves at the fair.[123]

Yet this still begs the question: What does it mean to exhibit works on the 1992 Los Angeles Riots at an art fair? How were these works read by viewers and other participating artists or gallerists? While very little criticism and reviews of the fair exist, perhaps underscoring the attendance problems ART/LA92 was experiencing, Kaufman's instinct to call up the fair organizers and call out their glaring exclusion led to an exhibition that brought three distinctive visual art perspectives of the 1992 Los Angeles Riots to the fair. From paintings that underscored the unseen makings for unrest to documentation of its destruction, from process art that tracked recovery efforts to assemblages and found objects that shed light on the false sense of modernity's progress, *The Antiphony of Anarchy* provided the only dedicated exhibit acknowledging that the devastating event had even occurred.

Absolut Billboard Art

In the fall of 1992, after securing the booth and his exhibition at the fair, Kaufman walked Sunset Strip in West Hollywood searching for the best vantage point to snap a few photographs of the newly installed Absolut Vodka billboard (Figure 2.5).[124] For nine years, Carillon Imports—the company that introduced Absolut Vodka to the United States—had commissioned artists to make billboards as an extension of its wildly popular international advertisement campaign, "Absolut Art."[125] The company contacted Kaufman after hearing about his recent work, and Kaufman immediately proposed a billboard series on the unrest made by a multicultural array of artists. Carillon Imports accepted the proposal but set parameters for Kaufman and all other participating artists: Each artist had to use the distinctive silhouette of the Absolut Vodka bottle as the basis for their work and include the name of the liquor brand to stay in line with its ad campaign.[126] The snapshots Kaufman took that fall captured the first of the two-part billboard series, which included five hand-painted, 25-foot-high by 8-foot-wide "bottles," each emblazoned with "Absolut Vodka."[127]

Installed on October 28, 1992, the first billboard displayed "bottles" made by Kaufman, Phoebe Beasley, Frank Gutierrez, Joel Nakamura, and

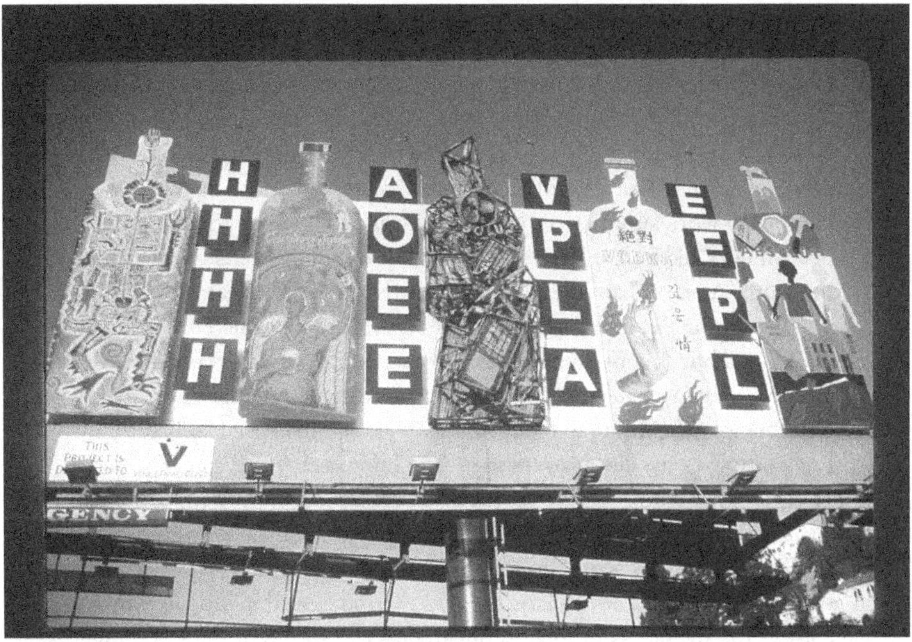

FIGURE 2.5 Joel Nakamura, Frank Gutierrez, Seth Kaufman, Hyesook Park, and Phoebe Beasley, *Absolut Hope*, 1992. Billboard at the intersection of Sunset and Crescent Heights Boulevards, West Hollywood, CA. Photograph courtesy Seth Kaufman.

Hyesook Park.[128] Between each artist's contribution were letters that formed a slogan conceived by Kaufman: "HAVE HOPE HELP HEAL." The alliterative phrase, inspired by artist Alex Echo's *Love Life Live Safe* (1992), communicated a theme centered on reunifying the so-called post-riot city, and Kaufman hoped to contribute to the restoration and reconciliation efforts with the public display of work made by artists who were white, Black, Latino, and Asian American.[129] Indeed, after the first few days of unrest, demonstrations and neighborhood clean-up campaigns began to take place throughout Los Angeles. With the racially charged and anti-immigrant looting, arson, and assaults, residents sought ways to mend, not just the physical damage of the city, but also the strained relationships between its diverse communities. Most notable was the Korean American peace demonstration, whose attendees offered pleas to stop attacks committed by and against Koreans while publicly expressing disapproval of the jury's acquittal of the police who battered and assaulted King.[130] Yet, while most of the artists' "bottles" used motifs that expressed notions of hope, love, unity, and restoration, the message behind Kaufman's was ambiguous.[131] His work, a three-dimensional assemblage in the shape of the bottle, resembled a building ravaged by fire. Using detritus that he took from properties burned down during the unrest and using skills he obtained building sets as a former actor, his contribution dramatically staged a scene evoking the city's freshly wounded landscape.

Kaufman built his "bottle" 3 feet deep and outfitted it with electrical components that controlled a large warehouse fan and lights. The top half of the work supported the slow spinning fan, which the artist backlit with fiery red bulbs. Dangling beneath it were blue letters that formed the word "Absolut," and below this the artist placed two barred windows at opposing angles and backlit them with yellow to further convey the illusion of a burning building. Between the windows, letters for the word "Vodka" spilled vertically, which underscored the sense that the scorched building was beginning to fail from the degradation caused by fire. Below the windows a backlit door dramatically hung askew and ajar. The background of the entire "bottle" contained corrugated sheet metal and large strips of wood that Kaufman sourced from actual burned-down properties and sometimes scorched himself for added effect. He then accented the charred materials with large strokes of bright paint in mostly primary colors. The overall assemblage appeared as if it was in imminent danger of total collapse—not only because of Kaufman's theatrical use of light and movement, but because he visually severed the top portion from the bottom by disjointing the outline of the assemblage and placing a large diagonal beam at its center.

During the daytime, *Absolut Triumph* resembled the numerous properties in Los Angeles that had been destroyed during the unrest. At night, when the lights shone brightly, Kaufman's assemblage seemed to be actively burning (Figure 2.6). As a work that recalled and was made from the buildings arsonists burned down, one might question whose triumph the title referenced.[132] At the time, Kaufman stated that he made the assemblage to demonstrate to audiences that "out of the ruin and ashes we can build something beautiful."[133] Yet the motif of the burning building, which evoked the thousands of properties lost to fire just months before, challenged, even contradicted, the artist's billboard slogan of unity and hope.

Though unintentional, the artist's symbolic destruction of the Absolut Vodka bottle could be read as a criticism of the brand and its commercialization of the unrest, as a critique of the proliferation of liquor stores over grocery stores in the working-class Black and Brown neighborhoods disproportionately affected by the unrest, or even as a warning of the destruction that could return if the city did not "heal." Today Kaufman embraces the alternative messages his work communicates about Absolut Vodka, the city, and the sociopolitical landscape. In our 2015 interview,

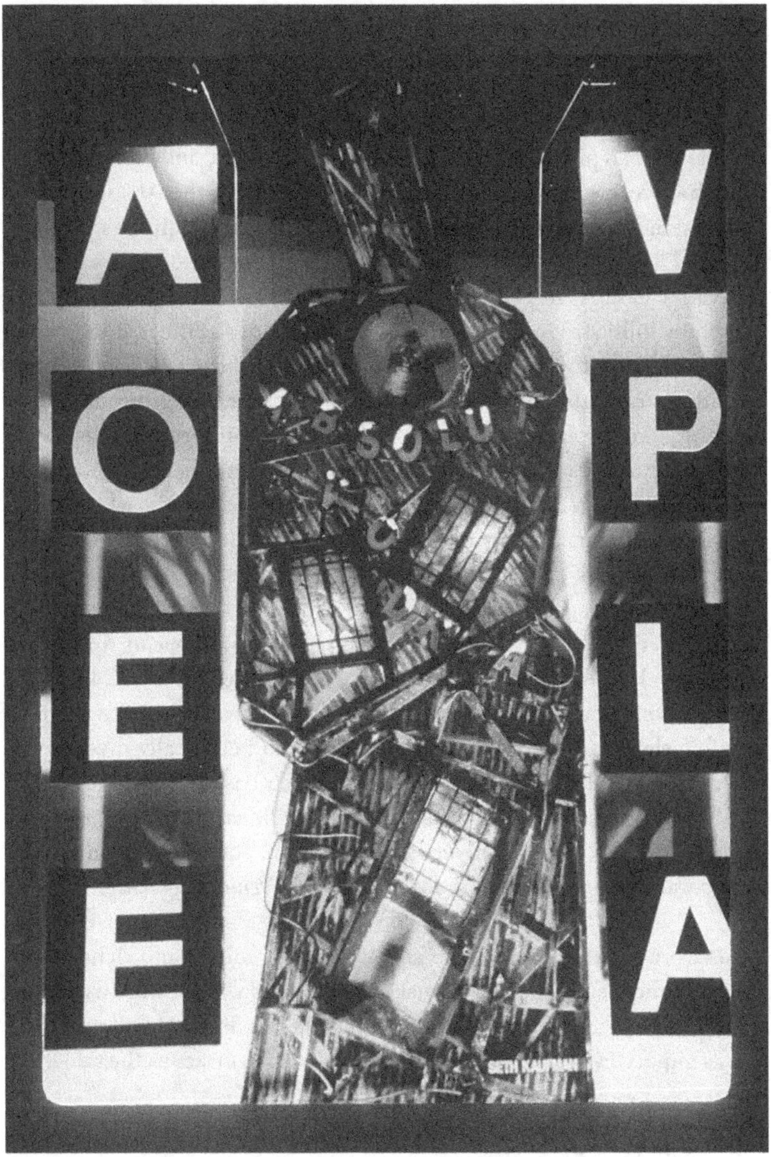

FIGURE 2.6 Seth Kaufman, *Absolut Triumph*, 1992. Courtesy the artist.

he stated, "I put the alcohol bottle in a negative light. It doesn't celebrate the bottle." Yet, returning to the hopeful message of the series, Kaufman continued, "Essentially, my idea was the fan moving at one or two rpms, very, very slowly, so that it was supposed to represent 'We're down, but we're not out.' And I painted it very colorfully and celebratory, but I also burnt it. It was a commentary on rebirth and rebuilding."[134] The paradoxes expressed in the work and cited in the interview defined the artist's practice during the time of the 1992 Los Angeles Riots.

Around the time Kaufman called the organizers of ART/LA92, an acquaintance had pitched his work to Carillon Imports, and he began planning the two-part billboard series on the unrest for the Absolut Vodka advertisement campaign. As previously mentioned, Kaufman's proposal included a multicultural slate of artists, which meant to convey the notion of racial unity in post-riot Los Angeles. Known as the *Absolut Hope* series, the billboard included large-scale silhouettes of the iconic Absolut Vodka bottle that were painted by two sets of five artists—each set representing nearly the same five racial and/or ethnic backgrounds.[135] The first billboard displayed hand-painted "bottles" by Phoebe Beasley (African American), Frank Gutierrez (Chicano/Mexican American), Kaufman (white Jewish American), Joel Nakamura (Japanese American), and Hyesook Park (Korean American) (see Figure 2.5).[136] The second in the series presented artwork by Bernie Casey (African American), Young Joo Choi (Korean American), Patti Heid (white American), Marc Katano (Japanese American), and Gronk Nicandro (Chicano/Mexican American) (Figure 2.7).[137] Also noteworthy is that the two sets of artists included four women total, two for each billboard.[138] However, unlike the purposeful selection of artists who were racially and ethnically diverse, it is unclear whether Kaufman explicitly chose artists based on their gender.[139]

Michel Roux, president and CEO of Carillon Imports, who spearheaded the "Absolut Art" advertising campaign, addressed the multicultural curation of the campaign for an article in *Venice* magazine.

> This work of art is symbolic of the diversity of culture and richness of spirit of the many groups who make up our nation. Our future has been entrusted to each of us, and that which makes us different will prove to be as important to shaping the future as that which makes us the same.[140]

In a 1993 article featured in *Print* magazine, Eric La Brecque criticized the billboard's slogan, "HAVE HOPE HELP HEAL," and the purported celebration of difference as one that bought into the "multicultural myth." La Brecque went even further, describing the billboard as "the graphic equivalent of Rodney King's well-intentioned but pathetic plea, Can't we all just get along?," implying that the cross-racial violence of the 1992 Los Angeles Riots and the events leading to the unrest demonstrated that the city was anything but the picture of racial harmony that the artists portrayed.[141] To be sure, La Brecque misquotes King. King's original public

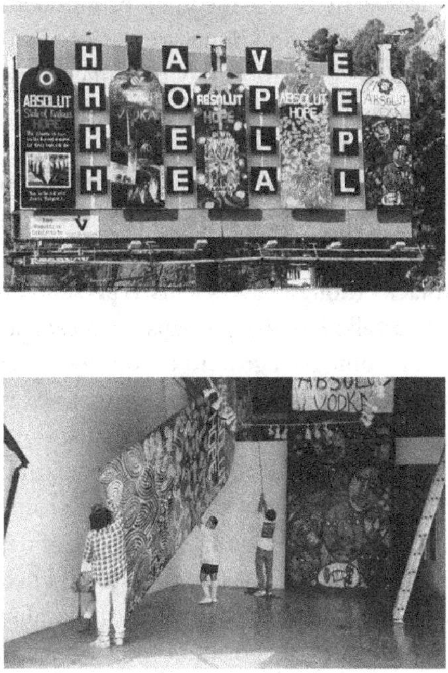

FIGURE 2.7 *Top*: Bernie Casey, Young Joo Choi, Patti Heid, Marc Katano, and Gronk Nicandro, *Absolut Hope*, 1993. Billboard at the intersection of Sunset and Crescent Heights Boulevards, West Hollywood, CA. *Bottom*: Installation for *Absolut Hope* (1993) reception at the Sharon Truax Fine Art Gallery in Venice, CA. Artwork by Marc Katano, left, and Gronk Nicandro, center. Photos: Nicole Katano. Courtesy Marc and Nicole Katano.

appeal included the repeated question, "Can we all get along?," which then morphed into his insistence that everyone must "try to work it out."[142] While deemed "pathetic"—both King's appeal and Kaufman's billboard message—the actionable effort, beyond words, is worthwhile.

For the first billboard, each artist's work was distinctive in style and ranged in content (Figure 2.5). Beasley's work included a collage of figures and objects that referenced cross-racial unity, clean-up efforts, new construction, and job development. Gutierrez's figurative work comprised an angel painting a rainbow within a dreamlike landscape of embers. Park's piece included red-orange flames that could be interpreted as threatening if it were not surrounded by a delicately painted hand whose touching fingertips recall the *vitarka* or *janan mudra*, which are ritualistic gestures of debate and knowledge in Buddhist practice. Nakamura painted a cartoonish creature whose body was made up of silhouettes of guns, hammers, flames, human figures, and bones that can be interpreted as an allegory of the unrest. The creature's belly contained an open mouth from which emerged a tall flower whose head was an open palm, which recalls the hamsa sign of protection.[143]

In the second billboard of the series, more of the "bottles" contained abstracted subject matter (see Figure 2.7). For instance, Katano's piece consisted of organic oval-shaped forms of various sizes in shades of white, red, yellow, and black. Though Heid's work represented a large diamond, she connected it to a yellow shape, perhaps a representation of a beam of light, set in front of a blue background of loosely rendered white polka dots. The pieces by Choi and Casey were less abstract, yet their contents were difficult to distinguish due to size and painting styles. Choi rendered a nighttime scene, with a full moon and a bird soaring through a dark blue sky with various figures set below—people, a car, plants, and other shapes. Casey's work depicted a bifurcated image of day and night with small, cursive, hard-to-read text written above and below it, which expressed a message about the need for love. Last, standing out from these works, was the painting of large, recognizably human figures by Glugio Gronk Nicandro, who goes by the mononym Gronk. The differently colored faces, which seemed to symbolize racial diversity, appeared as if they were submerged in liquid and crowded up against the "glass" of the Absolut Vodka "bottle."[144] Dubbed by the artist "pickled heads," the fifteen faces appeared wide-eyed but expressionless as they stared out at viewers.[145] Gronk's desecration of the liquor brand's iconic bottle with decapitated heads, like Kaufman's rendering of it as a burning building, could be read as a challenge to the billboard's overall message of unity and hope and, by extension, a criticism of Absolut Vodka's advertising campaign and the commodification of the unrest.

In a 1993 magazine interview, Kaufman explained the theme and slogan of *Absolut Hope* by hedging criticism through the personalization of his intentions. He stated, "I don't mean to promote a message of healing, I mean to be an example of healing."[146] At a time of high-profile cases of brutality, destruction, and loss, the placement of himself as a model for healing is offensive and gestures toward his co-optation of the period. The remark also countered his slogan, "HAVE HOPE HELP HEAL," which expressed the notion of community renewal.

Kaufman claims to have received other criticisms for the *Absolut Hope* campaign. In a 2015 interview, he stated, "Unbeknownst to me, there was a cultural discourse that surrounded liquor companies in the inner city and the lack of resources for fresh food. Not being a part of that dialogue, I wasn't aware of it."[147] He continued, "There was some consternation from the community regarding Absolut Vodka sponsoring a message of unification using the liquor bottle as a vehicle, being that there was this discourse about the lack of resources in the inner city, the predominance of liquor stores and alcoholism."[148] No published criticism could be found surrounding the role of the liquor brand's commodification of the 1992 Los Angeles Riots. However, protests against the preponderance of liquor stores in South Central Los Angeles did occur in the 1990s. Years later, Mark Bradford would make *Rebuild South Central* (2015), a mixed-media painting based on a photograph he took in 1992 of a protest sign emblazoned with the bilingual English and Spanish demand, "Rebuild South Central without liquor stores!"[149] While Kaufman admits to his ignorance then about "food deserts" and the contentiousness between low-income communities and liquor companies specifically, the symbolic destruction of the liquor bottle via *Absolut Triumph* harbors the potential to signify conflict with the company and gesture toward these issues whether or not the artist originally intended it.[150]

Although Le Brecque criticized *Absolut Hope,* he went on to praise Kaufman's artwork for the billboard campaign, stating, "If you took time to study it, [it] was different. It didn't represent anything easy. It *was* something in itself."[151] Indeed, Kaufman's 25-foot-high assemblage stands out among the other commissioned works—even Gronk's contribution. Whereas the other artists in the series made mostly one-dimensional compositions that tended to stay within the frame of the traditional bottle shape, Kaufman built a high-relief sculpture and dramatically altered the shape of the bottle's silhouette. The content of Kaufman's work—made from materials burned during the unrest and rebuilt as a burning building—allowed for a pessimistic interpretation of post-riot Los Angeles that could place Absolut Vodka in a negative light. Interestingly, the company severed its relationship with Kaufman. While the concept for the billboard campaign was largely based on his ideas and he selected the artists for both billboards, he claims to have been shunned by company representatives and was excluded from the second billboard's installation process and press. To this day, Kaufman is unsure why.[152]

Anniversary Exhibition

After a year of collecting materials from burned-down properties and making assemblages and found objects, Kaufman's work culminated in a solo exhibition. *Dwelling in Rebellion: A Year to the Day* opened at Zero One Gallery in the Melrose District of Los Angeles on Friday, April 30, 1993—just one day after the one-year anniversary of the 1992 Los Angeles Riots (Figure 2.8).[153] It included *Behind My Window Pain*, a filmed spoken word performance staged in the shell of a burned-down property, and about forty-four assemblages and found objects, some of which were also on view at ART/LA92. Unlike the art fair, Kaufman apparently sold about two dozen works at Zero One Gallery, which typically exhibited street art, graffiti, and other work by artists from the "underground" Los Angeles art scene.[154] It is unclear why he sold more works at the small gallery than at the art fair, especially since his "looted" materials were deemed marketable by the fair and Carillon Imports with their buy-in of his curatorial projects and gifts of free space. However, the solo exhibition had been what Kaufman originally hoped for but the fair organizers had denied.

While Kaufman whirled around the busy gallery on the opening night of his solo exhibition, Mr. and Mrs. Martin walked inside. In recollecting the event for me, the artist recalled greeting the owners of the destroyed furniture store where his project first began and thanked them for

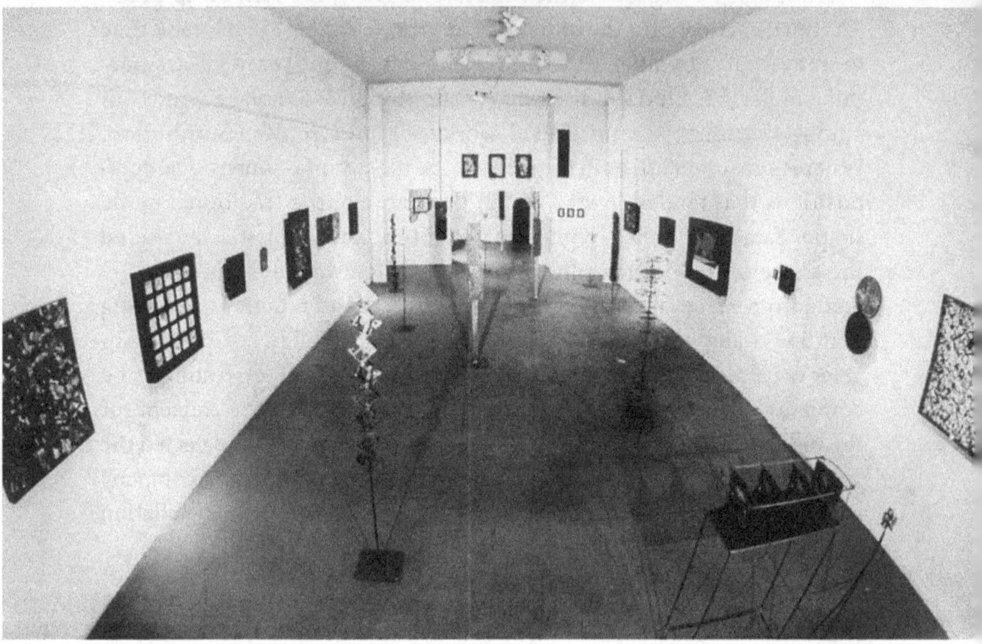

FIGURE 2.8 Seth Kaufman, Installation view of the exhibition *Dwelling in Rebellion: A Year to the Day*, April 30–May 29, 1993, Zero One Gallery, Los Angeles, CA. Courtesy the artist.

attending.[155] Watching them in the gallery, he remembered wondering if they would recognize the wood screws he found in copious amounts at their property and be surprised to see just how many he ended up using in his assemblages. According to Kaufman, if they did, they did not mention it to him. Instead, they spent their time at the gallery seeming to marvel at the burned objects.[156]

Notably, this exhibition became the last major presentation of his work from the *L.A. Rebellion* series. In 2002, Kaufman spoke with Christopher Reynolds, a staff writer for the *Los Angeles Times* covering the arts for the ten-year anniversary of the unrest. He explained, "I didn't want to become 'The Riot Guy.' I exorcised what I needed to get out of me, and it was time to move along," and continued, "I came out of that year broke."[157] Reynolds noted an "ambivalence" in Kaufman's recollection. Then the writer quoted the artist as stating:

> It was a very tumultuous and painful journey. . . . I came under attack in many cases, in fact, because I was a white guy talking about issues that had largely affected inner-city groups. But the fact is that we were all terrified as we drove around the city, and we all saw the buildings on fire.[158]

Reynolds ended the segment on Kaufman with this statement, allowing the uncomfortable and unequal comparison between what "inner-city groups" experienced and what others merely looked at speak for itself.

That Was Then, This Is Then

On August 11, 2015, Kaufman and I spent a total of four hours going through his personal archives at his Southern California home. He had several storage boxes filled with slides, photographs, magazines, videos, and various documents related to his artwork on the 1992 Los Angeles Riots. While the artist possesses slides and photographs of his work and still has some of the objects in his personal collection, many were sold to private collectors. At the time, Kaufman did not keep records of the transactions or a list of who collected his work. Thus many of the works are only accessible through photographs and slides. Due to the aging technology, we worked together that day with the intention of selecting images and other relevant documents to preserve digitally for future audiences and researchers.[159]

I organized photographs, press releases, artist's statements, and other ephemera from *The Antiphony of Anarchy*, *Absolut Hope*, and *Dwelling in Rebellion* in separate folders and envelopes while Kaufman examined hundreds of slides, filtering out doubles and poor-quality images from those he felt should be preserved. I came across old photographs from another billboard campaign the artist organized for President Bill Clinton's 1993 Summer of Service initiative, a national community service program to give youth job opportunities in exchange for educational and financial assistance. The photographs depicted the billboard's canvas splayed at the bottom of the Hollywood Athletic Club's unfilled pool. Numerous volunteers—artists, actors, youth, and a few elders and small children—held brushes and cans of paint as they colored in the figures and letters that spelled out the name of the community service program.[160] The photographs showed participants working closely together, painting, smiling, and having conversations with each other. For this project, Kaufman seemed to have genuinely developed a dialogue and creative exchange with residents, artists, and volunteers. It then occurred to me that this community-based project he led would not have taken place without his experience curating the Absolut Vodka billboard campaign or organizing the group show at the art fair the previous year.

I sorted through another stack of photographs. It included several polaroids of burned properties with the facades blackened and melted away. A couple other photos capture Kaufman digging through debris. They seemed staged, not only because a professional photographer took the photographs, but because of the forced appearance of the pose: the artist holding a found object and pondering it with a too-neat smear of dirt across his face. Then I came across other snapshots of Kaufman actively making the large-scale assemblage for the billboard and installation shots of his exhibitions. I continued sifting through the photos but paused when I came across a snapshot of a beautiful young woman. The image, taken from the inside of a pickup, captured the bronze-skinned Latina as she entered the vehicle with a large and colorful bouquet of loosely gathered flowers. Surprised by the camera, she smiled, and the spray of blooms complemented her equally beautiful smile. I showed the seemingly out-of-place photo to Kaufman. Taking it in his hands, he beamed. It was a photo he snapped of his then-girlfriend in the year or two after the completion of his projects on the 1992 Los Angeles Riots. Years later, they would marry and build a family. After sharing the flood of memories the photograph sparked, he set it aside for safekeeping. As we resumed the archival work, I thought of the Martins and the album of photographs that captured their early years of courtship in Cuba, which Kaufman found in the shambles of their business over two decades earlier. Kaufman had once thought of turning their keepsakes into art, but he eventually returned them—not only because it got him out of a conflict with Mr. Martin but also because

Mrs. Martin made him realize the significance of the photos beyond their mere art-making potential.

Kaufman's practice of "post-riot looting" led to one of the few series of art that contains materials collected from buildings that were destroyed.[161] After the city cleared out the damaged properties and eliminated many of the visible traces of rebellion from the streets, the found objects and assemblages from his series inadvertently became the few remaining collections to include physical relics of the unrest.[162] The artist's firsthand experiences excavating materials from the properties, his contentious interactions with the Martins, and the multiple exhibition opportunities he created for himself and other artists are also significant, especially in a sociopolitical landscape with deep divisions and during a period of multiculturalism that struggled to recenter diverse voices. Kaufman's art, his partnerships with commercial enterprises, and the projects he curated highlight understudied traces of the 1992 Los Angeles Riots and emphasize the need for ongoing examination, despite the contradictions and flaws.

✷ 3 ✷

Beyond Black and White

On July 21, 2018, at the Museum of Modern Art (MoMA), I stood in line anxiously waiting to enter *Black Box/White Box* (1992). I had recently studied photographs, reviews, and other documentation of the installation, which comprised two larger-than-life cubes that contained multimedia references to the 1991 videotaped police beating of Rodney King and the 1992 Los Angeles Riots; but this would be the first time I experienced the installation for myself. The artist-philosopher Adrian Piper originally completed the commissioned work for a 1992 group exhibition at Ohio's Wexner Center for the Arts, and after being acquired in 2003 by Austria's Generali Foundation and exhibited at several international venues, it had recently returned to the United States for the MoMA retrospective, *Adrian Piper: A Synthesis of Intuitions, 1965–2016* (Figure 3.1). Placed in the context of a career spanning over five decades, Piper's use of conceptual and minimal art strategies to tackle issues of race, gender, and xenophobia were clear, consistent, and powerful. I had initially been drawn to Piper's work for her specific cutting-edge combination of formal art strategies and multimedia to explore issues of race and racism, of which *Black Box/White Box* is an example. The long history of art critics' refusal to see her work for what it was—not a reflection of her but an opportunity for viewers to explore their perceptions and understandings of themselves and others—also intrigued me.

The MoMA installation of *Black Box/White Box* was different from the original. Apart from the wait, likely the result of the rave exhibition reviews and the last weekend to see the show, it was placed among other works by Piper, and, most notably, it was missing the atmospheric sound of fire and the gray-colored gallery walls that originally enveloped the stark black and white cubes at the Wexner Center. While these components may have been deemed unnecessary to its specific presentation in the MoMA retrospective, the absences led me to reflect on the 1992 installation and its

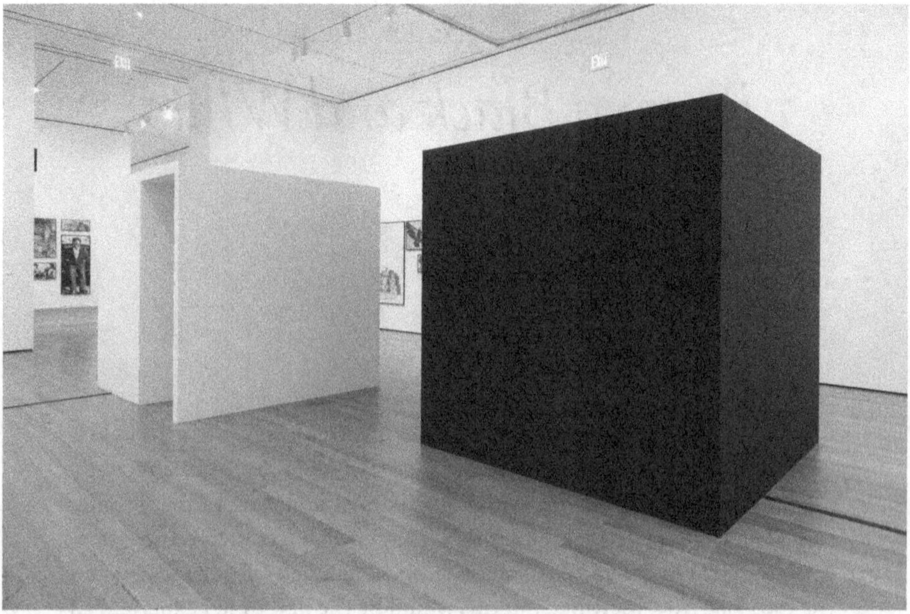

FIGURE 3.1 Adrian Piper, *Black Box/White Box*, 1992. Mixed-media installation. Video (color, sound; 00:30:00), with two constructed wood environments, monitor, four photographs, light box, audio, chairs, tables, tissue boxes, and trash baskets. Dimensions variable. Installation view of Adrian Piper: *A Synthesis of Intuitions, 1965–2016*, The Museum of Modern Art, New York, March 31–July 22, 2018. Photo: Martin Seck. Generali Foundation Collection Permanent Loan to the Museum der Moderne Salzburg. © Generali Foundation and Adrian Piper Research Archive Foundation. Digital image © The Museum of Modern Art. Licensed by SCALA/Art Resource, NY.

poignant immediacy in the aftermath of unrest. The context of the original installation also included both a Midwestern location and a group exhibition to address another major event that year: the five-hundred-year anniversary of Christopher Columbus's "discovery" of the "new world." How did the original components of *Black Box/White Box* work together, and how did this affect a viewer's understanding of the work, especially so soon after the widely disseminated footage of brutality and fires, far from the Los Angeles epicenter, and during the Columbus Quincentennial? How did the issues of race, racism, and violence register then and echo across time? One of the significant threads the 2018 retrospective of Piper's work highlighted is the frustrating and dangerous continuity of bigotry in American culture and society, including that within our very conception of race. Thus I understand the black- and white-colored cubes as visual metaphors for race and race relations in the United States—and as a critique of the rigid binary of race that "boxes" in our understanding and perception of others.

Piper's *Black Box/White Box* addresses the Black-white racial narrative with the use of aesthetic strategies she acquired and developed from minimalism and conceptualism, broadening the discussion of race, the systemic nature of oppression, and considerations of how society engages in xenophobic thought and behavior. While these attributes are present in numerous works in Piper's oeuvre, I argue that *Black Box/White Box* is a marked change in her practice in her use of the timely and vastly familiar video of the King beating. With the use of the King video, along with a formally rigorous and multimedia array of visual and sonic strategies, the issues of race and xenophobia advance from philosophical contemplation to a deepened viewer engagement, where viewers were confronted with their tacit consent of and role in state violence. Showing it outside of Los Angeles, in the Midwest and parallel to the Columbus Quincentennial, *Black Box/White Box* also ties the beating of King and the 1992 Los Angeles Riots to a longer and broader history of brutality and subjugation. In this way, I view the installation as a demand for us to push the discussion of race and xenophobia beyond the dominant dichotomy of racial discourse in the United States. This is not to ignore the specific history of racial violence that the King video captured but to recognize how it affects all those within and outside its bounds. Illustrative of unrest is Piper's unrelenting drive to make work that encourages viewers to challenge their perceptions of themselves and others, to take responsibility for changing the limiting and life-and-death consequences of racist and xenophobic conditions, and to use the heightened knowledge and awareness—an expanded understanding of our shared humanity—to end bigotry in all its forms.

Post-Riot at the Wexner Center

The alarming sounds of fire resonated through the Wexner Center for the Arts in the fall of 1992. Emanating from an exhibition space, the source of the crackling noise led the university museum visitors not to flames but to two monumental black and white cubes (Figure 3.2).[1] At approximately eight cubic feet each, *Black Box/White Box* (1992) was stark in appearance and presentation. The gray-colored walls and ceiling of the gallery referenced the smoke one might expect to see with the sounds of smoldering fire; yet the painted surfaces were sleek and unadorned, like the cubes.[2]

In the catalog essay for *Will/Power*, the group exhibition that included

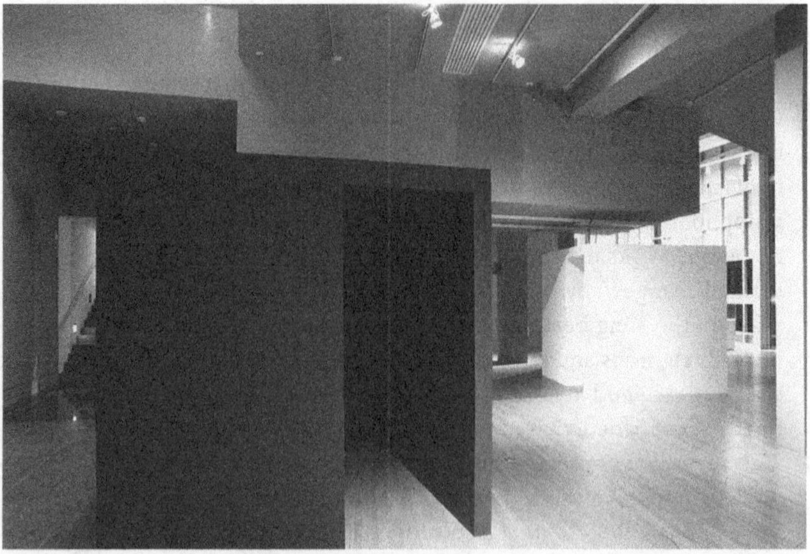

FIGURE 3.2 Adrian Piper, *Black Box/White Box*, 1992. Mixed-media installation. Video (color, sound; 00:30:00), with two constructed wood environments, monitor, four photographs, light box, audio, chairs, tables, tissue boxes, and trash baskets. Dimensions variable. Installation view of *Will/Power: New Works by Papo Colo, Jimmie Durham, David Hammons, Hachivi Edgar Heap of Birds, Adrian Piper, Aminah Brenda Lynn Robinson*, Wexner Center for the Arts, The Ohio State University, September 26–December 27, 1992. Image courtesy of the Wexner Center for the Arts. Photo: Richard K. Loesch. Generali Foundation Collection Permanent Loan to the Museum der Moderne Salzburg. © Generali Foundation and Adrian Piper Research Archive Foundation.

Piper's installation, the Wexner Center's assistant curator, Ann Bremner, remembers that the artist's April visit to the Columbus, Ohio, art institution coincided with the onset of the 1992 Los Angeles Riots.[3] News broadcasts of the unrest included aerial views of Los Angeles with thick, dense clouds of smoke rising from the raging fires.[4] The sounds the fires made as they consumed the buildings and their contents also stood out in Bremner's memory.[5] Piper, who traveled to the Wexner Center in preparation for the commissioned work, decided to capture the conditions of the unrest and strip down the fire and smoke to their most essential auditory and visual elements. This minimalist use of color and form for *Black Box/White Box* would focus viewers' attention on the materials she selected for scrutiny.

As Wexner Center audiences walked around each box, they encountered a built-in short corridor that led to a small interior core. In contrast to the stark exteriors, the cores of each cube contained an assortment of auditory and visual materials. Piper also constructed each of the cube's interior spaces in a way that restricted viewers' entry and movements. While each cube was around eight cubic feet, their cores were smaller in size due to the corridor and the inclusion of objects, furniture, and equipment (Figures 3.3 and 3.4). Thus the physically stifling interiors of *Black Box/White Box* allowed one viewer to enter at a time to take in and focus on the multiple forms of media intimately.

Inside the interior spaces, the viewer encountered one black leatherette chair that was flanked by a small table holding a box of Kleenex on one side and a wastebasket on the other. Behind each chair hung the same photograph of then-President George H. W. Bush shaking the hands of police officers. The Ben-Day dots that composed the image made clear its newspaper origins, and, indeed, Associated Press photographer Marcy

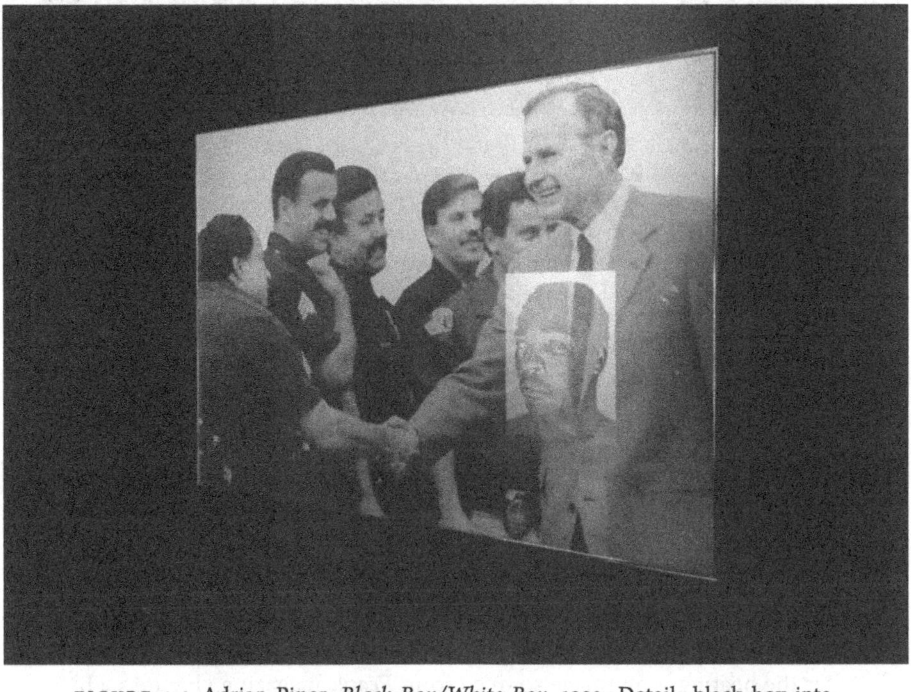

FIGURE 3.3 Adrian Piper, *Black Box/White Box*, 1992. Detail: black box interior. Installation view of *Adrian Piper: A Synthesis of Intuitions, 1965–2016*, The Museum of Modern Art, New York, March 31–July 22, 2018. Source photography: John I. Barr/ Gamma-Liaison and Marcy Nighswander/AP. Photo: Martin Seck. Generali Foundation Collection Permanent Loan to the Museum der Moderne Salzburg. © Generali Foundation and Adrian Piper Research Archive Foundation. Digital Image © The Museum of Modern Art. Licensed by SCALA/Art Resource, NY.

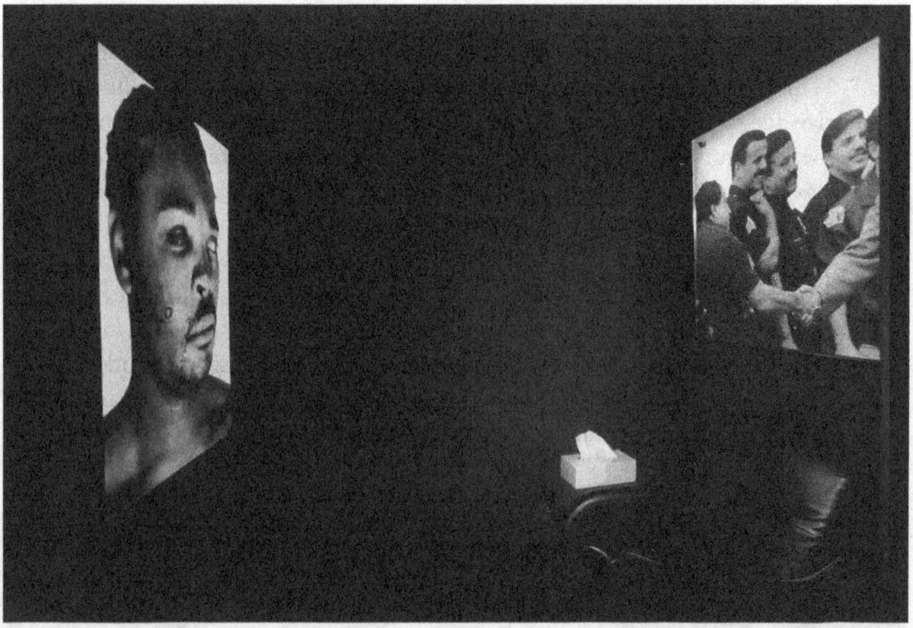

FIGURE 3.4 Adrian Piper, *Black Box/White Box*, 1992. Detail: black box interior. Installation view of *Will/Power: New Works by Papo Colo, Jimmie Durham, David Hammons, Hachivi Edgar Heap of Birds, Adrian Piper, Aminah Brenda Lynn Robinson*, Wexner Center for the Arts, The Ohio State University, September 26–December 27, 1992. Source photography: John I. Barr/Gamma-Liaison (*left*) and Marcy Nighswander/AP (*right*). Photo: Richard K. Loesch. Image courtesy of the Wexner Center for the Arts. Generali Foundation Collection Permanent Loan to the Museum der Moderne Salzburg. © Generali Foundation and Adrian Piper Research Archive Foundation.

Nighswander took the original image during the president's survey of Los Angeles "post-riot."[6] In front of each chair and press photo, the viewer faced what Piper called an "image screen."[7] In *White Box* this "image screen" was a television monitor embedded in the wall that played on a loop the video of King's beating. In *Black Box*, the "image screen" was a backlit portrait of King taken by photographer John T. Barr three days after the beating—an image sourced from *People* magazine (Figure 3.4).[8] Along with each "image screen," the viewer heard audio recordings of music and speeches that the artist meticulously edited to accompany the visuals.

Once the viewer exited the black cube and its white counterpart, she may have further reflected on the meaning of their colors. In fact, this was my experience of *Black Box/White Box* in 2018, and I have come to view the black and white cubes as allegories that signify them as Black and white bodies. I therefore suggest that the Black-white racial binary, together with the formal and multimedia components, encouraged meditation on the racial violence surrounding the King beating and the unrest in 1992. It also encouraged an acknowledgment of the historical and ongoing American tradition wherein this Black-white dichotomy drives national narratives, locates conflict, and favors particular racialized encounters and experiences over others. Yet one could not ignore the reference to the ubiquitous cubes found in minimalism. We encounter Piper's dynamic development of art strategies drawn from both minimalism and conceptualism, which help us understand more deeply her interest in engaging viewers to examine critically their perceptions of others.

The Influence of Minimalism and Conceptualism

The large cubes of Piper's *Black Box/White Box*, devoid of exterior decoration beyond their painted surfaces, evoke the minimalist sculptures of the 1960s and 1970s. In particular, the artist seems to harken back to the sleek, pared-down cubes made by artists such as Donald Judd, Robert Morris, and Tony Smith.[9] Although Piper was twenty years younger than Morris and Judd and thirty-six years younger than Smith, she began making minimal art not long after they began.[10] As explained by art historian John Bowles, the particular minimalism of Judd and Morris and the conceptualism of Sol LeWitt, an artist known for his serial structures and instruction-based large-scale wall art, deeply influenced Piper's early work.[11] Bowles explains how the minimal and conceptual strategies worked together: One brought to attention the materiality of construction and exhibition and the influence of space and time on viewer's experience of an object; the other "harness[ed] the contingency of the self-reflexive encounter to direct viewers' attentions beyond the artwork." Together, they allowed artists and viewers to engage in self-reflection, including a politicized one.[12]

Piper, who has described her work from the 1960s as "strictly minimalist," explains that minimalism and conceptualism provided her with new tools and intellectual freedom as an artist.[13] She found potential in their capacities to abstract content and obscure evidence of her hand and subjectivity in the art-making process.[14] At the same time, she found minimal artists insistence on specificity compelling. In a discussion of how many contemporary artists take as their charge the questioning and expansion of knowledge to remedy conventional or even narrowminded thinking, she explains, "The point of presenting geometrically, materially and formally reductive objects was to draw the viewer's attention away from extrinsic association and toward the specificity and materiality of the particular object itself."[15] She goes on to explain, "In its aesthetic strategies, Minimalism repudiated the imposition of abstract theory—psychoanalytic, social, or aesthetic—as cognitively inadequate to a full comprehension of the work. Instead it emphasized the uniqueness, singularity, and indexical immediacy of the art object itself."[16]

What became known as minimalism developed partly as a response to abstract expressionism, illusionistic qualities in painting, and the critic's increasing reliance on biography, psychology, and even spirituality to understand artworks. A younger generation of artists began thinking critically about the art object itself. That this so-called detached art, often historicized as being void of politics, developed during the civil rights era and the antiwar movement is significant.[17] I view as dubious the assertion that minimalism was apolitical or impersonal. That claim willfully closes its eyes to sociopolitical context. Furthermore, any claim that art is detached or removed from its social or political contexts is a politics in itself.

Soon after Piper's early art-making period, she began to realize that she could not maintain the intellectual freedom she had found. Her ambiguously gendered name and low visibility in the art world had initially, and inadvertently, veiled her identity as an African American woman.[18] However, as she became better known within the art community, she increasingly experienced sexism and racism.[19] These experiences followed her throughout her academic career as a philosophy graduate student and then a professor.[20]

The early experiences of discrimination in Piper's art and academic careers increased with her rising political consciousness in the context of the Vietnam War, the US invasion of Cambodia, and the shooting deaths of students by the National Guard at Kent State University and Jackson State College.[21] She became, in her words, "self-conscious."[22] But more than that, Bowles explains, the state's suppression of dissent and the mass actions that began to take place made Piper realize how "she had previously resisted and even consciously avoided recognizing art's potential to effect change in the viewer."[23] He shares that in a statement she made on the withdrawal of her work from a conceptual art exhibition in response to the student killings, she "declared abstract forms and ideas unsuitable for a moment scarred by violence and moral corruption."[24]

While Piper sardonically describes her art during the 1960s as "the work I did in the Garden of Eden, before I found out I was a black woman," she went on to use the strategies of minimalism and conceptualism to investigate the conditions of discrimination and oppression in the United States—forging a new methodological purpose.[25] While conceptual art came to be understood as art that could also be political, many historians came to use the term "post-minimalism" to describe minimalist works that reflected social and political concerns.[26] Yet many of these artists, including Piper, did not recognize their work as set apart from that of other minimalists, and I suggest that the separate category places practitioners in art historical ghettos that not only segregates them from colleagues and mentors, but fixes the development of minimalism in a particular time made by particular people—namely, a few straight white men.

What artists like Piper recognized was how the visual language could be developed further. Due to the currency of minimalism's visuality, her use of it could draw in viewers who recognized the style before they realized its content too. This became an artistic strategy that encouraged viewer engagement with unpopular sociopolitical issues, such as the ongoing prevalence of xenophobia and racism in the United States. Likewise, this strategy encourages the reevaluation of the visual language and its politics.

While, as Bowles underscores, minimal and conceptual strategies first gave her the means to avoid issues of racism and sexism, they subsequently gave her the tools to investigate them and engage viewers to consider these issues as well.[27] These histories and aesthetic strategies would continue to deeply influence Piper's body of work in the years and decades to come. *Black Box/White Box* carried on the artist's meditation on the concurrent art historical and political events of the mid-twentieth century. She also explicitly tied these developments to the 1991 videotaped beating of King and the 1992 Los Angeles Riots—two episodes that, for many, laid bare the ways in which the state and representatives of the law, like the police, violated and rendered precarious the civil rights of Black Americans. Thus the video and unrest provided Piper with a contemporary frame to explore the ongoing experiences of xenophobia and state-sanctioned violence.

The Significance of an Ordinary Place

The Wexner Center mounted *Will/Power* as a group exhibition of commissioned new works that explored the politics surrounding another major event, the Columbus Quincentenary. Locales across hemispheric America had planned celebrations, and the Wexner Center, located in the largest city named after the infamous explorer, sought artists from diverse backgrounds whose work touched on concerns surrounding the event.[28] These concerns were especially captured in many of the contributors' critiques of the city's civic events marking the Quincentenary, such as the replica of the *Santa Maria* that traversed the Scioto River in downtown Columbus and the tourist attraction AmeriFlora'92—the latter of which the exhibition's curator, Sarah J. Rogers, described as a "neo-Disney floral exhibition" that lost money and, worse, displaced Black residents.[29] Acting director William Box Cook shared that Wexner Center staff felt that they had a responsibility "to mark the occasion in a different way," one that would widen points of view and center issues of history and identity.[30] He explained that the artists' works "articulate concerns about self (personal and cultural), about viewpoint and representation of self, about the incompatibility between the canons of history and the realities of those who are exempt from canonical 'truths.'"[31] Yet, for *Black Box/White Box*, Piper did not address her "self" or her personal viewpoint as a Black woman, a racial identity that the artist identified with at the time but "retired" from ten years later—a decision I view as related to her criticisms of the Black-white racial binary.[32] She instead developed an installation that challenged viewers to consider *their* perceptions and subjectivities.

During Piper's April visit to the Wexner Center, the unrest in Los Angeles received continuous media coverage, which informed her decision to address the event in her commissioned artwork.[33] In fact, Rogers explains that Piper had initially planned a different project for the exhibition and that the original intention for her April visit was to help staff troubleshoot its installation. However, because of the unrest in Los Angeles and the artist's increasing desire to create a "truly meaningful intervention" for students at Ohio State University where the Wexner Center is located, Piper decided to stop the original project.[34] She then began developing *Black Box/White Box* as an installation that would encourage viewers to contend with their experiences of the 1992 Los Angeles Riots and their "forced awareness of individual responsibility."[35]

Such intentions are significant. They recognize how the unrest in Los Angeles affected people across the nation and shifted accountability for the events to everyone. To be clear, this is not to discount the real harm caused by actors, like the police officers who beat King, or to downplay the outrage caused by the jury's decision of acquittal. Instead, *Black Box/White Box* underscores how those who seem far from the events are nonetheless connected to them. More than passive viewers of the news or of the artwork, they are part of a system that reifies xenophobia and racial violence, *and* they have the ability to resist and change these behaviors. The presentation of Piper's work at the Wexner also deepens the purpose. It is located on the campus of Ohio State University, a major research institution not unlike those where state violence helped bring Piper to political consciousness in her earlier years. The Wexner, founded in 1989, was also a leading center in the Midwest for the exhibition of experimental and cutting-edge art.[36] The institution played a crucial role in education and the incubation of new ideas while actively displaying the academic and democratic commitments to open inquiry and freedom of expression. Furthermore, the development and presentation of *Black Box/White Box* at the Wexner highlighted how the Midwestern university and town were not immune to state violence and episodes of unrest like those that occurred in Los Angeles.

To this point, let us briefly consider *11777 Foothill Boulevard, Los Angeles, California* (1991) by Lewis Baltz. The large-scale 4 × 8 foot color photograph, commissioned by the Los Angeles County Museum of Art (LACMA) for his traveling retrospective *Rule Without Exception*, depicts what appears to be an everyday street scene of a few vehicles populating a paved road flanked by a gravel sidewalk, housing, streetlights, telephone poles, and a few green bushes (Figure 3.5).[37] It could be a depiction of any suburb in the United States—and that was the point. In a 1992 *Los Angeles Times* interview, Baltz explained that the ordinary appearance of *11777 Foothill Boulevard* was intentional. He purposefully searched the city for "completely generic locations."[38] He clarified:

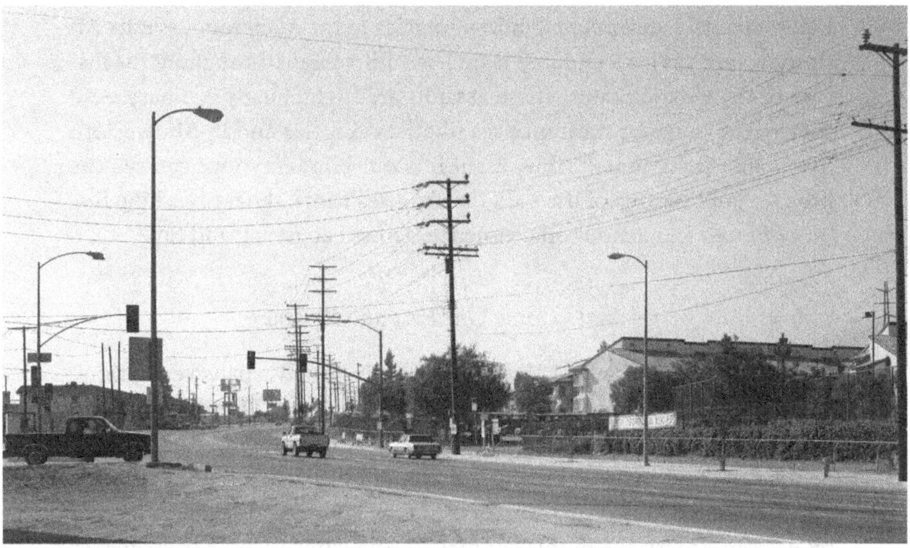

FIGURE 3.5 Lewis Baltz, *11777 Foothill Boulevard, Los Angeles, California*, 1991, printed in 1992. Photograph, Silver dye-bleach (Cibachrome) print, Unframed: 48 × 96 inches (121.92 × 243.84 cm). Los Angeles County Museum of Art, Los Angeles, CA, USA. Commissioned with funds provided by Michael R. Kaplan, M.D., Gary B. Sokol, and the Horace W. Goldsmith Foundation (AC1992.27.1). Digital image © 2026 Museum Associates / LACMA. Licensed by Art Resource, NY. © Copyright Theresa Luisotti Gallery.

> I suppose there's a kind of nostalgia in that, because Los Angeles is really becoming less generic. As it becomes more of a built city, it is taking on some sort of a flavor rather than just of being sort of the id of the Midwest. . . . [But] there are still vast tracts of featureless stuff in Los Angeles. I wanted to make up a photograph that looked easy and typical. Anybody can see that. It's something that's completely unextraordinary. . . . It looks like a skin graft from 50 other locations around here.[39]

Yet the title of Baltz's photograph, which is the street address of the pictured location, is not as "unextraordinary" as he suggests. 11777 Foothill Boulevard is the precise location where Los Angeles police officers beat King on March 3, 1991. Thus the street the photographer captured is at once ordinary and extraordinary. Indeed, without knowledge of the event the address references, the image appears commonplace because it could represent Anywhere USA. Its ordinariness also speaks to another situation: The police beating that took place at 11777 Foothill Boulevard in Los Angeles has been experienced similarly by numerous Black men across the country, at places that look as ordinary as the one in Baltz's photograph.

By presenting *Black Box/White Box* at the Wexner in Columbus, Ohio, Piper linked what happened in Los Angeles to the numerous assaults African Americans have endured from law enforcement throughout the history of the United States. These assaults are frighteningly ordinary. And they occur in major metropolises like Los Angeles and in Midwestern towns like Columbus.[40] Thus Piper lifts our blinders so we can see the broader implications of the 1992 Los Angeles Riots: the far-reaching history of racist and xenophobic violence, across geography and time.

What's Going On: Past and Present

In addition to Piper's work, *Will/Power* also included expansive multimedia installations by Papo Colo, Jimmie Durham, and David Hammons. While none of the other artists addressed the unrest in Los Angeles directly, Rogers compared Piper's and Hammons's artwork in her catalog essay, writing that both artists "focus on the contradictions encountered by African Americans in this country."[41] The comparison Rogers makes of the two artists' installations warrants further investigation. Considering the exhibition's historical and political contexts, how do these two cutting-edge artists harness the past to address the political climate of the present? *Will/Power* provides an organizing concept that we can identify in their works, from the capacity of an individual to influence others to one's ability to exert power over the self.

Rogers organized *Will/Power* in part as a counternarrative to the five-hundred-year celebration of Columbus's expedition to the Americas. Her hope for the exhibition was to respond to the Quincentennial programming happening in Columbus by contributing a celebratory event that brought artists of color together in a "still predominately white institution."[42] While she recognized that the exhibition could be misinterpreted as "one more attempt to 'ghettoize' artists of color as other" by a white curator, she hoped to provide a "forum through which it might become clear that knowledge, point of view, and power are not monolithic."[43] Thus *Will/Power* organizers recognized that the popular narrative of Columbus's voyage was problematic because it skewed and eclipsed the histories and experiences of Indigenous and other people of color. Citing recent debates surrounding multiculturalism, which were sparked by the Columbus Quincentenary, Rogers explains:

> A plethora of assumptions were set forth, beginning with the questionable viewpoint defining Christopher Columbus's adventure as a discovery and the ensuing colonization as progressive, and including the view that marginalization will magically cease if significantly acknowledged by the dominant culture.[44]

Yet she also suggests that the wide discussion of polarizing national accounts could possibly lead to their decentering. This would allow the United States "to move from acknowledgment to knowledge, from will to empowerment."[45] Hammons and Piper sought similar paths toward transformation in their works.

Many artists of the time were likewise attuned to the violence, bigotry, and fantasy surrounding Christopher Columbus's "discovery" of the "new world," its quincentenary celebration, and that which continued to exist through colonial legacies. Perhaps the most well known of such works is Coco Fusco and Guillermo Gómez-Peña's interdisciplinary art project and performance commonly known as *The Couple in the Cage* (1992–94), the documentary of which was screened at the Wexner in a film and video program to complement the art exhibition.[46] *The Couple in the Cage* parodied the "founding" of the Americas and critiqued the historical European and North American practice of exhibiting Indigenous people from not only the Americas but Africa and Asia too—a popular practice that, as Fusco points out, was pioneered by Columbus after the Spanish Court displayed one of the several Arawak people he returned with as evidence of his "discovery."[47] In the exhibition catalog, William J. Horrigan, curator of media arts, explained that the screening program complemented the art exhibition because they shared similar purposes, ones that had been driving the media arts for years: to "problematize and to throw into high relief . . . issues related to cultural hegemony, to empowering 'marginalized' voices, to broadening access to communication tools, and to questioning the discursive, social, and structural terms a culture uses to speak and define itself."[48] Yet, to be sure, the issues being problematized were not new to contemporary times. As Fusco said of her and Gómez-Peñas's project, the work is "much more about the present as it was about the past" in that the art was able to demonstrate how this past continues to exist in and affect our everyday lives and treatment of other people.[49]

Returning to the Wexner Center exhibition, Hammons made the 13-foot-high *Black Star Line* (Figure 3.6).[50] The large five-pointed, three-dimensional star referenced the 1919 shipping line of the same name that Pan-Africanist leader Marcus Garvey and other members of the United Negro Improvement Association (UNIA) cofounded. The UNIA's Black

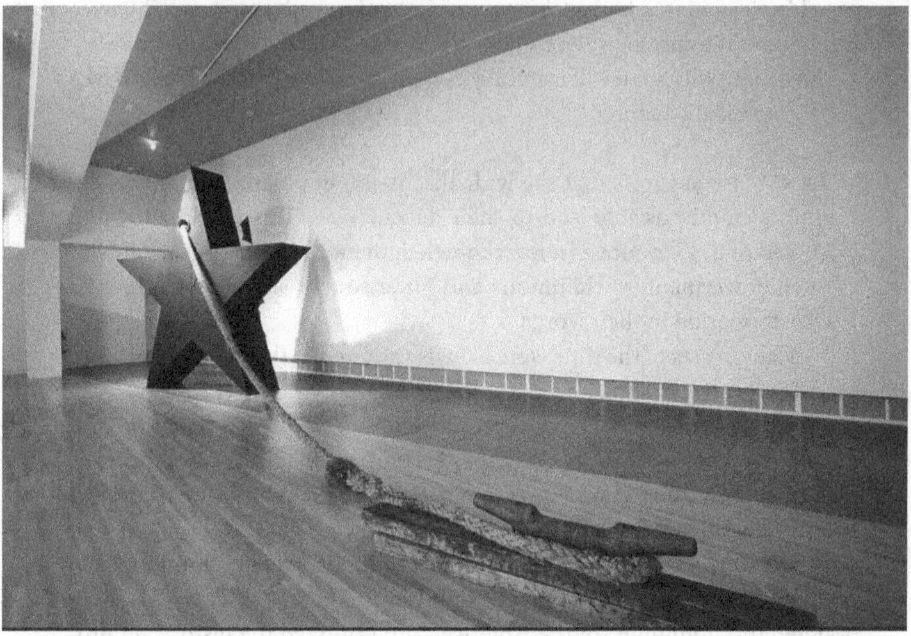

FIGURE 3.6 David Hammons, *Black Star Line*, 1992. Installation view. Mixed-media installation. Installation dimensions variable. Height of star, 13 feet (396.24 cm). Installation view of the exhibition *Will/Power: New Works by Palo Colo, Jimmie Durham, David Hammons, Hachivi Edgar Heap of Birds, Adrian Piper, Aminah Brenda Lynn Robinson*, September 26–December 27, 1992, Wexner Center for the Arts, The Ohio State University. Image Courtesy of the Wexner Center for the Arts. © 2025 David Hammons / Artists Rights Society (ARS), New York.

Star Line was a means to fund the organization, which promoted the idea of eventually transporting Black Americans to Africa—a plan that expressed the desire for Black liberation and the physical return to an ancestral homeland.[51] Though the works by Hammons and Piper drew from disparate historical periods, both focused on Black experiences to analyze the relationship between African Americans and the United States. Indeed, made during the year of the 1992 Los Angeles Riots and the Columbus Quincentenary, in a land whose colonial and slave histories are indelible vestiges that have continually limited the civil rights of Black people, their installations also explored, perhaps unintentionally, what it means to be Black in America.

Black Star Line was set catercorner in a gallery separate from Piper's. Hammons made the work's surface with bolted, charcoal-colored metal, which resembled the hull of a large seagoing vessel. From the top point of the star-shaped ship, a rope came out of a small opening in the hull. The rope, inconsistently dyed blue, stretched loosely from the hole and across the gallery floor to an anchor where Hammons tied its end. As viewers walked around the installation to the side that faced the white gallery wall, they encountered an altar. Centered and slightly recessed into the star was a black-and white photograph of Garvey and a small shelf that held slave shackles, candles, and other offerings (Figure 3.7). Instead of the bolted hull-like surface found on the opposite side of the star, the altar was surrounded by a patchwork surface of weathered siding sporadically decorated with dried bouquets tied with an orange ribbon. Thus Hammons transformed the ship into a homelike setting. Above the altar, Hammons mounted five miniatures of his *African American Flag* (1990), which were crowned by a tricolor flag created by the UNIA and commonly referred to as the "Pan-African Flag." Both flags' black, red, and green colors symbolized Black people, the blood of their shared ancestry, and the natural wealth and land of Africa. The artist's star/ship/shrine seems to reference simultaneously the slave ships that transported Africans to the so-called new world, the stars used by enslaved peoples to navigate their way to freedom, and the ships, like the Black Star Line, their descendants hoped would take them back to ancestral homelands. Thus it referenced previous struggles for liberation and recognized that the fight is ongoing. While the struggle for liberation might be carried into the future, Hammons's *Black Star Line* suggests that its destiny, which has yet to be charted, will be anchored by the past and guided by the light of future generations.

In the exhibition catalog, Rogers includes an excerpt of a speech given by Garvey in 1924 at Madison Square Garden. In it, Garvey appeals to white audiences and sets forth grounds for why Black separatism, or Black

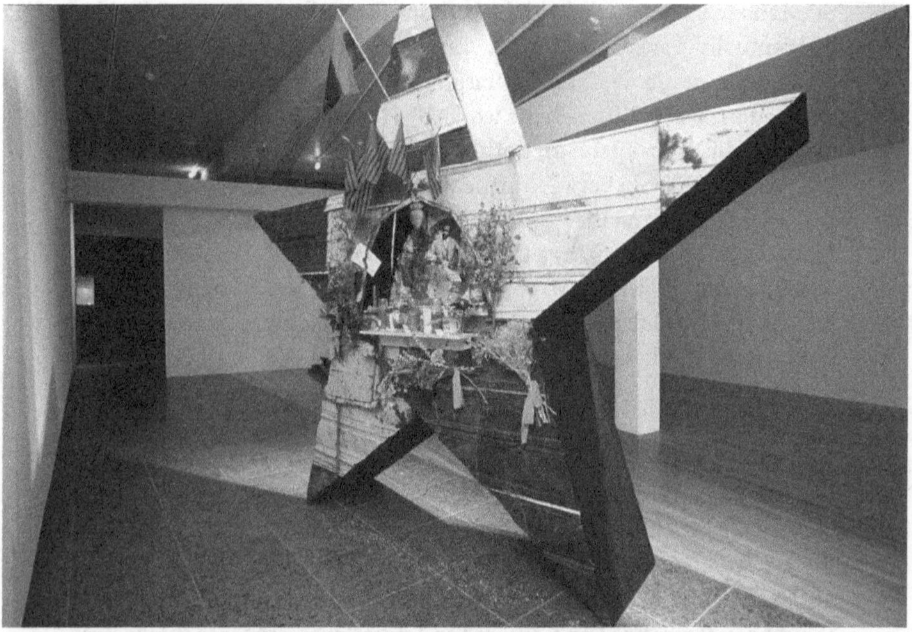

FIGURE 3.7 David Hammons, *Black Star Line*, 1992. Installation view. Mixed-media installation. Installation dimensions variable. Height of star, 13 feet (396.24 cm). Installation view of the exhibition *Will/Power: New Works by Palo Colo, Jimmie Durham, David Hammons, Hachivi Edgar Heap of Birds, Adrian Piper, Aminah Brenda Lynn Robinson*, September 26–December 27, 1992, Wexner Center for the Arts, The Ohio State University. Image Courtesy of Wexner Center for the Arts. © 2025 David Hammons / Artists Rights Society (ARS), New York.

culture making and the return to Africa, should not be challenged.[52] With an examination of Garvey's longer original speech, we can find a deeper intergenerational understanding for both Hammons's and Piper's works. In the speech, Garvey goes on to challenge claims to white racial superiority by arguing that it has been determined simply by who is in power and who inflicts the most violence on others.[53] In other words, Garvey insists that white racial superiority is not a biological fact. Instead, it has been asserted and maintained by the cruelty that whites wield against others. Garvey then insists that "our highest purpose should be to love and care for each other."[54] He continues:

> Our desire is for a place in the world; not to disturb the tranquility of other men, but to lay down our burden and rest our weary backs and feet by the banks of the Niger, and sing our songs and chant our hymns to the God of Ethiopia. Yes, we want rest from the toil of centuries, rest of political

> freedom, rest of economic and industrial liberty, rest to be socially free and unmolested, rest from lynching and burning, rest from discrimination of all kinds.[55]

By citing the intergenerational violence Black people have experienced in the United States, Garvey attempted to gain support for his movement and share the UNIA's committed struggle against systemic violence and institutional discrimination. Hammons's reference to Garvey for his Wexner Center installation thus becomes a portal that traverses the waters of time to tie the history of Black struggle and liberation to recent events like the 1991 beating of King and the 1992 Los Angeles Riots. If our "highest purpose" is met, as Garvey suggests, love and care would guide us into a thriving future civilization where "rest from" violence and the "rest of" freedoms can be obtained—not only for Black people, but for all people. In the same speech, Garvey warns that "the white man's standard" of racial superiority is "too inhuman and dangerous to be permanently helpful." Thus the continuation of faulty racial logic would ensure the oppression and limitation of freedom, and, as a result, unrest will be maintained. Exemplifying the fallout of this faulty logic during the time of *Black Star Line*'s exhibition were the racial violence displayed in the King video, the xenophobia and racism expressed during the police trial, and the unrest sparked by the jury's acquittal of the officers. The lack of rest from violence and the holding back of the rest of freedom also contributed to the unrest the verdict sparked.

In *Black Box/White Box*, Piper addressed similar issues of ongoing violence and discrimination; yet her installation stands out from Hammons's work. While *Black Star Line* paid homage to a past Black leader who, as Rogers suggested, may not have been familiar to many Wexner Center viewers, Piper offered an installation that incorporated contemporary figures and referenced directly the police beating of King and the unrest, which every viewer would readily recognize.[56] In addition, Piper created a work that provided an immersive and interactive experience for each viewer that sought both a conceptual and concrete "move from acknowledgment to knowledge, from will to empowerment."[57]

Inside the cramped confines of the white cube, the black leatherette chair beckoned the viewer to sit. From it, the viewer watched the looped recorded beating of King, which the bystander George Holliday videotaped on March 3, 1991, and soon after was screened on news outlets across the nation—a video that countless Americans viewed on their living room TVs, perhaps while seated in upholstered chairs similar to the one provided in *Black Box/White Box*. The looping of the King video also seems to be a metaphor for its heavy rotation on national television and during the state trial of the police who brutalized King. Yet, unlike the at-home living room experience, Wexner Center audiences could not watch the video with family or friends. Nor were they able to turn the TV screen off. Instead, each viewer watched the video alone, and to stop seeing it, she had to make the decision to leave the core of the cube. Otherwise, as long as she sat in the chair, the image of King being beaten repeated, again and again.

While the viewer in *White Box* watched the King video, two soundtracks played in the background: President H. W. Bush's May 1, 1992, national address and Marvin Gaye's 1971 hit song, "What's Going On." As the viewer watched officers assault King with their batons and kick him, President Bush outlined his plans to "restore order" in Los Angeles.[58] In the original address, Bush notes that 3,000 National Guardsmen are already on duty and another 2,200 National Guardsmen and 1,000 law enforcement officials are on standby. He discloses that he has ordered the Justice Department to dispatch 1,000 federal law enforcement officers, including FBI SWAT teams, US Marshals, and the Border Patrol, and that he has directed 3,000 members of the Seventh Infantry and 1,500 Marines to stand by. Finally, he explains that he will federalize the National Guard and instruct General Colin Powell, the highest-ranking officer in the US Armed Forces at the time, to place the troops under a central command. Then the president shares his personal assessment of the unrest and delivers a promise and a threat.

> What we saw last night and the night before in Los Angeles is not about civil rights. It's not about the great cause of equality that all Americans must uphold. It's not a message of protest. It's been the brutality of a mob, pure and simple. And let me assure you: I will use whatever force is necessary to restore order.[59]

Piper's use of President Bush's address as a soundtrack for the beating of King underscores the violence of hypocrisy and the cruelty of paradox. On the one hand, the 1992 Los Angeles Riots erupted after the acquittal of the law enforcement officers who brutalized King—representatives of the state who were tried for excessive use of force and assault with a deadly weapon, among other offenses. On the other hand, the president promised the nation that he would use whatever force is necessary to quash dissent, and it seems he planned to use every armed force at his disposal. In *Black Box/White Box*, Piper's use of the King video with the president's national address as its voice-over makes evident a shocking irony: the use of state-sanctioned violence to nullify unrest, which police violence and the state's failure to hold them accountable triggered.[60] Thus the artwork stages the cycle of violence.

Presenting a stark contrast to the president's 1992 national address was Marvin Gaye's "What's Going On." Written in support of Vietnam War protesters who endured police brutality, the song was originally released several years after the death toll of African American soldiers in Vietnam peaked.[61] From 1961 to 1966, Black Americans made up approximately 13 percent of the US population but accounted for almost 20 percent of all combat-related deaths.[62] After 1966, army and Marine commanders worked to lessen the number of Black casualties, and their death rate began to fall in line with population data. Yet, in 1968, African Americans frequently contributed half the men in front-line combat units.[63] The fact that Black people bore a heavy share of the fighting burden intensified war protests. This led civil rights leaders to speak out against what was perceived as a racist war—one that Martin Luther King Jr. described as "a white man's war, a black man's fight."[64]

While Gaye's lyrics describe the antiwar movement of the 1960s and 1970s, they also spoke to the period's countercultural emphasis on love and posits love as the antidote to war and hate.[65] The original recording opens with chatter among band members before the soft crooning of a saxophone cuts through and introduces Gaye's velvety voice as he sings:

> Mother, mother there's too many of you crying.
> Brother, brother, brother there's far too many of you dying.
> You know, we've got to find a way to bring some lovin' here today.
> Father, father, we don't need to escalate.
> You see, war is not the answer.
> For only love can conquer hate.
> You know we've got to find a way to bring some lovin' here today.

Played as a soundtrack to the King video in Piper's installation, the soul music took on renewed meaning. It spoke to a war that Black men like King continued to experience—not abroad, but at home. The ongoing war in the United States was defined by racism and anti-Black violence; yet, as Gaye's song suggests, love could defeat this hate. At the same time, played in the installation, "What's Going On" conveyed confusion, even disbelief, over the images of police brutality in the King video and the continuity of state-sanctioned violence since the song was first released thirty years earlier. As police struck King with their batons and kicked him, Gaye sang-talked in staccato, "Picket signs. And picket lines. Don't punish me.

With brutality. Talk to me. So you can see," before belting out, "Oh, what's going on!" As the assault continued, backup singers and Gaye took turns crying, "What's going on, what's going on. What's going on, yeah, what's going on. Oh, what's going on . . ." With the footage of police brutalizing King, the repeated cry seemed to accent each baton blow to his body. Piper's editing and collaging of visual and sonic materials intensified the familiar media and made it anew, drawing attention to the ongoing and sometimes paradoxical horror of state and racial violence.

Repetition and the Power of Art

Piper's use of repetition, like that of Gaye's chorus and the looping of the King video, is a significant artistic strategy in *Black Box/White Box,* and it is found in the practice of minimalism. Even her construction of two cubes for *Black Box/White Box* conveys minimalism's tenet of seriality with what is arguably the art movement's most common structure: the cube. As an aesthetic strategy, repetition or seriality allows artists to investigate form and space. By repeating a structure over and over, artists study the nuance of the serial object and the space it inhabits, which was a dominant characteristic in much of the work made by Judd, Morris, and LeWitt—those artists whose practices influenced Piper early in her career as an artist.[66] Thus the use of repetition in *Black Box/White Box,* of the violence captured in the video and expressed in the audio and musical accompaniment, could be understood as a study of the media at hand. However, edited and played together, the work moves beyond contemplation to one that strives to change perception about what was seen and understood in the video and during the 1992 Los Angeles Riots. What the installation does not do is attempt to portray some sort of equivalency in the repetition caused by traumatic experience. Repetition, in this form, is a behavior that might develop after experiencing a traumatic event, which the American Psychiatric Association defines in its *Diagnostic and Statistical Manual of Mental Disorders (DSM-5)* as an experience in which one was exposed to "death, threatened death, actual or threatened violence."[67] Instead, we might understand Piper's installation "in terms of its capacity . . . [to] tell us about the lived experience and memory of trauma" and not its ability to "reflect predefined conditions and symptomologies," as scholar Jill Bennett stated about the work of other artists who drew on similar subject matter.[68] A better fit yet is Bennett's overarching argument in *Empathic Vision,* which stressed how such artworks elicit critical thought and inquiry in viewers.[69] Indeed, Piper's use of repetition and her specific combination of edited media, inside the confines of the cube, create an affective experience for critical thinking. On the surface, the effort might seem to mimic the repetition of trauma or even simply be a symbol for the repeated screening of the video on television, which certainly happened; however, what *Black Box/White Box* really does is encourage a critical awareness of the act of seeing and understanding the larger structure of violence at play. With this, the shifting of perception, the police beating of King moves beyond a singular, confined—extraordinary—incident and becomes recognized for the pervasive and dangerous problem it is for us all. In this sense, the repetition acts as a mode of unrest—the inability to rest in the face of injustice in the form of ongoing violence and the enduring work it takes to shift passivity into action.

Still, what does it mean to use the video of a Black man's beating by police for art? While such discussions often veer into ethical dilemmas that limit artistic freedom and misplace moral responsibility away from King's perpetrators, it is worth noting two things. First, organizers of *Will/Power* seemed to be aware of this dilemma, and Bremner addressed it head-on, stating that Piper "[did] not intend to borrow Rodney King's suffering" and underscoring that the work instead insisted that viewers reflect on their "acquiescence in racism and its manipulations" and "get beyond a recitation of simplistic reactions." She then explains that Piper's work "is to turn the numbing evidence of violence into a wake-up call."[70] Thus she redirects criticism onto the viewer, the viewer's complicity, and the need to make pivotal and lasting change to end such violence. Second, the use of the videotape is found across artistic media and the arts, not to mention its general influence. From being used in the opening credits for Spike Lee's biopic *Malcolm X* (1992) to influencing rock and hip-hop songs published shortly after the unrest, the videotape of King's beating found currency beyond the news and legal circuits and across the arts and popular culture. Within the visual art world, the inclusion of the King video stood out in the controversial 1993 Whitney Biennial. The biennial included many artists from underrepresented backgrounds in the art world, including people of color and queer people, and art critics widely criticized the artwork and its exhibition—for being too didactic or too political and for lacking artistic rigor or merit, among other things. Interestingly, nearly half of the biennial artists contributed artwork that comprised or included film and video. Nevertheless, Holliday's uncut and unedited ten-minute version of the videotaped beating was conspicuous. It was made by someone who was not an artist or a filmmaker, yet it was arguably the most familiar and widely seen piece in the entire show.

The Whitney's curator of film and video, John G. Hanhardt, took credit for including it in the biennial. In a *Los Angeles Times* article, he described it as representing "a new way of seeing what is around us" and likened it to "an emerging practice within video to rethink the medium and address public issues."[71] Then, after framing it as a work of art, Hanhardt suggested that Holliday "revealed something about the world, the police brutality which we have heard about but most of us haven't seen."[72] In the same article, Holliday's lawyer, Robert W. Grigg, speaking on Holliday's behalf, expressed his client's excitement at having "created something unique" that increased attention to important issues.[73] It was undeniable that the video brought issues of racial violence and policing to the forefront of national discourse. It deeply resonated with politicos, general audiences, and artists alike. And, as Hanhardt suggested, it visualized violence many people had not seen—or, perhaps better said, it made unavoidable prevalent violence that some have had the privilege to long ignore.

In the biennial's exhibition catalog, Hanhardt describes the King video as a "home video" and then as a possible precursor of "a new form of documentary," claiming that Holliday made it with intention as if to support Holliday's merit and shield the video from criticism for being included in the exhibition.[74] While the intention behind Holliday's fortuitous recording is suspect, Hanhardt is better at relating the video to the others in concluding general remarks on media arts.

> The media arts are part of a theoretical and conceptual framework in which working methods and art works are overcoming the teleology of art as a constant advance on high culture and avant-garde models and precedents. In its place, a new generation of artists is confronting the idea of art, the viewer, and the creative self, and identifying new communities of reception and production. The result is a dynamic, fluid, and challenging art world.[75]

The inclusion of the King video makes sense under the rubric of challenging previous notions of art, its viewers, and the communities that media arts can reach. This is what the King video did and what Hanhardt accomplished by deciding to include it in the biennial.

Curiously, in the artist listing of the exhibition catalog for the 1993 Whitney Biennial, Holliday's section includes a selected bibliography of eight news articles on the videotape of the police beating: five about Holliday suing others for its use without permission or proper compensation and at least three that directly reference a lawsuit against Spike Lee. Lee, who Hanhardt also included in the biennial with the short video *Money Don't Matter* (1992), settled out of court with Holliday by paying the bystander for the use of a clip in *Malcolm X*.[76] Lee opens the film with a clip of the King beating, underscoring what art historian Eddie Chambers has characterized as "the brutality of 'white' America towards its black citizens, and the impunity with which that brutality was meted out."[77] In the film, the clip is interspersed with cuts to an image of an American flag. As the video and image switch back and forth, audio of a speech by Malcolm X, played by actor Denzel Washington, condemns the violence whites have inflicted on Black people throughout the history of the United States. Near the end of the speech, the flag begins to burn until it forms the shape of an "X," the civil rights leader's insignia. The wails and crashing sounds of a saxophone and cymbals close out the scene. Lee's opening connects the past with the present—a present very palpable for his moviegoing audiences during its November 1992 release and just six months after the unrest caused by the acquittal of King's assailants. Piper's use of the King video for *Black Box/White Box* similarly stands out for its connections across history, her meticulous editing of the clip, and its combination with other multimedia components. Lee's and Piper's use of the King video demands the attention of audiences and attempts to create an emotional response in ways that guide them to a critical introspection and critique. While Holliday's video helped bring the police to court and ignited national discourse, it could not convince a jury of legal wrongdoing. Nor could any art. However, I maintain that the skilled artistic use of the video, as seen in Lee's and Piper's works, became a strategy to hold viewers' attention, provoke an emotional response, and underscore the misconduct and historical impact beyond the trial, news cycle, and even the video's specific moment in time. This is the power of art. And, at its best, such art can help viewers see themselves and the world in new light—lifting the cover of complacency and indifference.

In the small confines of the white cube, with video and audio, Piper created a scenario framed as an aesthetic experience that pressed the viewer to revisit recent events and connect on an emotional level to the violent images—images that they had already encountered numerous times since the 1991 dissemination of the King video in news broadcasts, newspapers, and magazines. Next to the black leatherette chair, Piper left a box of tissues for the viewer. Was the viewer moved to tears and compelled to wipe them? Or was the viewer numbed to the played-out images of violence? Piper's gesture seemed to suggest that the emotional responses of viewers, as tracked by their use of tissue, conveyed information about their sensitivity to the violent imagery. According to art critic Brian Wallis, when he visited the Wexner Center the tissue boxes in *Black Box/White Box* were completely emptied and the trashcans filled.[78]

Oppression and Freedom

In addition to inciting an emotional response, the scenario Piper created challenged viewers to look inward and question whether they tacitly consent to violent acts like the beating of King through their participation in societal structures that support such behavior. When the viewer stood to exit the interior space of the white cube, vinyl wall text installed at eye level was seen across the interior opening. It read, "Once you have taken everything away from a man, he is no longer in your power. He is free." Piper credited her edited quotation to Alexander Solzhenitsyn's *The First Circle* (1968).[79] While the artist says she had found the original passage in a *New York Review of Books* article on Solzhenitsyn's novel and did not read the book until years later, the premise of the story provides a relevant scenario about state oppression and violence for us to consider.[80]

Solzhenitsyn's novel is set in a Moscow prison camp where intellectuals and technicians work on projects to serve the Stalin-led state in exchange for less harrowing prison conditions for themselves. Like the first circle of hell in Dante's epic poem *Inferno*, those condemned to the camp are not egregious sinners. The Russian author's "first circle" also similarly acts as a limbo, though one between harsher conditions and freedom. While many of the inmates recognize that they are better off than those at typical prisons, some struggle knowing they are aiding an oppressive system that terrorizes and harms others. In the context of Piper's *Black Box/White Box*, the literary reference elicits several meanings. First, *The First Circle* serves as a metaphor for oppression that we can apply to the moral and ethical dilemma of bigotry, such as that of racism or xenophobia. Like the Solzhenitsyn characters, viewers of *Black Box/White Box* might have wrestled with the knowledge that they are complicit with state-sanctioned violence either directly via bigotry or indirectly as a passive observer of its violent enactment against others. Viewers also could have left *Black Box/White Box* knowing that they contributed to conditions that oppress or harm other people, indeed that they might even benefit from the situation. *The First Circle* speaks to the ways in which oppression imprisons both people and their perceptions of others. One can hardly ignore the cramped interior spaces of *Black Box/White Box*, a confined space we might interpret as a physical expression of the "prison" bigotry creates for all members of society.[81]

Piper's altered Solzhenitsyn passage provides further meaning. It seems to warn that once one is stripped of all dignity, of humanity and hope, there is no longer anything left to lose. In the first *New York Review of Books* article on Solzhenitsyn's novel, writer V. S. Pritchett poignantly describes a character's understanding of the unending sentence he and others have been subjected to in the prison camp: "He has understood the awful words 'For ever' as few of the others have; they mean 'You have exhausted your power to hurt me.'"[82] Many initially saw the King video as a form of evidence that promised justice in court; however, that optimism quickly dissolved with the 1992 acquittal of the law enforcement officers who brutalized him. If anything, the verdict seemed to prove that one cannot rely on the state, especially given its unjust history, or on camera-generated images as verifiable evidence, particularly in such a society. The structure of unrest is one that appears as though it is unprecedented even as it should have come as no surprise. As I discussed in chapter 1, Martin Luther King Jr. observed in his statement, "A riot is the language of the unheard," that unrest occurs at times of desperation, after those who have the official authority to incite change have continually ignored demands for justice.[83] Thus King's quote with Piper's altered Solzhenitsyn passage, "Once you have taken everything away from a man, he is no longer in your power. He is free," underscores the illegitimacy of abusive authority and the liberatory potential of self-determination even under oppressive conditions.

Piper similarly used and installed the altered passage in the black-colored cube, which the viewer would see on her way through its corridor. After entering the small interior, she found and seated herself in the familiar black leatherette chair. At eye level in front of her, she encountered an "image screen" of Rodney King's visage (Figure 3.4). As she confronted the backlit portrait of King, she registered the visible lacerations, swelling, contusions, and bloodshot eye, which were caused by the baton blows of police. As in the other cube, she also encountered sound, though it instead was a recording of Rodney King's May 1, 1992, televised plea to residents.[84] In Piper's edited recording, as in the original version, King's defeated voice desperately tries to find the words to urge residents to stop the shootings, assaults, looting, and arson that characterized the unrest. First he assures listeners, "We'll get our justice; they've won the battle, but they haven't won the war. We—we'll have our day in court, and that's all we want."[85] Despite his hopefulness, the image of King's face contradicts his message. His injuries convey a counternarrative, one of injustice and the facts of his brutal beating by police and their not guilty verdict. Stacey Koon, Laurence Powell, Timothy Wind, and Theodore Briseno, the four police officers who assaulted him, were acquitted of charges in the 1991–92 state trial. In 1993, although the officers were tried for a second time in federal court and Koon and Powell were convicted, the two did not repent for the serious harm they caused.[86] Instead, Koon and Powell repeatedly asserted that they acted "properly" in the beating of King. Likewise, they suggested that they were being "sacrificed" to maintain peace in Los Angeles.[87] Even as King went on to win a civil lawsuit against the City of Los Angeles in 1994, in the end it didn't bring about the LAPD reform some had hoped for.[88] In fact, corruption within the LAPD would publicly resurface only a few years later with the numerous counts of police misconduct during the 1997 Rampart Division Scandal, which included unlawful beatings, shootings, and tampering with evidence.[89]

As Rodney King's address continued, the tone of his voice changed from one of hope surrounding a new "day in court" to one of desperation regarding the ability of the city to "get along." Again, with the image of his beaten face acting as visual counterevidence to his message, he gave the plea:

> And I mean—please, we can get along here. We—we all can get along. We just gotta—we just gotta, you know—I mean, we're all stuck here for a while. Let's, you know, let's—let's—let's try to work it out.[90]

Suddenly, the lighting behind King's portrait dramatically switched off and the room went dark. Then, just above the "image screen," a spotlight turned on. It shone brightly in the viewer's face like an interrogation light, causing momentary disorientation. Once the viewer's eyes adjusted to the stark change in lighting, she realized that the mirrored surface of King's portrait now captured her own reflection. In effect, she replaced King as the victim of police brutality.

Piper's descriptor "image screen" for the reflection device is significant. "Image" denotes a visual representation, such as a portrait, and it can be understood as a copy too, like the duplicate of the original photograph of King. Yet "image" can also mean to imagine something or, as a noun, an idea. "Screen" is many things as well: a monitor, as that of the television in the black cube; or an action, as in to broadcast, shield, or inspect. Thus we may understand "image screen" here as that which encapsulates both the representation of King and the ability of Piper's device to project his image and then conceal it and reflect that of the viewer. The hope here seemed to be that viewers would have assessed what they saw and what they now see. Thus describing the "image screen" as a mere portrait or mirror is insufficient.

While inspecting her face in the "image screen," the viewer then noticed the reflection of a photograph hanging on the wall behind her. It was the Associated Press photo of President Bush shaking the hands of police officers in Los Angeles after the unrest (see Figure 3.3). The president's gesture suggested "a job well done." Having just examined King's beaten face, the viewer might have wondered if the president was congratulating police on their handling of the unrest or on the brutalization of King. Given the widespread condemnation of police operations leading to and during the unrest, the former seems less likely. Due to the reflective device Piper used, the viewer could have read the inclusion of the photo-op as implicating her—both at the literal and the metaphorical level—as a possible or potential victim of police violence, an accessory to King's beating, or an unwitting partner in state-sanctioned violence more broadly.

King's plea for audiences to "try to work it out" seems to urge viewers of *Black Box/White Box* to figure out whose side they are on: that of the victim or that of the state. This situation evokes the one found in Albert Camus's "Second Letter," which I discussed in chapter 1, where a German priest chose to side with the Nazi state instead of with God or his children and thus helped condemn an innocent, imprisoned boy to death. Because bigotry is a form of imprisonment for everyone, even those who benefit from it are never truly free. They too can suffer the brutality of state violence at any time. Thus *Black Box/White Box* provides a scenario that invites viewers to consider how it behooves us all to fight bigotry in all its forms.

In Wallis's review of *Will/Power*, he suggests that Piper "linked the issue of race directly to the presidential election," which was to take place during the run of the exhibition in November 1992.[91] To be sure, near *Black Box/White Box*, the artist set out a voter registration table.[92] As previously mentioned, during Piper's emerging artistic practice in the late 1960s and early 1970s, the student antiwar movement left an indelible mark on her growing political consciousness as a young adult. Given this experience, it may not be surprising that Piper sought to connect with the students at Ohio State University. Interestingly, this engagement took the form of registering voters in the gallery space of *Black Box/White Box* during the first two weeks of the exhibition.[93] The Wexner Center helped ensure Piper's vision by having staff, docents, and other volunteers run the voter registration table. It also connected with the university's Undergraduate Student Government, which administered a voter registration campaign on campus.[94]

Piper's gesture of including the voter registration as part of her installation suggested a hope that all viewers would enact their right to vote and use it as a means for political action. Rogers confirms, "Piper continues to believe in democracy's inherently optimistic invitation to everyone to participate in change, just as she believes that the overt messages or subtle cues of her work can effect changes in her viewers."[95] While registering people to vote would not, on its own, ensure that state-sanctioned or racial violence would end, what Piper's gesture does is invoke the civil rights history of those who fought for the right to vote and also fought to protect it. The voter registration table should not be read as some sort of passive or "liberal" solution to the violence and injustice shown in the King video or the jury's acquittal of the police who beat him. Instead, it is a reminder that while one must critically analyze their own behavior and change it, changes must take place at a national, societal scale. The voter registration table underscores how precarious citizenship rights have been for countless people in the history of the United States, and because forms of precarity continue, no one can afford to take civil rights like voting for granted. Registering students to vote also acknowledged the concerted, intergenerational endeavor required to exercise liberty and ensure justice, placing young people at the forefront of that endeavor as they have been throughout civil rights history and liberation movements. Those who registered to vote just months after the 1992 Los Angeles Riots, one of the most devastating and widely documented episodes of unrest in the nation's history, likely included people who would vote against President Bush's reelection. In fact, he was unsuccessful in obtaining a second term.[96]

Precedents and Flying

Piper's use of minimalism for the multimedia installation at the Wexner Center and her use of the voter registration table were ideas she had explored before *Black Box/White Box*. Two artworks, made during the two years preceding *Black Box/White Box*, deepen our understanding of Piper's use of visual language and media to create interactive works that address issues of racism and xenophobia.

Piper used the American convention of the voting booth and the visual language of minimalism to make *Vote/Emote* (1990) (Figure 3.8). The installation comprised four connected, black-colored booths, each outfitted with a three-quarter-length door. Installed inside each booth was a different backlit image screen on which was shown a black-and-white photograph of Black marchers, which, from the clothing styles and signage, appears to have been taken during the civil rights era. Piper framed each photograph with a wooden grid that cut it into six squares, which in effect resembled six-paned windows that looked out onto each group of people.

Upon entering any one of the four booths and perhaps closing the door for privacy, the viewer looked out the "window" and realized that the demonstrators seemed to be marching toward and, in many cases,

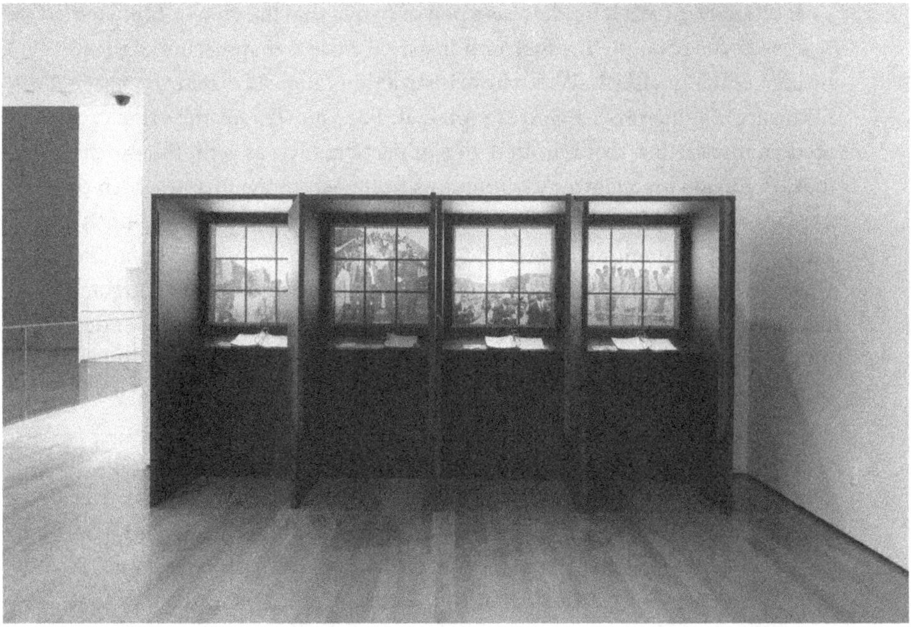

FIGURE 3.8 Adrian Piper, *Vote/Emote*, 1990. Mixed-media installation. Four constructed booths with swinging doors, each containing notebook with preprinted pages, pen, transparent photo prints, light boxes, framed windows. 84 × 164½ × 48¾ inches (213.3 cm × 417.8 cm × 123.8 cm). Source photography: Kristine Larsen, *Village Voice* (1988; Brooklyn, NY); Dick Durrance II, *National Geographic* (1977; Cape Town, South Africa); Bruce Davidson-Magnum, *Newsweek* (August 29, 1963; Washington, DC); Alon Reininger, *Village Voice* (January 14, 1980). Installation view of *Adrian Piper: A Synthesis of Intuitions, 1965–2016*, The Museum of Modern Art, New York, March 31–July 22, 2018. Photo: Robert Gerhardt. Private collection. © Adrian Piper Research Archive Foundation. Digital image © The Museum of Modern Art. Licensed by SCALA/Art Resource, NY.

looking directly at her. Lying under the "window" and on top of a ledge, the viewer saw a three-ring binder. All the binders contained white sheets of paper with one of four instructions printed on the heading: "List the fears of what we might know about you"; "List the fears of what we might think of you"; "List the fears of how we might treat you"; or "List the fears of what we might do with your accumulations." The "we" seemed to refer to the group of Black demonstrators represented in each photograph, and because of the proximity of the photographs to the directives inside the binders, it appeared as if they, not Piper, were directing the viewer's participation. Furthermore, their seeming proximity and eye contact with the viewer dissolved the sense of privacy the booth otherwise may have provided.

Included with each binder was a pen or pencil that the viewer could use to answer the prompt. The instruction-based work is reminiscent of those by conceptualists like LeWitt whose instructions allowed others to engage in the art-making process and complete it. For *Vote/Emote*, the artist created an installation that required viewer participation as well. But participation hinged on a viewer's willingness to reflect on the image screen to express—"emote"—the "fears" that might arise in the presence of the image of Black demonstrators. Did viewers follow the instructions? Did they feel comfortable enough to truthfully share their fears or thoughts? Did they feel confronted by the seeming onlookers? *Vote/Emote* depended on viewer participation to enact the extent of Piper's concept for the piece. How viewers activated the installation also depended on who they were, and it seemed to many that Piper's intended viewer was white.

In a write-up on a 2011 presentation of *Vote/Emote* at the Elizabeth Dee Gallery in New York, art critic Katie Kitamura recalled that viewer responses to Piper's directives were varied: "self-indulgent, flippant, earnest and new age."[97] Describing an earlier installation of *Vote/Emote* at Ikon Gallery in 1991, writer Ewan Morrison notes with more detail that the UK viewers' replies were made by people of "varying ethnic backgrounds, who felt that they had either been excluded as subjects of racist oppression or falsely defined within the context of the oppressors."[98] That is, according to Morrison's observations, the image of Black people in Piper's installation limited the cross-racial scope of those who have experienced bigotry. Morrison also observed that the "you" in the directives of the *Vote/Emote* binders was interpreted as a white subject who was inherently racist, which alienated nonwhite audiences. While the context of a gallery in the United Kingdom differs, viewers of *Black Box/White Box* at the Wexner Center might have had a similar response, especially since each cube seemed to stand as a metaphor for race. This begs the question: Did Piper intend the content in each box to correlate with either a white or a Black experience?

Morrison described the Black-white opposition that Piper created for *Vote/Emote* as a "deliberate overstatement intended to provoke a personal response" and a means of "tak[ing] racial division to crisis point rather than using the gallery as a potential site for integration and cultural plurality."[99] Of all the various points Morrison touches on in his review of the exhibition, from audience interpretation versus the artist's intention to the assumption that one cannot be an ethnic minority *and* racist, his statement above is particularly significant. The apparent goal of creating a "crisis point" in lieu of developing a harmonious multicultural unity in an art institution not only misjudges Piper's intention, but forces one on her. It also overlooks the artist's experience and denies her awareness of the potentiality that art and art spaces encompass. This is to say, the critic's statement is as reductive of her as he claims the artist is of her work's audience and location.

Vote/Emote physically recalled the pared-down sculpture and grid work that came to define minimalism and conceptualism beginning in the 1960s, of which she was an early practitioner. At the same time, it evoked the structures used to enact one's right to vote in the United States—a right that was not federally protected for racial minorities, like African Americans, until the 1965 Voting Rights Act.[100] Thus *Vote/Emote* implemented visual art languages that became popular during the mid-twentieth century and were concurrent with the rise of the civil rights and antiwar movements. The convergence of these art and sociopolitical histories expands our understandings of Piper's specific selection of subject, form, and style and helps us recognize them as deliberate and mindful decisions in her art-making practice.

Morrison's recognition that Piper's installation included a "deliberate overstatement" to prompt a viewer response is apt, for her oeuvre includes many works that attempt to encourage responses from viewers that call for sociopolitical thought, self-reflection, and action.[101] In a 2000 interview, Piper addresses the question of audience participation in her work.

> There's no reason for me to ever put the work out in the world unless I want someone else to receive it, so in a way, I'm always thinking about audience. There was a period before I got rehabilitated in the 1980s when I basically was working for kind of an ideal audience, people who understood exactly what I was doing and really appreciated it. And now that I'm kind of having my 15 minutes and I'm finding out . . . what I can expect from the real audience. It is a real education[.] [. . .] I think about the real audience when I give talks and I show these images and I get feedback from the audience, and that's really interesting, I learn a huge amount by doing that. But when I actually make work, it's harder.[102]

Piper admits to how she once took for granted her viewers' comprehension of her work and then recognized the difficulty of successfully communicating her intent through her art, especially when it began reaching broader audiences.

She experienced similar difficulty with the earlier installation, *Four Intruders Plus Alarm Systems* (1980). Like *Black Box/White Box* (1992), viewers could enter the 6 × 7–foot cylindrical work, though unlike the 1992 installation, they could do so in small groups. The installation included music and contained four evenly dispersed silkscreened lightboxes. The only light sources in the room were emitted from behind the eyes of Black men pictured in the image screens that hung at eye level (Figure 3.9). As viewers entered the darkened cylindrical room, the men's faces glowed and seemed to be staring at the viewers while the slow funk jam of "Night People" (1979) by War played in the background. Over the bouncy rhythmic bass and guitar lines, viewers heard War's vocalists sing about the imagined behaviors of "night people": "Somehow they all look the same / Fun'n and run'n their game / Dealin' and feelin' no shame / They never give the right name / Niiii-ght people . . ." Underneath each of the silkscreened portraits the viewers found headphones that played one of four different monologues spoken by Piper. The monologues questioned the artistic validity of the portraits and commented on the Black men with

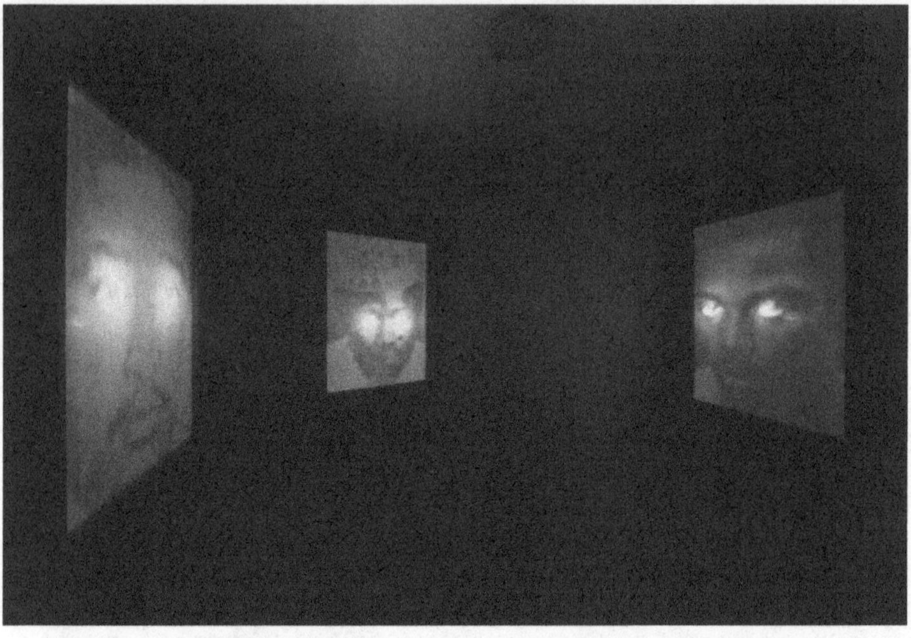

FIGURE 3.9 Adrian Piper, *Four Intruders Plus Alarm Systems*, 1980. Interior detail. Mixed-media installation. Constructed wood environment, four photographs, light boxes, audio, and headsets. Dimensions variable. Installation view of *Adrian Piper: A Synthesis of Intuitions, 1965–2016*, The Museum of Modern Art, New York, March 31–July 22, 2018. Photo: Martin Seck. Collection of The Ohio State University. Courtesy Wexner Center for the Arts. Gift of the artist. © Adrian Piper Research Archive Foundation. Digital image © The Museum of Modern Art. Licensed by SCALA/Art Resource, NY.

statements that ranged from dismissive to paternalistic and from biased to explicitly racist.[103] In a 1995 essay on her installation, Piper explains:

> Here I was concerned with articulating and isolating certain racist stereotypes of black men (aggressive, hostile, malevolent), and also a set of paradigmatic racist responses to those perceived stereotypes, among which I now include the *aestheticizing* response (avoidance or suppression of one's racist responses to blacks by simply changing the subject, just as we avoid our own gut responses to the pervasive political issues raised by art, by talking about form and color instead).[104]

Comments that dismissed the artistic validity of the men's portraits and her work were at best attempts to avoid the sociopolitical message of the work or at worst a tactic to hide one's racism. Piper found that some viewers interpreted the monologues that were blatantly racist or that promoted stereotypes about Black people as confirmation of the hegemonic racial imaginary. Indeed, the artist encountered viewers who felt that her work supported their bigoted worldviews.[105] In the same essay, clearly troubled by this experience, she describes her intention as opposed to the audience's interpretation.

> From the perspective of my experience (and, I venture to add, that of most blacks in this country), it was impossible to regard the content of the monologues as anything other than objects of ridicule, scrutiny, and self-examination. That is, I took it to be impossible to take them at face value, as expressions of the artist's advocacy of the values they voiced. Wrong. While the black audience, and some members of the white audience understood the devices used immediately, others thanked me for expressing their views so eloquently.[106]

The experience drove her to contemplate the responsibility of the artist in such a situation, especially when she had thought, perhaps idealistically, that there was no room for misinterpretation.[107] Piper concluded that "no artist with political concerns is required by a viewer's ignorance to make simplistic art," meaning that artists should not be expected to tailor their work for bigoted viewers.[108] Indeed, how would one always and correctly anticipate or predict the perception of every individual—not to mention the grossly skewed perception of racist ones? She then asserted that "there is no excuse" for the ignorance and racism of "any adult American."[109] Piper's statements are not intended to license artistic carelessness.

Instead, they underscore how white supremacy shifts responsibility away from those who practice it, like the racist viewers of *Four Intruders,* and back onto the communities targeted with racism and xenophobia. Thus white supremacy shields itself from criticism and protects its practitioners.

Yet the shift in Piper's work from *Four Intruders* to *Vote/Emote* ten years later reflects a marked change in the way she addressed the problem of artistic intent with the requirement of viewer participation to complete the work. Morrison, who misjudged the intent of *Vote/Emote,* otherwise deftly articulates the general significance of Piper's installations. He explains, "The reading of the work is then not concerned with objectifying and displaying the oppressed for the anonymous viewer, but with challenging the distance between the viewer and the work—showing that detachment is an act of complicity."[110] In *Black Box/White Box,* Piper immerses her viewer in this notion with multimedia—video, photos, and audio—and various objects, including the boxes of tissue and the voter registration table.

In the 1991 group exhibition *Dislocations* at MoMA, Piper introduced another minimalist multimedia installation.[111] *What It's Like, What It Is, #3* was a tall white rectangular box centered in a large white room reminiscent of an amphitheater. In the top portion of the box, on all four sides, sat television monitors that were infinitely reflected in mirrors located directly across from them (Figure 3.10). The monitors showed a video of a Black man, from the neck up, as he negated racial stereotypes. After every fourth statement, he took a quarter turn, and each monitor exposed a different aspect of his head to viewers. As the man spoke and turned, the mid-tempo Commodores R&B ballad "Zoom" (1977) played in the background, with Lionel Richie singing about wanting to fly away, where he could "find the love I long to see, where people can be what they want to be," and wished "the world could live as one and how freedom would someday come."[112]

In 1987, Piper wrote an essay describing a recurring dream in which she flies.[113] Although she characterized the dream as one of her "most treasured," she described the immense anxiety it caused her—anxiety caused by the heights at which she flew and those who threatened to keep her grounded by trapping her indoors and pulling at her ankles.[114] She explained how she struggled against their attempts to pull her down and after escaping the grasping hands and flying back into the open air, how the fear dissipated and she felt "invisible, disembodied, [like] pure sexual desire."[115] The artist then connected the experience of flying with the artistic strategy of abstraction. Piper wrote, "Abstraction is flying. Abstracting is ascending to higher and higher levels of conceptual generalization; soaring back and forth, reflectively circling around above the specificity

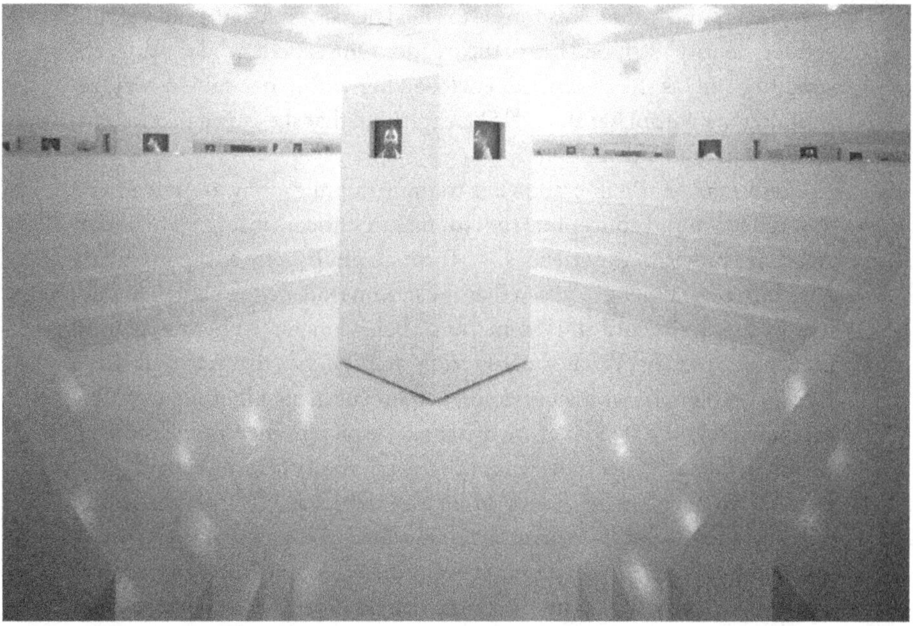

FIGURE 3.10 Adrian Piper, *What It's Like, What It Is #3*, 1991. Video installation. Video (color, sound; 00:12:30), constructed wood environment, four monitors, mirrors, and lighting. Dimensions variable. Installation view of *Dislocations*, The Museum of Modern Art, New York, October 19, 1991–January 7, 1992. Collection of The Museum of Modern Art; acquired in part through the generosity of Lonti Ebers, Marie-Josée and Henry Kravis, Candace King Weir, and Lévy Gorvy Gallery, and with support from The Modern Women's Fund. © Adrian Piper Research Archive Foundation. Digital image © The Museum of Modern Art. Licensed by SCALA/Art Resource, NY.

and immediacy of things and events in space and time."[116] She continued by stating that abstraction is also freedom. She explained that it is "freedom from the immediate boundaries of concrete subjectivity, freedom to imagine the possible and transport oneself into it."[117] But she admitted, "Abstraction is a solitary journey through the conceptual universe, with no anchors, no cues, no signposts, no maps, no foundations to cling to. Abstraction makes one love material objects all the more."[118] She explained how she came to adopt abstraction in her art and how it transformed with time, beginning with her abstraction of materiality in 1967–72, which was "strictly minimalist," then her experimentation with her own objecthood via public and durational performances, such as those of the *Catalysis* series (1970–73) for which she rendered herself unusual or repulsive physically in highly populated areas.[119] Yet the women's and antiwar student movements and "others' responses to [her] perceived social, political, and gender identity" stripped her of the freedom she experienced through abstraction and, as she described, enclosed her within her subjectivity, restraining her within her skin.[120] She explained that she "struggled to transcend both" and failed.[121]

From 1972 on, Piper credits her training in philosophy as giving her a new reflective and conceptual tool to "make political sense" and to understand her previous experiences.[122] Through philosophy and particularly *Four Intruders*, Piper explained that those who ridiculed her and her work with racist, sexist, and elitist remarks or behaviors forced her to see from their point of view. What she saw from their perspective was that she, a racially ambiguous woman of color, is their "ultimate nightmare."[123] She explained that the "fear, fantasy, mistrust, suspicion, anger, confusion, ignorance obstructs [her transcendence], [her] ability to lose [herself] temporarily in the other, in the world, in abstract ideas."[124] Thus the loss of freedom and the imprisonment she experienced within her subjectivity—the imposed barriers that kept her from flying—are reflected in her artwork. She elaborated, "I am no longer drunk on abstract theory, because the sobering facts press in on my daily life too insistently."[125] Philosophy, she explained, disciplined her flying and direction, but she was quick to clarify that this freedom is temporary. While philosophy might have helped her sometimes soar over "moral cretins," it could not change the behaviors of other people.[126] Piper explained, "So they always bring me down again eventually. And there is no escape: I know I will find such individuals in every institution in this society."[127] Still, she asserted, "my art practice . . . holds out to me the promise of release into the night."[128] She continued to soar, experiencing and reveling in freedom no matter how fleeting it might be and despite attempts to control and oppress her.

In contrast to the Commodores' lyrics about freedom and as a form of testimony to Piper's discussion of that which kept her from soaring, the Black subject in *What It's Like, What It Is, #3* cannot be who he wants to be, nor is he free. Instead, he is consumed with the work of negating racial stereotypes. With "Zoom" playing as a soundtrack, the man recites four groupings of four different stereotypes each, such as "I'm not vulgar. I'm not rowdy. I'm not horny. I'm not scary."[129] As Piper described in her essay on flying, the stereotypes restrict the man within his subjectivity as a Black person. It is also significant that he makes the statements encased in a box in a mirrored room via infinitely reflected monitors. The minimalist box imprisons his image both literally and symbolically. Indeed, the man's quarter-turns resemble those taken in police mugshots.[130] His anonymity and perpetual reflection in the space also mark him as a stand-in for all Black men and the seemingly endless oppression, bigotry, and racism they must counteract.

Similarly, *Black Box/White Box* references oppression and discrimination. It also acts as a form of confinement but with one stark difference: It confines the audience. Moving from the confinement of a generalized Black male to individual viewers allowed Piper to create an opportunity for audiences to reflect more deeply on their positionalities and experiences as both participants in the artwork and consumers of media. It also encouraged participants to further empathize with the prejudice Black males experience by attempting to incite an emotional reaction from them, whether that is in the form of outrage, sadness, or another feeling, in the presence of the all too familiar video of violence. To recall, the artist achieved this by creating a situation in *Black Box/White Box* where the viewer repeatedly watches King's beating with the accompaniment of President Bush's threat of more violence and Gaye's plea to end brutality with love. The artist also seemed to have sought an additional empathetic response by using the image of King's beaten face and his message of love and hope for justice along with the mirror device that enables the viewer to see herself in his former position, which might then invite the viewer to imagine herself as him.[131]

In a 1992 review of the MoMA group exhibition, art critic and historian David Deitcher asserted that Piper's *What It's Like, What It Is, #3* confronts and deconstructs the art history most comfortable to museums and claims that she uses the "museum-ready aesthetics" of minimalism "just as the ancient Greeks did their wooden horse at Troy."[132] In her own words, Piper stated that one of the major drives of minimalism is the focused attention on the individual, the specific object, and the reduction of that object to a set of properties, which reveal it simply as "what it is."[133] She added:

> If you think that xenophobia can be overcome by focusing on the specific, unique, concrete qualities of individuals, then it would make sense to think of Minimal Art decision-making as a kind of aesthetic strategy for drawing attention to the concrete, specific, unique qualities of individuals; this is what my work does.[134]

More than using the style of minimalism to draw viewers in or to lure viewers into a dialogue about racism, like a Trojan horse, as Deitcher suggested, *What It's Like, What It Is, #3* served as a meditation on how one might use the very tenets of a visual art language to contest xenophobia or other forms of bigotry. Yet while Piper saw potential freedom in the decision-making aesthetic strategies of minimalism, in *What It's Like, What It Is, #3* her use of them also conveyed a symbolic form of imprisonment. Many modern art principles, like those of minimalism no doubt, compelled numerous artists, critics, and historians to ignore sociopolitical issues and politics inasmuch as they were believed to be extraneous to art. However, I suggest that Piper's use of minimalism's principles reveals how oppression and racism exist and, importantly, how the nature of such violence and bigotry is inherently illogical. *Black Box/White Box* could be understood similarly; however, with its numerous devices, such as the reflective image screen of King, the boxes of tissue, and the voter registration table, I contend that they heighten the potential for viewer interaction, empathy, and change proportional to her art and writing practices, which stage and theorize emancipation from oppressive forces—no matter how fleeting.

Breaking the Black and White Binary

Having experienced *Black Box/White Box,* the minimalist exteriors and multimedia interiors, viewers at the Wexner Center may have interpreted the colors of the boxes as being more than skin deep. As allegories of race, they stand in as symbols for Black and white people and the experiences of violence Piper referenced in the installation. The use of the colors black and white as shorthand metaphors for racial difference prompts us to meditate on how the Black-white binary marks past and present experiences of oppression and violence, as well as how it has framed discussions and coverage of the police beating of King and the 1992 Los Angeles Riots. In this regard, it is important to note that Briseno, one of the police officers tried for beating King, is not only white (as he was and still is overwhelmingly described) but also of Mexican American descent.[135] Many media outlets and city authorities also dismissed the fact that more than half of those arrested during the five days of unrest were Latino and that Latinos made up the second largest ethnic group to lose property from looting and arson—the single largest ethnic group being Koreans and Korean Americans, as I discussed in chapter 1.[136] Moreover, while the media recognized the immense property loss Koreans and Korean Americans experienced, the emphasis of a "Black-Korean conflict" by media and authorities ignored Black-Korean solidarity and arguably incited increased instances of cross-racial tensions.[137] Scholars Nancy Abelmann and John Lie explain:

> To emphasize the "black-Korean conflict" only diverts our attention from more pressing problems. The interethnic conflict, outside of its historical and political economic context, misses the central problems facing both ethnic groups and South Central Los Angeles [the epicenter of the unrest]

at large. The "black-Korean conflict," in spite of prejudices and tensions, is ultimately beside the point in the central concerns of most African Americans and Korean Americans.[138]

Recognizing the racial and sociopolitical complexities surrounding the police beating of King and the 1992 Los Angeles Riots does not minimize the important and devastating role racism played. However, it does point to the ways in which nuance is needed to understand the experiences that these histories comprise. Simply put, the King beating and the 1992 unrest are much more multifaceted than the Black-white binary allows.

While Piper's *Black Box/White Box* acknowledges a history wherein the Black-white racial split drives national narratives and locates conflict, it also demonstrates how certain racial narratives are favored over others. In this way, I suggest, the work invites us to question what narratives are missing in our national remembering of the King beating and the 1992 Los Angeles Riots and in our assessments of oppression, racism, and xenophobia in the United States at large.

Asserting the importance of the Black-white binary, legal scholars Roy L. Brooks and Kirsten Widner have argued that it provides important context for race discourse.[139] Even as the authors have claimed that the binary does not diminish the experiences and needs of other marginalized groups, other scholars disagree.[140] For instance, law and critical race studies scholar Juan F. Perea argued in "The Black-White Binary Paradigm of Race" (2013) that the continued emphasis on the racial dichotomy interferes with liberation and equality.[141] He used Toni Morrison's 1994 essay, "On the Backs of Blacks," as a case in point. Perea criticized the Nobel laureate for pitting Latinos and Asian Americans against African Americans. Although he agreed with her claim that "American 'whiteness' is often achieved through distancing from blacks," Perea disagreed with her assertion that African Americans are, as she stated, "the real aliens" and cited legislation that has denied Latinos and Asian Americans rights.[142] To be clear, he did not assert that Latinos or Asian Americans are "the real aliens." On the contrary, he argued that emphasizing conflict, prioritizing the oppression of one people over that of others, and ignoring the lived experiences of all marginalized groups in the United States impede the struggle for liberation. Speaking as a member of the Latino community, Perea explained:

Our claims can be ignored by whites, since we are not black and therefore are not subject to real racism. And our claims can be ignored by blacks, since we are presumed to be not black and becoming white, and therefore

> are not subject to real racism. Latinos/as do not fit the boxes supplied by the paradigm.[143]

Perea also stated that the Black-white binary and studies with only minor acknowledgment of other people of color "marginalize all people of color by grouping them, without particularity, as somehow analogous to blacks."[144] Here Perea saw an inherent conundrum: Non-Black people of color are either ignored in racial discourses or conflated with whites or Blacks.[145] Sánchez has argued that Asians and Latinos are shaped by racialized white and Black stereotypes, respectively. Yet he foresaw a further problem regarding the ways in which racial discourses in the United States marginalize Asians and Latinos: "With the white-black discourse increasingly metamorphosed into the national discourse defining the contours of race in America, it is not unreasonable to predict that Asian and Latino immigrants will be increasingly vilified as the ultimate racial 'others' in a society bent on sustaining national borders."[146] With ongoing immigration and new immigrant populations from Latin America and Asia, Sánchez argued, Latinos and Asian Americans will always be othered in the United States and never truly fit into the Black-white paradigm. He concluded, "It is clear that all Americans can get caught in the white-black paradigm of race relations, a model that relies on opposites, opposites which too often substitute for the complexity and diversity of social and ethnic relations."[147]

Despite their acknowledgment of such counterarguments, Brooks and Widner asserted that although incorporating non-Black histories in African American scholarship might "enrich" one's perspective on racism, it is not necessary to understand civil rights or the Black ethos or to address "black issues."[148] They also argued for the recentering of and the value in studying the Black-white binary in African American history. They wrote:

> In a world of limited resources, achieving progress in one group's agenda can come at the expense of that of another. The game is, indeed, often zero sum. The racial dynamic between blacks and Latinos/as, the latter being the most persistent critics of the black-white binary, well illustrates this point.[149]

They then hedged their bets. They stated that they do not argue against coalition between Black and Brown or other racial groups. Instead, they believe "racial problems facing particular groups must be analyzed separately to arrive at an accurate, undiluted understanding of the problems before we attempt to form coalitions."[150] They continued, "Hence African American civil rights interests should take priority only in those instances in which African Americans are statistically worse off than other racial groups."[151] Unintentionally, these assertions demonstrate how the Black-white binary serves to exclude others and to summarily disregard critique so that divisions remain in place. Such assertions also assume that "Latinos" does not also include Black people and descendants of Black people. The politics of race does not have to be a "zero sum" game.

Piper has written provocatively on the Black-white racial binary, describing it in one essay as a "two-dimensional binary fiction" that "stigmatizes" and "flattens" all and asserting that "no racial stereotype is cruder than this one." She then quickly underscores how the binary operates, not as a social construct, but as a "*political instrument* for allocating power and status so as to maximize the perceived advantage of the speaker."[152] She goes on to outline how the Black-white binary operates as a caste system, organizing people hierarchically based on their perceived racial, ethnic, and gender identities to control power, status, and advantage and enforcing it via harassment, coercion, and violence. She then goes on to explain the difficulty of eradicating such a political instrument.

> Unfortunately, having cultivated the practice of racial styling without regard to its self-defeating consequences, Americans now find it impossible to reverse without exacerbating those consequences. For they have so oversimplified the available vocabulary for naming the enormously varied multitude of ethnicities that in fact constitute the population of the United States as to leave no viable alternatives to the essentialist fiction of Black and White for conceptualizing them; and therefore no viable strategy for extricating themselves from the centuries-old caste system that fiction has configured.[153]

Here Piper highlights several important features of the racial binary: the seeming catch-22 of its existence and control over our understandings of race and ethnicity, its quintessential Americanness, and its dependence on a fiction. This fiction I surmise to mean that of the pseudoscience that asserted racial difference, promoted white supremacy, and created racial categorization and types. While the scientific world began to publicly reject such false science in the mid-twentieth century, its effects, including its influence on policies and laws, continue to harm and limit the lives of the historically oppressed and marginalized by white supremacy, bigotry, and xenophobia.

The Gray Zone of Unrest as Clarity and Purpose

To be sure, we should not dismiss the resonance of the Black-white binary throughout American history. Our very understandings of race, racialization, and racial violence in the United States are driven by the dichotomy, as demonstrated even in arguments for and against it. Piper's *Black Box/White Box* illustrates this reality. By using tools to reflect us back to ourselves, we can begin to realize, if we have not already realized, that violence and racism seep beyond the singular episode of the police beating of King or the 1992 Los Angeles Riots and that we often become so acculturated to xenophobia and complacent that we do not recognize or really care about the inhumanity we see in our everyday lives—even when it is broadcast into our living rooms. For the 1992 Los Angeles Riots, which were cross-racial and multiethnic in scope, gradation beyond black and white thinking is needed to describe the realities of one of the most devastating episodes of unrest in the history of the United States. If we do not shift the limited perspectives of the Black-white binary and black and white thinking, we essentially box in our understandings of ourselves, each other, and the world. With that said, perhaps the gray-colored walls and ceiling of the Wexner Center gallery, which Piper accompanied with the crackling sounds of fire, can become a metaphor for us to expand the Black-white binary. This "gray zone" of unrest is not defined by a lack of clarity, as the idiom is often used, but instead is crystal clear. We only refuse to recognize the complexity at hand.

The flames of arson in 1992 caused immense damage, consuming the businesses, property, and livelihoods of numerous Angelenos and rendering buildings and their contents into charred carcasses. As parts of the city burned and then smoldered, the smoke and ash traveled across the skies, shrouding Los Angeles and touching parts of Southern California that were otherwise seemingly unaffected by the unrest. Through the physical destruction of both the human body and the cityscape in the form of beatings and arson, brutality was laid bare and raw across the city and broadcast on television screens across the world. The dark gray—of the smoke and the ubiquitous concrete that paves much of Los Angeles—is so omnipresent that we either do not recognize it for long or do not ever really notice it—just like the gray-colored walls and ceiling of Piper's installation in 1992 or their absence in 2018. This gray surrounded the original installation of *Black Box/White Box*, enveloping the cubes and its viewers. But, like smoke, it seemed elusive, dissipating into the atmosphere the artist created. Together, though, the colors black and white make gray.[154] If we can grasp the grayness that makes up the history of the 1992 Los

Angeles Riots and that which surrounds us in the world in which we live, then perhaps we can see how far-reaching the unrest really is. This realization is the first step in resisting and then addressing the vast harm caused by white supremacy, xenophobia, and racial violence, which has affected generations. Yet this harm continues. In response, Piper has continued to address it through her work.

In 2013, after George Zimmerman, a racially mixed white-Latino, was found not guilty in the shooting death of the black teenager Trayvon Martin, Piper made *Imagine* (Figure 3.11). Available to download at no cost on her website, the work features a faint image of Martin set under round red crosshairs and within a black-bordered square frame, reminiscent of the minimalist paintings of Jo Baer. Piper sourced the portrait of the boy from a popular black-and-white photograph of him wearing a hoodie that

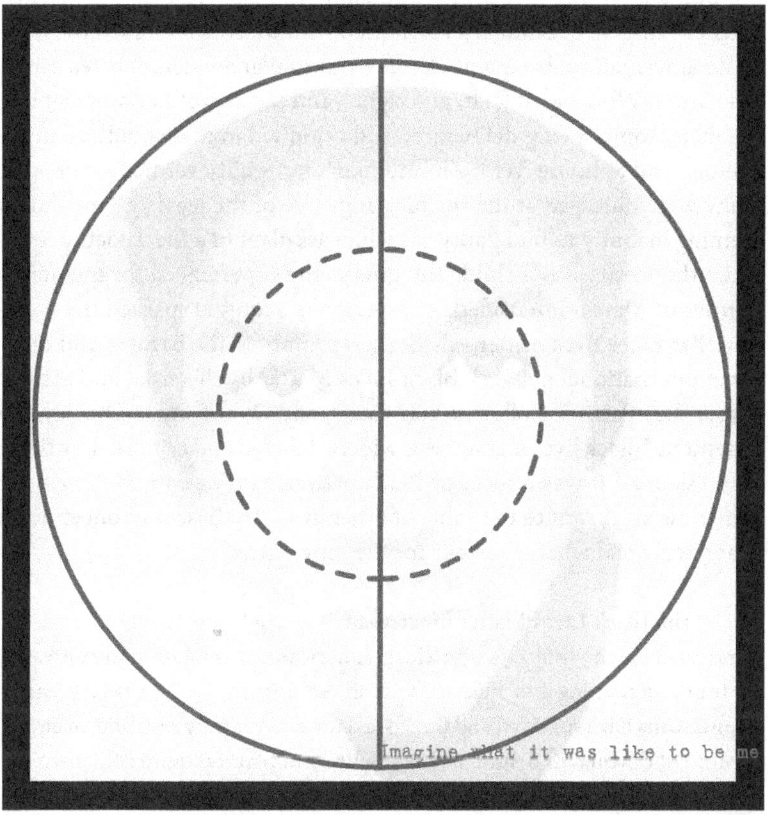

FIGURE 3.11 Adrian Piper, *Imagine [Trayvon Martin]*, 2013. Digital PNG formatted image. 10⅞ × 10¾ inches (26.49 × 27.33 cm). 300 DPI. Available for free download at http://www.adrianpiper.com/edinburgh/art/index.shtml. Collection of the Adrian Piper Research Archive Foundation. © Adrian Piper Research Archive Foundation.

circulated in the media but edited and altered the saturation of color so that the portrait comprises a white background and gray tones so light we must focus our eyes and attention to fully see Martin. As we perceive Martin, we begin to realize that his image fits almost perfectly within the sightlines. This near-perfect placement of the youth's face makes clear how he is ideally proportioned—a signature of beauty. Simultaneously, he is almost perfectly sighted by the crosshairs and, consequently, sighted as a target by viewers. In blue typeface located at the bottom right of the image are the words, "Imagine what it was like to be me."

In 2012, Martin was walking to his father's home in Florida after buying candy and a soft drink from a convenience store. Zimmerman, a member of a neighborhood watch committee, followed Martin, later claiming he did so because the Black boy looked suspicious. To be clear, Martin was not doing anything illegal. After pursuing the teen against a police dispatcher's directive, Zimmerman clashed with Martin and killed the boy.

Zimmerman's subsequent charges and trial generated debates across the nation. Who was at fault, gun rights, and racial profiling were among the many topics being deliberated and critiqued in media outlets, in academia, and at home. With Zimmerman's not-guilty verdict a year later, many were outraged at the ongoing injustice of the legal system and its seeming inability to find guilty the white assailant of a Black victim, even when the victim was a child. The grief many experienced for the unjust murder of Martin intensified. Zimmerman's acquittal sparked the assertion that Black lives matter, which then prompted the hashtag and organized international network Black Lives Matter by the artist and activist cofounders Patrisse Cullors, Alicia Garza, and Opal Tometi. Quickly, the statement "Black lives matter" was widely debated and criticized by those who assumed it was a form of Black nationalism or anti-whiteness, or somehow an affront to the value of other lives. To these misconceptions, Piper explained what is at stake for the movement.

> [. . .] the Black Lives Matter movement is not fighting merely to protect and advance the interests of African-Americans. It is fighting to cultivate a fundamental level of humanity in all Americans. [. . .] That African-Americans have survived and flourished for 400 years by resisting an environment devoted to dehumanizing them demonstrates quite conclusively how highly their capacities for transpersonal rationality are developed. The statement that black lives matter is a reminder to those whose perpetuation of that environment has effectively dehumanized *them* to develop those capacities just as highly; i.e. that their own humanity also matters.[155]

Piper underscored how critics fundamentally misrecognized the statement and the call to value black lives as equally as those of others. Indeed, this is a tenet written into the US Constitution, that all men are created equal; yet it is a value that has been historically debated and limited for the unfree and women; has been repeatedly compromised by state legislation and policy that limits the rights of Black people, other people of color, immigrants, women, and the poor; and has not been upheld in both the legal system and the assessment of videotaped police brutality and extrajudicial cases, like Zimmerman's vigilantism and killing of Martin. Our inability to reflect critically on the statement, history, and ongoing state violence and oppression renders us all dehumanized. The red, white, and blue colors of *Imagine* may signify for some viewers the colors of the American flag, and with that interpretation we must also consider how violence and oppression is an American tradition.

In response to the not-guilty verdict of Zimmerman, many artists like Piper made visual art. For instance, Juan Capistrán, discussed in chapter 1, created *Still I Rise Above* (2013) (Figure 3.12). The title combines Maya Angelou's "Still I Rise," a poem about African American resiliency, and Black Flag's "Rise Above," a punk song of resistance. The image contains a figure set within an expansive white space. Dressed in black and wearing a hoodie, the person holds onto a pole—in essence becoming a black flag, a symbol of anarchy. The hoodie is particularly significant. Martin not only wore this article of clothing in the image that Piper uses for her work; he also wore a hoodie when he died. Media pundits, namely, Geraldo Rivera, blamed the garment for Martin's death, which deflected Zimmerman's xenophobic surveillance of the child and his vigilante behavior. On social media, in response to debates, numerous users began to take photos of themselves wearing hoodies as a form of critique and a symbol of solidarity with the Martin family in their fight for justice. The hoodie-wearing, back-facing figure in Capistrán's work, obscures the individualism of the person pictured. This allows viewers to envision the figure as anyone or to even project themselves onto it, as the hoodie wearer, as Martin, as a banner of rebellion against injustice.

In memory of Martin, those like Piper and Capistrán, those working to have us change our perceptions of these events, ourselves, and others, urge us to imagine. So, as Piper implores, we must imagine ourselves as Martin. Indeed, we must imagine ourselves as Latasha Harlins, Tamir Rice, and Michael Brown. For some, this might be a leap. For others, this is hardly a jump. Still, for many, there is nothing to be imagined because it is already a reality, made tangible by those that have targeted them or their loved

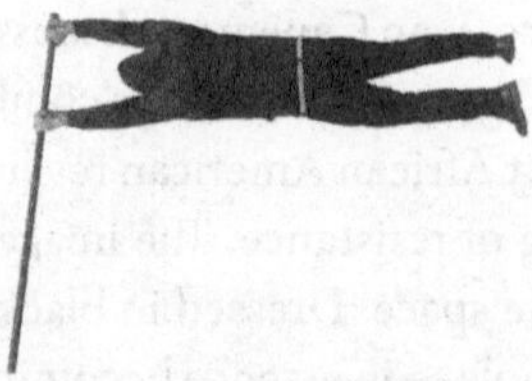

FIGURE 3.12 Juan Capistrán, *Still I Rise Above*, 2013. Archival pigment print. 27 × 30 inches (68.5 × 76.2 cm). Courtesy the artist.

ones with racism and other forms of bigotry and violence. Then, as Capistrán's title suggests, we must rise. And we must rise together, allowing our unrest to drive us as long as racial violence and xenophobia continues to limit and harm Black lives and, thus, humanity at large.

In 2018, at the MoMA retrospective of Piper's artwork, I sat in the black leatherette chair of the black box. Amid King's public plea to work things out, his bruised visage suddenly disappeared. I then saw myself reflected in the image screen, seated in front of the photo-op image of the first President Bush shaking hands with law enforcement officers. The photo was positioned in such a way that the image was not simply behind me but perfectly centered so that my body was wedged in front of the handshake and in the middle of the commander in chief and the uniformed officers. It seemed to imply that I, and any other viewer who sat in the chair, was part of the group of men. It also seemed to clearly correlate the brutalization of King via his devastating portrait to that of this group. Next, in the white box, I saw the police beating played on a loop and heard Gaye's song play and then become only faintly audible under President Bush's address to the nation. There I recognized a powerful correlation. Shortly after Gaye attests that "only love can conquer hate," the LAPD officers encircle King and two of them beat him with their batons just as the president states, "It's been the brutality of a mob. Pure and simple. Let me assure you, I will use whatever force is necessary to restore order." Piper repurposes the president's words so that they become both a criticism and a description of the police beating King endured. In this way, the police beating of King is the "brutality of a mob" that will be stopped with "whatever force is necessary." The failure of "the law" is acknowledged, and Piper helps us see our roles and potential in conquering it.

While *Black Box/White Box* challenges viewers to consider the 1991 videotaped police beating of King and 1992 Los Angeles Riots, it also encourages viewers to recognize the long legacy and ongoing experience of state violence, xenophobia, and racism, especially in light of the Columbus Quincentenary and the presidential election. Piper uses the tools of minimalism and conceptualism, and her use of familiar and timely media requiring viewer participation and engagement—intellectual, emotional, and physical—marked a shift in her oeuvre. The viewer's participation included the decision to stay within the core of each box and to engage with the materials she offered for scrutiny. The demands on the viewer's body involved the visceral reaction and emotional response to what was seen and heard after having decided to stay and engage with the work. While Piper does not have the power to control or ultimately change a viewer's perception and worldview, her impressive multimedia and visual art strategies are aimed at waking viewers up, if not by logical means, then through the heart. Thus Piper encourages the viewer—us—to contemplate the ongoing legacy of violence, challenging us to consider our roles within it as complicit spectators or tacit participants. Ultimately, her work underscores the choice and responsibility we each have in enacting change and combating white supremacy and the violence it generates, of acting with love and recognizing the humanity in ourselves and each other.

✷ 4 ✷
Vision in Ruins

"From the Future, I See It"

During the last segment of Latipa's three-channel video installation *Civil Society* (2008), a cityscape darts across the window of a moving train (Figure 4.1). The blur of buildings and other structures moves across the three screens in sequence, but each image is slightly delayed, making it more difficult for my eyes to focus on the fast-moving footage. So instead I shift my attention to Latipa's soft-spoken narration. Over the quiet rumble of the train, she reflects on the past fifteen years since the 1992 Los Angeles Riots, struggling to understand herself within the discord of declarations she has internalized. From the claim, "We have healed, we have mourned, we have moved on," to attempts that try to differentiate "those people" from "us" and "us from them," and finally to the appeals she should make in light of this history and her positionality as "a woman of color, the child of immigrants, issued out of colonialism," I hear the frustration, anxiety, and pain. Then, with unexpected clarity, she explains, "Fifteen years have passed, and I see ruins. The ruins have nothing to do with cities, structures, streets, fire, ashes, smoke, hints of an orange sky. The ruins are myself. Part of myself, I leave for the wind. I am in ruins." With these last words, my vision blurs with tears. Latipa continues with certainty, "1992, Los Angeles. There is in fact nothing to see." Nothing but also everything: our memories and experiences of unrest. As my tears further dissolve the cityscape into a haze of sorrow, childhood memories of violence and death take shape.

I remember my mother kneeling over a teenage boy as she desperately tries to stop blood from spilling out of the bullet wounds that ruptured his body. His bike lays beside him on its side and the tire spins. With a rush of confusion, so does my head once I realize that the crowd gathered around us is unwilling to help. Is it the shock of seeing someone dying that freezes them in place? Or is it the sight of an African American in our Latino neighborhood? My heart races. I cannot breathe. His death marks the moment I realized how Black people, even children, are especially vulnerable

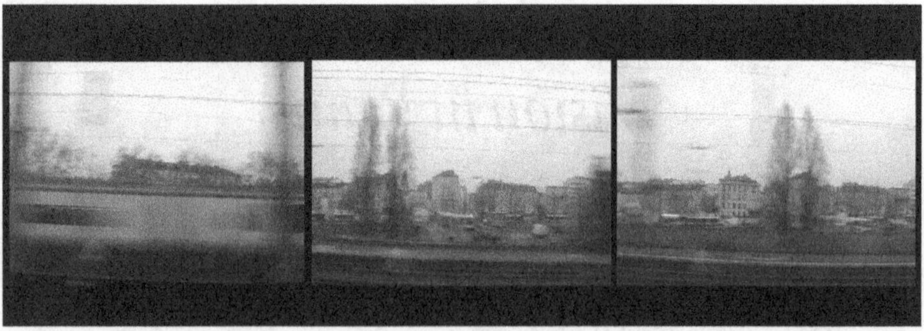

FIGURE 4.1 Latipa, *Civil Society*, 2008. Three-channel video, 37-minute duration. Courtesy the artist.

to hostility and cruelty. I then remember the video of police beating Rodney King. They hit him, over and over, as he repeatedly tries to crawl away. But he cannot escape. Evidence of the disproportionate brutality that Black Americans experience was not enough to convince a jury to convict King's uniformed white and Latino attackers. The crowds chant outside the courtroom, "No justice! No peace!" We then take cover from the bullets being shot outside our home. With my face pressed against the rough brown fibers of the carpet in my grandmother's living room, I watch live news coverage of lootings and beatings morph into panoramic views of our neighborhood engulfed in flames. Thick plumes of smoke rise into the sky, and my throat burns as I struggle against the visceral response to weep. *I am in ruins*. These words echo over and over in my head along with memories of the dead and beaten. *I am in ruins.*

I am in ruins I

am

in

ruins

Then, from the unrest, I hear Latipa's voice: "To remain looking toward the past would mean to let this past die. And no, every part of me says, it must live on." I can no longer hold back the tears. As they silently fall, my blurred vision clears, and suddenly I can see even though the city is still distorted and out of sync. With the sound of the train wheels hitting the tracks like a steady heartbeat, Latipa concludes, "You tell me, you understand, I've created a space to grieve." I am in ruins. But from ruins our unrest and grief can drive us forward—it must because, as Latipa poignantly promises, this is how what has been lost can live. It is then, from the future, I see it: the embrace of our roles as the ruins of so-called civil society, undermining, demanding, and seeing to the end of racial violence, xenophobia, and oppression. "Civil society" is a vision *in* ruins, a monument already and always in decline.[1] And ours is a vision *of* ruins—ruin-nation: the unrest that recognizes the end as beginning.

* * *

"From the future, I see it," a curious phrase Latipa uses throughout the film, now resonates with me in new ways like that of ruins. The phrase underscores what we did not—could not—see in the past due to traumatic experience or the pressures to forget and move on to survive and maintain the facade of peace and a status quo that polices what it means to be a good citizen. The phrase also signals the structure of white supremacy that aims to limit our understandings of the world, each other, and ourselves to consolidate power—to control vision—so that we do not recognize the coercion or the misdirection of blame onto the individual or the other. Still, the phrase recognizes that we can find clarity and focus despite or because of the grief-stricken past and present, sometimes achieved with the help of distance in time or location, as for Latipa as she rode the train or in my experience of her work. Our unrest can drive us forward, not away from the past, but with it.

Civil Society, a thirty-seven-minute, three-channel video installation by the Los Angeles–based artist Latipa (née Michelle Dizon) emerged from a place of sorrow (Figures 4.1–4.3). She began making *Civil Society* in 2005, shortly after Hurricane Katrina and the French unrest occurred within two months of each other.[2] Both events involved state-sanctioned violence inflicted on poor Black and immigrant populations and were documented extensively in photographs and video footage. The dissemination of the highly mediated images triggered a series of near-forgotten memories for the artist, who had witnessed the racialized violence of the 1992 Los Angeles Riots as a teenager.[3] Indeed, at the 00:05:50 mark of *Civil Society*, Latipa describes the experience, speaking over three black screens before a hazy Eiffel Tower appears at the center in an extreme panned-out view of Paris, a midrange view, and a close-up across each screen.

> The vision of ruins arise for me just as televisions announce the fires that cover the outskirts of Paris. I was young, but I wasn't that young. Did I see

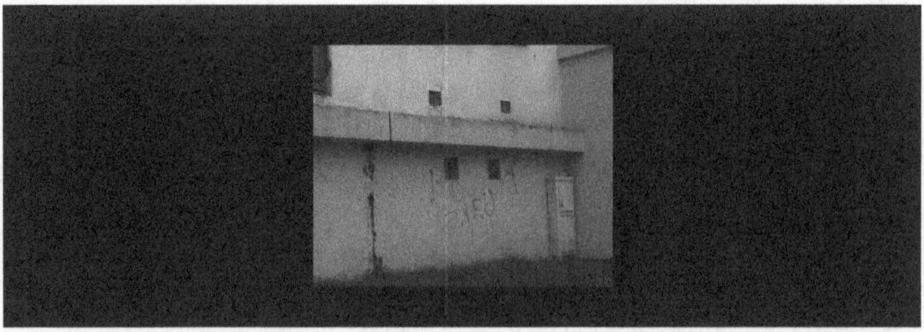

FIGURE 4.2 Latipa, *Civil Society*, 2008. Three-channel video, 37-minute duration. Courtesy the artist.

> nothing because I wanted to see nothing? Or did I see nothing because I was taught to see nothing? To see would mean to put something at great risk, but what was it? No answer comes easily.

The experience compelled her to research seemingly disparate episodes of unrest throughout the twentieth and twenty-first centuries, and for *Civil Society* specifically, she explored the 2005 French unrest, the 1992 Los Angeles Riots, and the 1965 Watts Rebellion. While the events are separated by decades, geography, and national borders, Latipa drew compelling links that spoke to the ways that xenophobia and racism surrounded them, demonstrating how distance does not mean disconnection and how distance ("From the future . . .") can bring clarity. With the use of a three-channel presentation of her video, she edited together original footage, found images, and archived recordings through a process that deconstructs traditional forms of storytelling and film montage. With the combination of historically disparate images and her editing methods, she reveals the interplay of reportage and predetermined racial narratives with the dialectics of seeing and not seeing.[4] In addition, she weaves in recollections of personal and intergenerational experiences of colonialism, immigration, and citizenship that underpin the histories of unrest. *Civil Society* would go on to become her master's thesis project at the University of California, Los Angeles (UCLA), and would later inform the topic of her doctoral dissertation at UC Berkeley.[5]

In this chapter, I argue that Latipa has developed a phenomenological space that invites viewers to see historical events anew, through what she has called both "vision of ruins," as referenced by her in the film, and "vision in ruins," as employed in her writing and interviews.[6] For the artist, "vision in ruins" denotes the inability to fully comprehend what is recorded by video, film, or similar forms of visual technology, which transmit and condition narratives and experiences from the past that remain to be seen today.[7] She has also explained this vision as not only the "mechanics of sight" but also "the West's Enlightenment," by which, through our many conversations, I take her to mean the philosophical and political project of imperialism whose xenophobic and racist underpinnings continue to affect societies across the world.[8] Thus *Civil Society* examines both the power and failure of vision.

I weave in the analysis of other artists' videos, films, and use of images to contextualize *Civil Society* in an art historical legacy that echoes across time and to provide insight into a lineage of art-making that deploys similar conceptual and technical devices to address the police beating of King, the 1992 Los Angeles Riots, and other episodes of state-sanctioned violence. While Latipa's three-channel video is not unique in content or technicality, her combination of editing, sound, and oral and visual storytelling styles creates an effective emotional and meditative space to tell the experience of unrest anew.

With her use of three screens, original and archival footage, manipulation of film speeds, and incorporation of sound, Latipa makes viewers of *Civil Society* aware of the process of seeing, how visual technology mediates vision, and how our knowledge of these processes are often delayed—that is, if we become aware of them at all. Her use of audio in the form of news reportage, voice-over, and music amplifies the roles of xenophobia and racism in the historical events, and, at times, the audio underscores the intergenerational experience of violence, tragedy, and loss surrounding the unrest in France and the United States. Because of this, I also maintain that *Civil Society* creates an important space for viewers to recognize how bereavement, in all its experiential registers, from sorrow to anger and frustration to love, drives unrest and how the ruins of grief can be a place of resistance and transformation.

Origins of Civil Society

After Hurricane Katrina hit the southern seaboard of the United States on August 29, 2005, the lack of federal, state, and local government preparedness left tens of thousands of residents stranded in flood waters without food, drinking water, or shelter. More than a thousand people died, most of whom were poor and Black.[9] Media coverage included portrayals of the flood waters' devastation. It also presented racially biased portrayals of the stranded Black residents that sometimes disregarded their suffering and emphasized stereotypes of criminality. In one of the most widely circulated and controversial representations, the Associated Press (AP) published a photograph of a Black man carrying a case of soda and a trash bag through chest-high waters; the corresponding caption described the man as "looting" a grocery store.[10] In contrast, a similar photograph released online by the Agence France-Presse (AFP) captured a white woman in chest-deep waters; the caption described the woman as "carrying" a plastic bag filled with food.[11] A couple of days after the release of the photographs, hip-hop artist Kanye West, now known as Ye, seemed to reference them on live television during a Red Cross fundraiser for Hurricane Katrina. Surprising his cohost and the national viewing audience with an off-script speech, West expressed with notable distress, "I hate the way they portray us in the media. If you see a black family, it says, 'They're looting.' If you see a white family, it says, 'They're looking for food.'" West then declared, "[President] George Bush doesn't care about black people."[12] In both statements, West voiced an indictment of the way news outlets portrayed Black people and how the government neglected them in times of crisis.

On October 27, 2005, two months after Katrina, three youths fled from police in the Paris neighborhood of Clichy-sous-Bois. After running into a power substation for cover, they were accidentally electrocuted, and two of them, Zyed Benna and Bouna Traoré, died. The third boy, Muhittin Altun, was hospitalized with severe injuries. The boys were the children of North African immigrants, and their deaths exacerbated long-existing tensions between French law enforcement officers and the immigrant community in which they lived.[13] Protests broke out and quickly escalated, spreading beyond the Paris city limits. For nearly three weeks, France experienced nationwide unrest. An estimated ten thousand vehicles were burned, and international media outlets focused on the images of arson.[14] Inflaming tensions between protesters, immigrant communities, and law enforcement, Interior Minister Nicolas Sarkozy publicly made baseless claims that illegal immigration and Muslims, among other factors, were to blame for the unrest, even though most participants were French citizens.[15]

For months, audiences across the world fed on the images and footage of anguish.[16] The onslaught of the news compelled Latipa to recall her own experiences of unrest in Los Angeles in 1992; however, she realized her recollections were defined not by her own lived experience but by her memory of the 1991 video recording of police beating Rodney King.[17] She then turned inward to understand further how the video had eclipsed her own memories of the 1992 Los Angeles Riots, including the fact of her family's participation in looting. Making the King videotape a primary research document for *Civil Society*, Latipa reflected on her positionality at the time of the unrest as a teenage daughter of working-class Filipino immigrants and a resident of the Westside of Los Angeles.[18]

Her parents were born in the Philippines and migrated to the United States by way of Guam and citizenship her father earned via US military service.[19] The Disneyland promise of "the happiest place on earth" influenced Latipa's parents to move to the Los Angeles area. Then, two years after Latipa was born, they settled into a ten-unit apartment complex in Culver City, a suburban-like community perhaps most well known for its film and television studios but one the artist describes as "quintessential multicultural L.A." for its ethnic diversity. At the apartment complex where she and her parents lived, their neighbors were from a variety of places across the globe: Mexico, Costa Rica, Barbados, Pakistan.[20]

Like many working-class immigrants who are part of an active diaspora, Latipa grew up often hearing her parents strategize on how to bring family members to the United States. When extended family members successfully migrated, Latipa and her parents often shared their two-bedroom apartment with them until they could earn money and transition to a place of their own. The bustling family home, at one time housing nine family members, encompassed what Latipa described as the profound sadness and pressures of leaving the Philippines behind and making a new life in the United States. The sadness arose not only from the physical distance from home, but from what Latipa explains as "the forgetting that goes into becoming a member of society," how one loses sight of her past to safeguard her belonging in a new nation—a notion Latipa would go on to contend with in *Civil Society* but not until after years of experimenting with video and film.[21]

Latipa's experiments in video began during the time of the 1992 Los Angeles Riots when she attended the Los Angeles County High School for the Arts. While video courses were not an official part of the curriculum, Latipa gained access to video cameras and other equipment during these formative teenage years.[22] She continued working with video through her tertiary education, from Santa Monica College and her part-time job at Hennessey + Ingalls, an art and architecture bookstore that gave her access to critical texts, theory, and catalogs, to UC Berkeley, where she earned bachelor's degrees in English and art history, and then the Philippines as a Fulbright Scholar, where she filmed *My Child Anak* (2001).[23] Yet she repeatedly experienced what she describes as "coming against the limits" of the documentary style of filmmaking.[24] Latipa's navigation of the documentary filmmaking process brought forth ethical and formal questions that, as a result of her sensitivities and critical view of the practice, made it difficult for her to deliver what is typically expected of the genre. By the time she began to make *Civil Society* during her graduate studies at UCLA, she had begun, in her words, a "process of unraveling" wherein her subjectivity began making itself seen in her videos and films.[25] Her analyses of past and current events in the context of a critical and deep reflection on the self, family, art, video, and film led to Latipa's examination of the roles race, citizenship, and visual imagery play in the history of unrest.

The King Video: Time, Perception, and Art

During her research for *Civil Society*, Latipa examined the King footage and how it had been used in the trial of the four officers who beat him.[26] She found that the police officers' defense team presented the video to the jury in three different speeds: real time, 12 percent of real time, and 6 percent of real time.[27] Furthermore, they dissected the video frame by frame and freeze-framed the content during the trial.[28] The slow-motion screenings and still images abstracted the actions of the police and de-emphasized the severity of their assault.[29] A juror stated to Ted Koppel, anchor of ABC news program *Nightline*, "A lot of those blows, when you watched them in slow motion, were not connecting." He is then quoted as saying, "Those batons are heavy, but when you looked at King's body three days after the incident, not that much damage was done."[30] Yet police hit King over fifty times.[31] The prosecution presented medical evidence of the injuries he sustained from the police assault, which included a broken cheekbone, several fractures to his face, lacerations to his forehead, a fractured right leg, and various contusions and abrasions on his body.[32] The manipulation of the video resulted in a systematic distortion and removal of content and meaning, which allowed the beating to be reframed by the defense and then reinterpreted by the jury.

Latipa references the manipulation of the trial video by including a slow-motion clip of the footage in *Civil Society*. Shortly after the 9-minute mark, the center channel projects a blurry recording that comes into focus on the police as they encircle King. The reduced speed and unidentifiable noises make it difficult to understand what one is seeing. However, given the familiarity of the beating for American audiences who saw its repeated play on the news in 1991 and 1992 and/or its portrayal in popular culture, as described in music and seen in Hollywood movies, documentaries, and even video games, they might expect to see the police begin to beat King.[33] Instead, the lens of the camera veers away from the men to the street. The image and noise then suddenly cut to a darkened silence. The cut to the mute black screen acts as a visual and auditory device that emphasizes the illegibility of the slow-motion scene before it. Indeed,

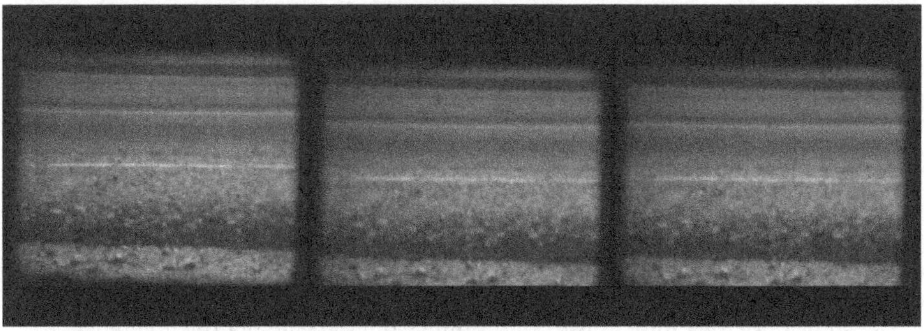

FIGURE 4.3 Latipa, *Civil Society*, 2008. Three-channel video, 37-minute duration. Courtesy the artist.

the only decipherable information in the specific scene of the King video that Latipa chose for her film was the passage of time as captured in the time stamp at the bottom of the footage. It registered that the 2-minute, 20-second segment contained only 8 seconds of real time.

In her 2011 dissertation, "Vision in Ruins," Latipa discusses the video of King's beating via the technology that captured it. She explains, "What this event reveals about video is that video alone, in fact, sees nothing. Video is not a device for seeing, nor is it an image produced from this seeing, but it is deployed as a proposition to the veracity of an event of vision."[34] Thus the King video, even when played in real time, cannot speak for itself. It requires human interpretation, as with all video and film.[35] Recognizing this, the defense asserted authority over the narrative of the King video, controlling the jurors' understanding of it and convincing them that the police used reasonable force when they beat King.[36] Not only that, but with their specific manipulation and interpretation of the video, they also convinced the jury that King—not the police—had control over the assault. They claimed that King could have ended the beating if only he had stopped moving.[37] This disregards the fact that King's writhing was an involuntary response to the pain caused by the officers' blows to his body with their batons. The defense team's argument fed into xenophobic and racist stereotypes of Black criminality, aggression, and superhuman strength, and their visual strategy supported this skewed logic.[38]

Black Panther leader Huey P. Newton once wrote, "For us the true definition of power is not in terms of how many people you can control, to us power is the ability to first of all define phenomena, and secondly the ability to make these phenomena act in a desired manner."[39] Newton made this statement to expound on the need for the Black community to use both theory and action in their efforts to control their destiny. He also explicitly expressed that "it is incorrect to seek power over people" and tied this wrong to the centuries of "dehumanizing power of exploitation and racism" that Black people have endured.[40] While Newton outlined a different form of power for the Black community, one in opposition to the type of power wielded through anti-Black racism and capitalism, he also pinpointed an incredible insight about white supremacy. As demonstrated by the defense team's use of the King video, tapping into xenophobic and racist logic to control perception and the understanding of it became a form of power. It is a type of power routinely wielded to oppress and abuse the Other, those seen as unlike oneself whether the difference is actual or perceived. While the skewed logic of xenophobia and racism often is rooted in fear or panders to it, there is no fear of consequences once the control of perception is established. Others now see the world, not necessarily as those in power see it, but as those in power envision it. In the case of the King beating, this strategy helped prove to the jury the innocence of King's uniformed assailants. It also recast blame onto King, seemingly proving his guilt as a criminal even though he was not on trial but the victim of a brutal assault by those who were on trial.

The King video drew the attention of numerous artists who, like Latipa, were interested in how it was mediated and then perceived by various audiences. An early example of this is found in *No Justice, No Peace: Young, Black, ImMEDIAte* (1992) by interdisciplinary artist Portia Cobb, who explored how the media's use of the video affected audiences' perceptions of Black males and their sensitivity to the racial violence they endured. Cobb's single-channel video, which has a run time of less than 14 minutes, begins with text from a statement by CNN news correspondent Bernard Shaw with an audio track of the artist counting in 5-second intervals. In white font over a black background, Shaw's quotation reads: "If television has an impact on people's perceptions . . . then yes television does have a measure of responsibility . . . for white people's fear of the black male" (Figures 4.4, 4.5).[41] As Cobb's viewer looks over the statement, she simultaneously hears Cobb slowly and evenly counting, "one 1,000, two 1,000s, three 1,000s, four 1,000s, five 1,000s. One 1,000, two 1,000s, three 1,000s . . ." After the quotation fades and the video's title page appears, Cobb cuts to a television screen playing a blurry clip of police beating King. She repeats a new phrase: "Fifty-six times in eighty-one seconds. Fifty-six times in eighty-one seconds . . ."[42] Then she layers another voice track over the first, which states twice, "Television. Multiply that by the number of times you saw it on television. Fifty-six times in eighty-one. On videotape. On videotape. On videotape." While the first voice track conveyed a measured tone, the layering of voices over the distorted clip

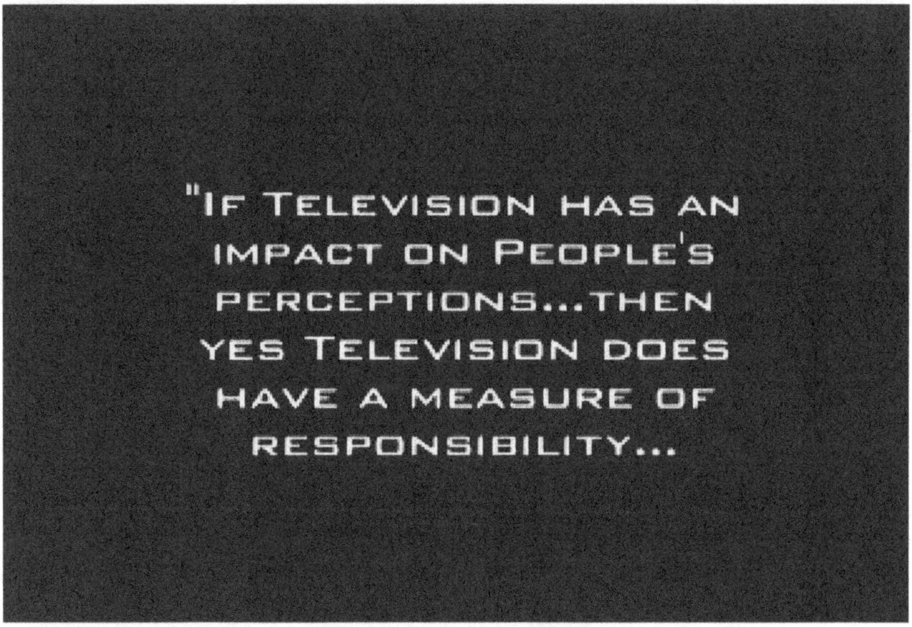

FIGURE 4.4 Portia Cobb, *No Justice, No Peace: Young, Black, ImMEDIAte*, 1991–92. Single-channel video, 14-minute duration. Courtesy the artist.

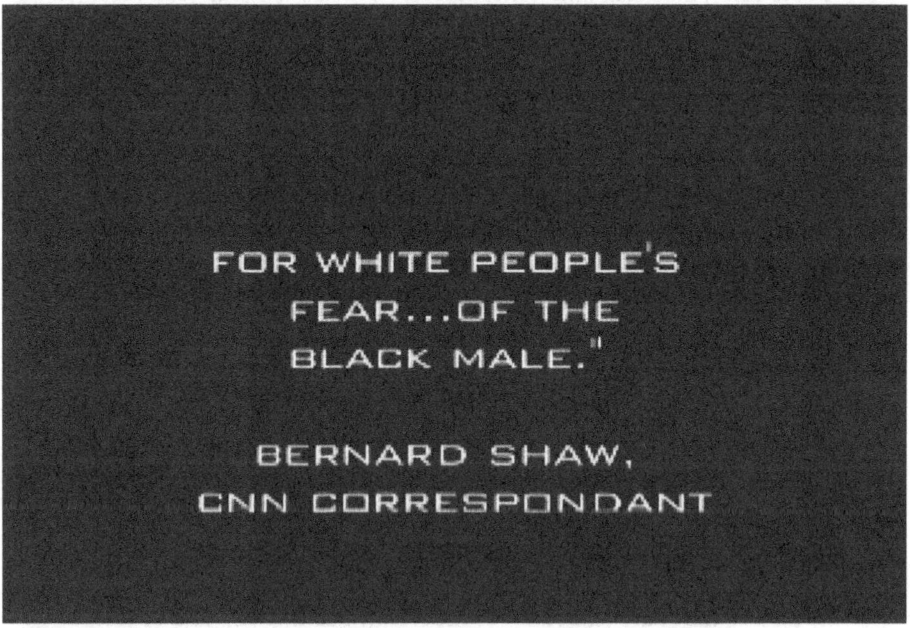

FIGURE 4.5 Portia Cobb, *No Justice, No Peace: Young, Black, ImMEDIAte*, 1991–92. Single-channel video, 14-minute duration. Courtesy the artist.

of the beating becomes disorienting, forcing the viewer to pay closer attention and make sense of both the sound and the image. In just a minute and a half, the seeming cacophony leads to clarity. With the layered voice-over and footage, Cobb expounds both the sheer number of times police hit King and the number of times viewers had watched the beating on television. She also seems to stress that fear of a Black man led to an unbridled act of violence that viewers readily consumed and that this behavior is perhaps incalculable because of its ubiquity in society. The layering effect of her voice tracks with the clip of King's beating to underscore these disturbing details and the addition of repetitious counting and fragmented sentences convey a sense of anxiety in the struggle to make sense of the senseless.

Throughout Cobb's film, segments of the King beating and its news coverage are intercut with a staged scene of a child watching television and interviews the artist conducted with young Black men at college campuses in Oakland, California, and other parts of the San Francisco Bay Area, where she had been a local radio deejay and a graduate student in film production at San Francisco State University. The interviews include the men's responses to the portrayals of Black males in the media and their lived experiences of being stopped by police. One interviewee, a young Boots Riley, musician and writer-director of *Sorry to Bother You* (2018), recalls a statement shared with him: "A teacher once said to me that power is the ability to define reality and to have others heed to that definition."[43] The quotation, similar to the Newton quotation above, could define the overarching theme of Cobb's film.

At the 00:07:15 mark, Cobb redefines perceptions of the King beating with the inclusion of a clip showing the televised beating of the white truck driver Reginald Denny. Black residents of South Central Los Angeles pulled Denny out of his truck and brutally beat him on the first day of unrest, April 29, 1992, which helicopter cameraperson Marika Gerrard and reporter Bob Tur captured live for television audiences.[44] In Cobb's use of the clip, Tur describes the Denny beating as "attempted murder." When Denny brings his arms up toward his face, Tur explains, "You see that, he's reaching up for help." Suddenly, Cobb cuts to a clip of the King video just as he raises his body up from the ground and an officer lunges toward him with a baton (Figure 4.6). The viewer continues to hear Tur's narration. Here, through editing and the intentional interchange of sound, the artist counters any argument that King was a threat to police. Instead, by pairing the audio and visual of the Denny beating with that of King's assault, Cobb powerfully suggests that the police were a threat to King's life, that they were committing "attempted murder," and that King was

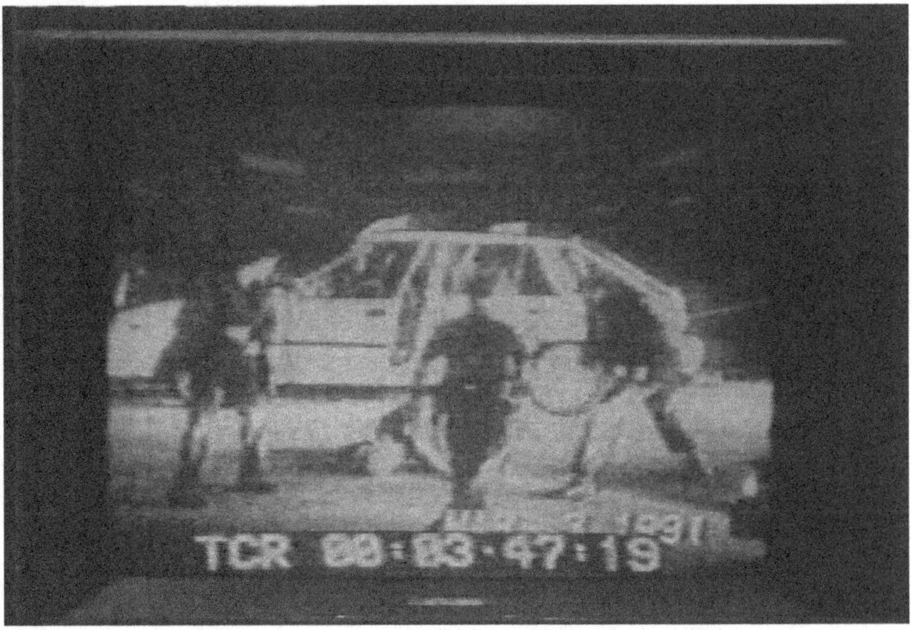

FIGURE 4.6 Portia Cobb, *No Justice, No Peace: Young, Black, ImMEDIAte*, 1991–92. Single-channel video, 14-minute duration. Courtesy the artist.

not resisting arrest but was "reaching up for help." Cobb then layers text over the clip of King's beating as it fades to black, asking, "Are these examples of high-tech lynching?" (Figure 4.7).[45] Then, as if answering the question, Tur exclaims, "That's right. This is attempted murder!" Explaining the artist's intention, film and television scholar Frances Gateward states, "Even as Cobb comments on mediated reality, she also informs us that she is aware that by constructing the video, she too is mediating reality[,] . . . reminding us that we are not watching privileged and objective truths."[46] Thus Cobb reframes the portrayal of the two beatings, one of a white truck driver and the other of a Black motorist, as equally horrific and unjust. Her comparison also encourages viewers to contend with how Denny's assault was immediately understood as wrong, yet King's was a matter of dispute.[47]

Like Cobb, Latipa came to understand the King video as more than a mere recording. She explains:

> I started to think about the Rodney King tape, not so much as [an] eyewitness or as the truth to an event, but rather, as a kind of repository for cultural memory. In this repository lay not only the event of the Rodney

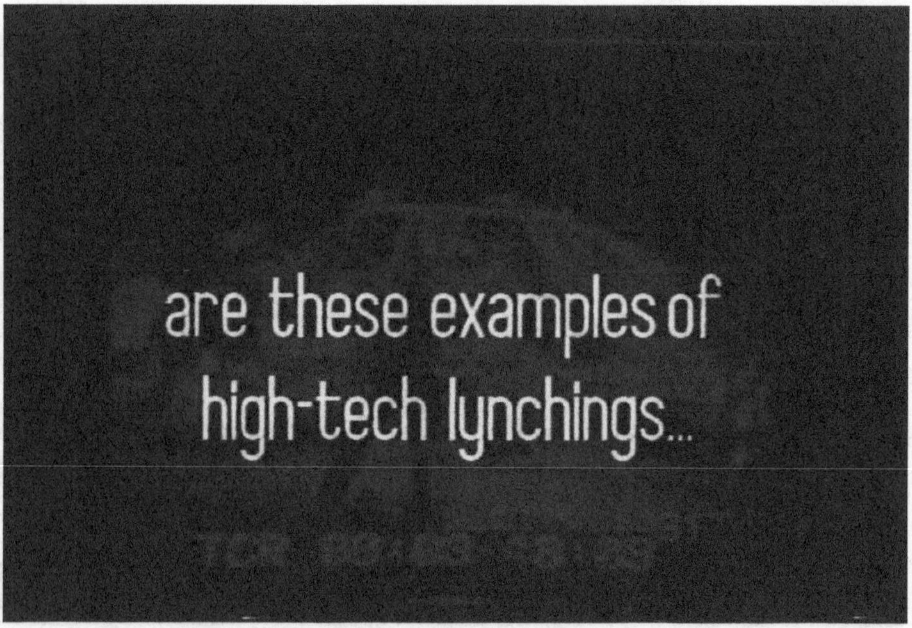

FIGURE 4.7 Portia Cobb, *No Justice, No Peace: Young, Black, ImMEDIAte*, 1991–92. Single-channel video, 14-minute duration. Courtesy the artist.

> King beating caught on video, but a whole set of apparati like the technology of video, the juridical and legal frameworks through which video was used, and the fundamental question of interpretation that cuts through all understandings of how it is that we think that we know something.[48]

Still, as Cobb insinuated in *No Justice, No Peace*, there was a rupture in the collective understanding of what the video portrayed. Latipa states, "If the jury could say that 'we see innocence' then those in the revolts could say that 'we see brutality.' In this difference lay the fact that one way of seeing could become universalized."[49] The 1992 Los Angeles Riots ignited out of widespread public condemnation of the jury's decision to acquit the police. There was a deep divide between the court's and the public's interpretations of the video, which had been regularly screened on television in the year leading to the unrest. What this contradiction revealed is not that one way of seeing would become universalized—either by a court's ruling or by unrest—but that vision itself is not universal at all. Instead, it must be systematically asserted and held by others as truth. Yet, as Cobb revealed in her video, especially in the pairing of the Denny and King beatings, vision and perception in matters of race often favor whiteness.

In other words, it is whiteness that is most often privileged as universal.[50] Artists like Cobb and Latipa have sought other means, not toward a universalism, but toward justice, one that critiques white supremacy, xenophobia, racism, *and* vision while centering the experiences of Black and other marginalized people.

Latipa's use of the King videotape in *Civil Society* triggers a rupture in storytelling. The blurred scene of police officers surrounding King, which led to an abrupt cut to blackness, is then layered with the off-camera sounds of someone walking across the hard floor of an unseen room. Soon a film projector, identifiable by its distinct clicking noise, projects close-up 16mm film footage of a street as vehicle tires zoom across the frame. The image of the street refers to the previous King clip, when the camera veered away from the beating to the road. The footage plays for just a few seconds before the filmstrip comes loose, registered by a flapping noise. The unseen projectionist makes sounds of struggle with the equipment before rethreading the filmstrip. It begins to click and project the footage of the road, but then the filmstrip flaps off the reel again. After two failed attempts, the projectionist successfully screens the film (Figure 4.3). In this segment, mostly through sound, the artist emphasizes the technology of film, the human hand behind it, and the failures of both.[51] The footage, which Latipa filmed at the exact location where police beat King, also signals an urgency and simultaneous struggle to capture the past in the present.[52] As Juan Capistrán once said, the landscape is forever scarred.[53] While Latipa also seems to assert this, the repeated failure to represent the scene, years later, suggests a paradox in our ability to see and not see such scars. This recalls the back-and-forth opening dialogue in Alain Resnais's *Hiroshima mon amour* (1959) where a Japanese man denies a Frenchwoman's ability to truly know the bombing of Hiroshima. Back and forth they state, "You saw nothing . . . I saw everything . . . You saw nothing . . ." Can we really know the painful pasts of others? But does this mean we should not try despite the impossibility? And how do we carry this past forward into the present?

Lewis Baltz similarly addressed the notion of capturing the past in *11777 Foothill Boulevard, Los Angeles, California* (1991).[54] As discussed in chapter 3, the large-scale color photograph's depiction of an everyday street scene could be any suburb in the United States; yet the photo's title is the address for the precise location where Los Angeles police officers beat King on March 3, 1991 (see Figure 3.5). The pictured street references that specific police beating, as well as the similar violence other Black men have endured in places that look as ordinary as Baltz's photograph. Thus Baltz's depiction symbolizes a frighteningly ordinary history. This is similar to a point made in Cobb's *No Justice, No Peace.* At the 00:09:30 mark, text reads, "What is the black male experience in America?" Then the video cuts to a clip of the King beating. Quickly, the scene fades to archival footage of the Watts Rebellion and police beating Black men, which is laid over an interview of a young Black man who answers the previously screened question: "The black male experience is to find a way to rise up in unity. A black man goes through a lot. [...] People just don't know that [police brutality] goes on all the time." The scene cuts to archival footage of police escorting Black men to cars and scenes of fires as Cobb's voice repeatedly counts in five-second intervals, "one 1,000, two 1,000s, three 1,000s . . ." Then, overlaying the archival footage, Cobb inserts text that reads, "56 times . . . still counting . . ."

Latipa also conjures the history of violence that Black men have experienced. Like Baltz, she records the street where police beat King. She also evokes the past with her use of vintage film technology. Similar to Cobb, Latipa points to the overwhelming absence of cultural memory regarding the brutality Black men have long faced. All three artists' works indicate that the police beating of King was not new. Yet Latipa's use of film footage also emphasizes the developments in film and video technology, such as the Sony Handycam Holliday used to record the King beating, that could finally capture police brutality and incite nationwide dialogues in ways previously unavailable.[55] In fact, decades after Holliday recorded the King video, it still resonates in our collective national memory and continues to be invoked in recorded instances of police brutality against Black people.[56] In this way, through its ordinariness and ubiquity, the King incident became and still is a stand-in for the many cases of brutality that have occurred.

Montage and the Anxiety of Chronology

Following Latipa's 16mm recording of the street, she includes three successive segments of black-and-white archival footage. The harmonium, violin, and viola soundtrack of sustained single notes returns, creating a solemn ambience for these segments. The first segment portrays aerial film footage of Los Angeles from 1960, which the artist gleaned from the Film and Television Archive at UCLA (Figure 4.8).[57] Though the three channels project the same footage, which includes a stadium, a freeway, and a building whose distinct structure identifies itself as Los Angeles City Hall, they are never in sync. Just when it appears as if two of the projected reels will coordinate, one screen suddenly cuts to a different view. This discordant portrayal of the same footage forces the viewer's eyes to dart

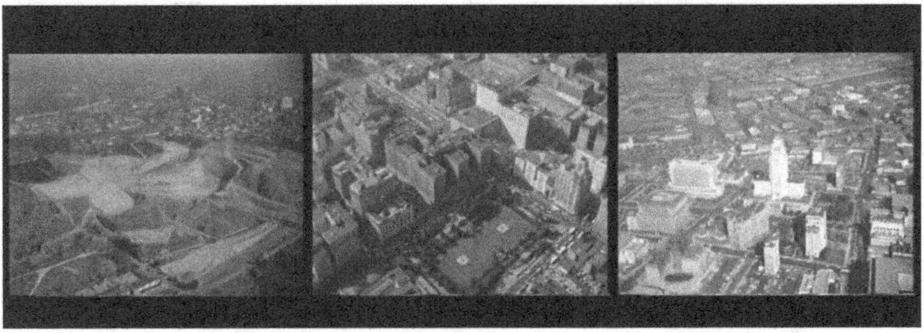

FIGURE 4.8 Latipa, *Civil Society*, 2008. Three-channel video, 37-minute duration. Courtesy the artist.

across each of the three screens in a futile attempt to capture the different perspectives of the city and match them with each other. Thus, these segments transport the viewer back in time while challenging her ability to master what she sees.

Latipa has described this out-of-sync portrayal as an "echo."[58] An echo, typically understood as an auditory phenomenon, occurs when sound waves bounce off hard surfaces and reflect the sound back with a delay and in a manner that distorts its source location. For example, if one were to yell "Hello!" into a large empty room, the hard floor, ceiling, or walls would reflect the sound back to the person as if someone were responding to the initial greeting with the same salutation. The experience of an echo can be disorienting, especially when it is unexpected. Like an echo, Latipa's three-channel presentation and editing technique distorts time and place. Time is distorted through the delayed start of the same footage across each screen, which disrupts the expected representation of place. The artist uses this phenomenon and experience to disrupt the viewer's expectations of temporality and chronology, distorting vision by taking the viewer out of time and disrupting the easy consumption of the footage as a whole.

The next segment begins when, one at a time, the three channels cut to a black screen. Over the continued solemn music, Latipa recalls in present tense, "You tell me: 1965, the heat will lay a pall over everyone, everything, inside and out."[59] The three screens begin flashing film footage of the National Guard, military aircraft, buildings on fire, and broken windows taken during the 1965 Watts Rebellion, with black screens sporadically dispersed among the cuts (Figure 4.9).[60] The clips play at random intervals through each channel, again challenging the viewer's ability to master what is being seen. Over the montages, Latipa makes a prediction

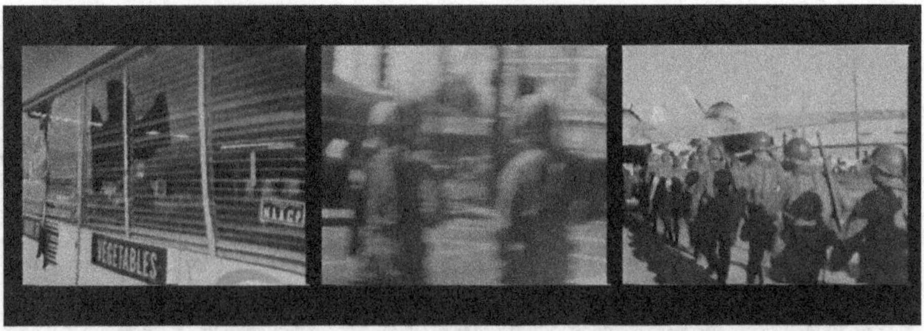

FIGURE 4.9 Latipa, *Civil Society*, 2008. Three-channel video, 37-minute duration. Courtesy the artist.

for a past that has already occurred: "A state of emergency will be called. A layer of ash will cover the neighborhood—a layer of ash over the year." Then, as if directed at the viewer, Latipa demands, "What's left, at least what's not in ruins, you tell me." With the last three words, each channel cuts to black again. In the darkness, Latipa explains, "A few months later, there'll be a program on TV. It'll be like looking at yourself through another's eyes. What stays with you are not the images but the voices." The film then projects, one at a time, three unique clips from a 1965 news broadcast on the unrest: a news studio with three white male anchors, an aerial view of a building on fire with several black residents walking near it, and a field interview with a white male reporter and resident.[61] The clips then play their original sound; yet because the sound from each clip plays one after the other without pause, the viewer's eyes struggle to match the images with each voice the viewer hears, much like an echo where the source location becomes distorted. Latipa then seems to explain the dissonance of the situation: "Each time he says us, you are them. And each time he says them, you grow numb." What's left and not in ruins, what the viewer struggles to grasp, are fragments of the past in the present, like visual representations of memories one struggles to fully recall—and they represent everything and nothing at once, bringing with them unease for both the narrator and the viewer. Through Latipa's specific use of montage paired with an affective narration and soundtrack, she portrays the past in ruins while conveying the unrelenting experience of unrest.

In "The 'Between' of Cinema," Pavle Levi explains that "films built on the principles of fragmentation, elliptical structuring, and disjunctive montage—films that highlight the existence of crevices, holes, and precipices in the fabric of their images"—reveal most acutely a viewer's cinematic desiring and a radical disruption of that desire.[62] Latipa achieves this with the use of disjunctive montage and the seemingly sporadic intervals of film footage, upsetting what Levi describes as the "normativized . . . desire for a flow of images—a desire for a film to 'take place.'"[63] The disruption of the "flow of images" in *Civil Society* is found in its interstices, what Gilles Deleuze defines as an editing operation of differentiation or disappearance between two images that "will be productive of a third [image] or of something new."[64] Deleuze asserts, "It is not a matter of following a chain of images, even across voids, but of getting out of the chain or the association."[65] It also is a matter of recognizing what Deleuze and Levi stress as the *between* of two images.[66] Latipa seems to recognize this with her use of three channels and the incorporation of black screens, which further disrupt the normative and binary relationships found in the flow of one image after another and the cuts between the two.

Latipa's *Civil Society* finds its lineage in the Dziga Vertov Group, of which Jean-Luc Godard was part, with the use of the interstice and black screen. As explained by Levi, "The interstice . . . became an expression of the Group's desire to enact a political demystification of the cut in a thoroughly *cinefied* world."[67] In 1970, when shooting and editing footage of Palestinian guerrillas in Jordan, Lebanon, and Syria, the Dziga Vertov Group experienced "a serious creative and ethical crisis" that ultimately informed a new direction for their footage.[68] As Levi had questioned, could the French filmmakers "credibly speak" for the Palestinian people and edit footage back home in Western Europe?[69] Then, after most of the Palestinians they filmed were killed by the Jordanian army, were they "still to appear as actors in a film made by and belonging to someone else?"[70] Five years later, Godard, Jean-Pierre Gorin, and Anne-Marie Miéville made *Ici et ailleurs* (1976), also known as *Here and Elsewhere*, discussing the war and using what Levi has explained as an "unsparing" auto-critique to confront "the filmmakers' desire to use moving images to simulate life where there was now only death."[71] Their strategy of critique used a combination of disjunctive montage, black screens, voice-overs, and multiple projector and monitor presentations to critique, not only themselves, but Israel and the involvement of the United States in the taking of Palestinian land, as well as the impact of capitalism and cinema on perceptions of the self and others.

By closely analyzing *Ici et ailleurs* and the editing techniques and statements deployed together in the film, we begin to understand Latipa's concept "vision in ruins" on a deeper aesthetic and political level. In under thirty seconds, *Ici et ailleurs* opens with the two French-speaking narrators, Godard and Miéville, taking turns stating the original title of the film in 1970, *Victoire* (Victory), and its change to *Ici et ailleurs* in 1974.

They emphasize "et" (and) in the title by verbally repeating it and cutting to footage of a 3D statuette of the word, which reappears throughout the film (Figure 4.10). As they state the title, text that reads "MON, TON, SON IMAGE" (my, your, his image) appears on the screen, with the last two words blinking, which emphasizes them visually, before cutting to Palestinian guerrillas training in the field and then a white French family watching television. A montage of footage of Palestinians shortly follows, interspersed with black screens that interrupt the flow of images and emphasize the cuts in the editing process, perhaps also signaling the gaps in the film's ability to fully capture the experience. Shortly after the 10-minute mark, text against a black screen reads, "LA MORT EST REPRESENTEE DANS LE FILM PAR UN FLOT D' IMAGES" (Death is represented in this film by a flow of images). "La mort" and "images" repeatedly blink, emphasizing the words and their relationship to each other. The filmmakers use this textual strategy several more times with other statements before returning to the physically materialized "ET" inserted between cuts to images representing the French and Arab Revolutions,

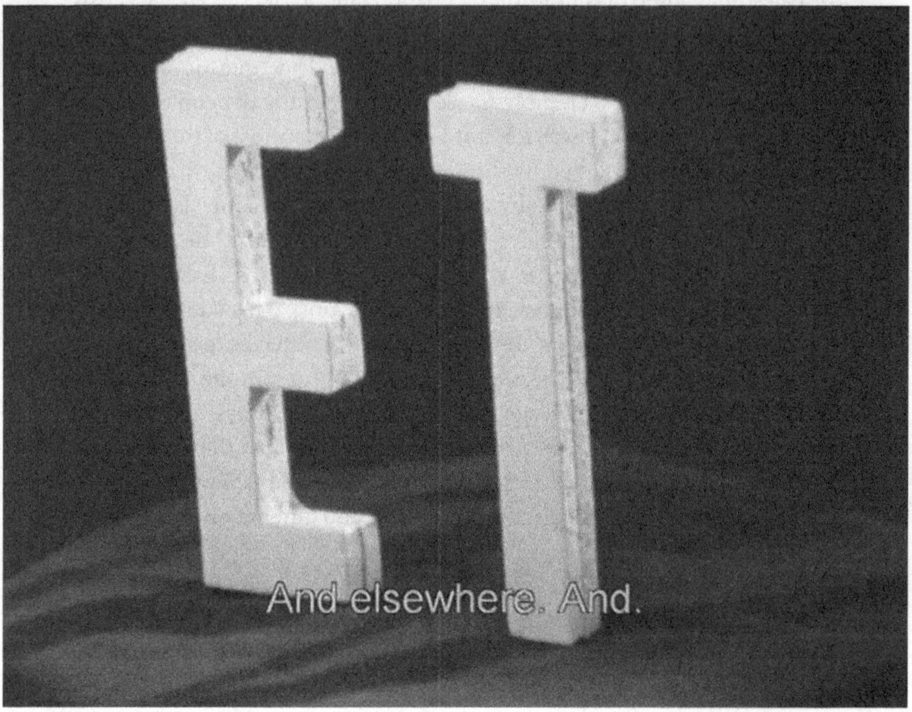

FIGURE 4.10 Jean-Luc Godard, Jean-Pierre Gorin, and Anne-Marie Miéville, *Ici et ailleurs*, 1976.

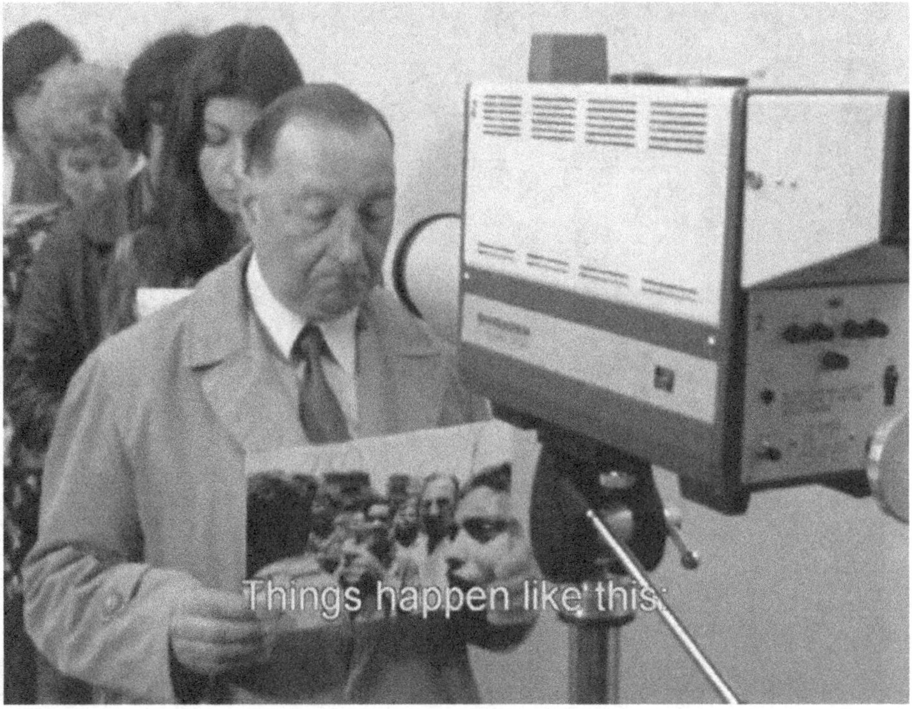

FIGURE 4.11 Jean-Luc Godard, Jean-Pierre Gorin, and Anne-Marie Miéville, *Ici et ailleurs*, 1976.

creating a comparison of the two events, yet simultaneously emphasizing the "ET" between them. About 12 minutes later, in a staged and didactic scene, people hold photographs and a poster from the war and pin them to a wall, with Godard critiquing the hidden process of cinematic montage. Then, one at a time, each person holds up a still in front of a movie camera (Figure 4.11). The scene deconstructs montage in a symbolic, yet literal performance, physically demonstrating the chain of images in space and time as well as the decisions made in the editing room. This didactic scene is echoed in the following segment where a narrator asks in French, "How do you use your time to occupy your space? How do you organize a schedule? How do you organize a chain?" Then a montage of cars, violent death, imprisonment, and commerce appear, before cutting to a scene of three slide projectors where a hand inserts various images into each slot and removes them at seemingly random intervals, simulating the process of montage. The filmmakers use multiple pairings of projectors, monitors, and projected images, in either a 2 × 2 or a 3 × 3 format, in several following scenes. After the 36-minute mark, as four monitors portray

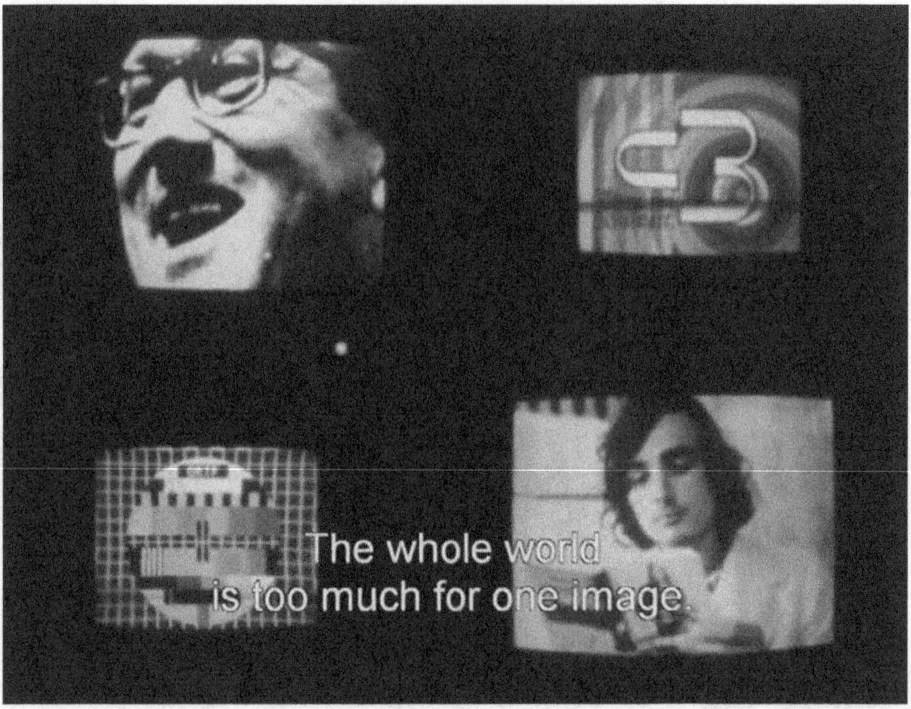

FIGURE 4.12 Jean-Luc Godard, Jean-Pierre Gorin, and Anne-Marie Miéville, *Ici et ailleurs*, 1976.

various images of people, graphics, and combat while a reporter shares an update on the war, Godard explains in French, "The whole world is too much for one image" (Figure 4.12). Then he quotes a counterstatement: "No, it's not, says international capitalism, which builds all its wealth on this truth." Godard continues, "There are no more simple images. Only simple people, forced to be as good as gold." Then, as the French family watches TV, he states, "That's how each of us becomes too many inside ourselves. But not enough outside."[72] Shortly after, a hand turns on and off the volume of a stereo playing a song as Godard lists nations and cities across the world that have recently experienced or are currently undergoing unrest. Through interstices, montage, voice-over, text, and sound—as well as critiques of some of these methods—the filmmakers challenge viewers to see the world anew, both the struggles of Palestinians and the imperialist impact on the visual field, which, as they seem to suggest, ultimately controls and clouds one's understanding of oneself and others through the uncritical consumption of the flow of images. Latipa shares this critical view, deploying similar filmic strategies in *Civil Society*. Latipa also understands the interstice as harboring the potential to disrupt time and space.[73]

Together, the three successive segments of fragmented archival footage in Latipa's video form a disjunctive montage sequence. In film, montage is a device that typically condenses time and moves a narrative forward. It was also, as Latipa has emphasized, once thought of as a "revolutionary" film technique, especially as used by Sergei Eisenstein or the Dziga Vertov Group.[74] Yet Latipa's use of montage instead propels the viewer back in time by following the 1991 King video with the 1965 Watts Rebellion sequence. The artist also blurs the visuals and sounds of the archival footage. Thus the scenes become a remnant of a past that cannot be fully realized. The inability of the viewer to fully comprehend what she is seeing symbolizes a "vision in ruins" and points to those stories from the past that continue to remain untold.[75]

The harmonium, violin, and viola score of solemn, sustained single notes also relates to this notion. First, it is important to understand the process of making the score. Latipa commissioned musicians Gabriel Will, Ian Ackerman, Warren Lee, and Joseph Kuta to help her create the composition. Intention was put into the selection of the specific instruments the musicians played and how they tuned them. As Latipa has explained, it was important that the instruments were "embodied," meaning that the musicians' bodies and awareness of their movements and effects on the instruments were necessary to the playing and achievement of sound.[76] Purposely avoiding the dominance of Western scales, which are often used to tune the instruments and create film scores, they consciously chose to tune the instruments using Asian and Indian scales. After they set that foundation, the process of composing the score included collaboration and comprised conceptual, formal, and emotional registers. Latipa would "communicate a feeling," the musicians would then translate that with their instruments, and together they would discuss the sounds before finalizing the notes and the duration in which they would play them.[77] In a 2015 interview, Latipa states that, according to the musicians, the sustained notes of the harmonium, violin, and viola reflect the time it takes to "open up" sound in infinite ways.[78] In an earlier 2013 lecture, Latipa explained:

> Something that is one can open up infinitely with time, for me, has very large ramifications, political ramifications if you want to call it that. . . . [H]ow is it possible for us to break out of ways of thinking, ways of seeing that have become normalized, what our knee-jerk reactions are. . . . Through their music I've learned that this—that time—might be that linchpin, that space for that which is infinite.[79]

The musical accompaniment, which is present through almost the entirety of *Civil Society*, sonically parallels Latipa's efforts to create a transformative space that disrupts normative thinking, automatic responses, and mainstream conceptions of art, time, and the world. With these considerations, we might think of Latipa's use of disjunctive montage, the black screen, and the three-channel projection as a visual method that recognizes how the past continues to unfold in infinite ways.

Repetition and the Mastery of Vision

The Tony Cokes video *Black Celebration (A Rebellion Against the Commodity)* (1988) incorporates similar black-and-white archival footage, accompanied by industrial music, to address episodes of unrest across the United States in the 1960s (Figure 4.13).[80] Opening with a Universal Pictures Newsreel logo, Cokes's video appears as if it is an official form of news like that often played before a narrative film in the days when movie theaters acted as sites for current events bulletins. After the logo, the pulsating sound of a keyboard introduces a title screen that reads, "TROOPS PATROL L.A. Damage Heavy In Coast Riots," with Ed Herlihy, a veteran newsreel narrator, listed as the speaker. Yet the sonic entrance of heavily distorted electric guitars and harsh grating vocals by the industrial band Skinny Puppy signals a foreboding alternative version of news for the viewer.[81] The soundtrack plays over archival footage of both the 1965 Watts Rebellion and the 1967 unrest in Boston and Newark, which Cokes intersperses with text drawn from song lyrics by English rock bands the Smiths and Depeche Mode and essays by conceptual artist Barbara Kruger and avant-garde political group Situationist International (SI).[82] Cokes especially draws heavily from the 1965 essay, "The Decline and Fall of the Spectacle-Commodity," by SI cofounder Guy Debord.[83] The essay theorized the unrest in Watts as a reaction to capitalism, and the sentence that Cokes cites in his video reads, "The Los Angeles rebellion was a rebellion against the commodity, against the world of the commodity in which worker-consumers are hierarchically subordinated to commodity values."[84] The artist's use of the essay and lyrical excerpts frames the pictured unrest as not only politically radical but also unified in purpose. Moreover, and like Cobb's intentions for *No Justice, No Peace*, Cokes creates a counternarrative to that which the media, such as the Universal Pictures Newsreel, had portrayed to the public. The artist has stated, "The intent of the piece is to introduce a reading that will contradict received ideas which characterize these riots as criminal or irrational."[85] Thus the unrest Cokes

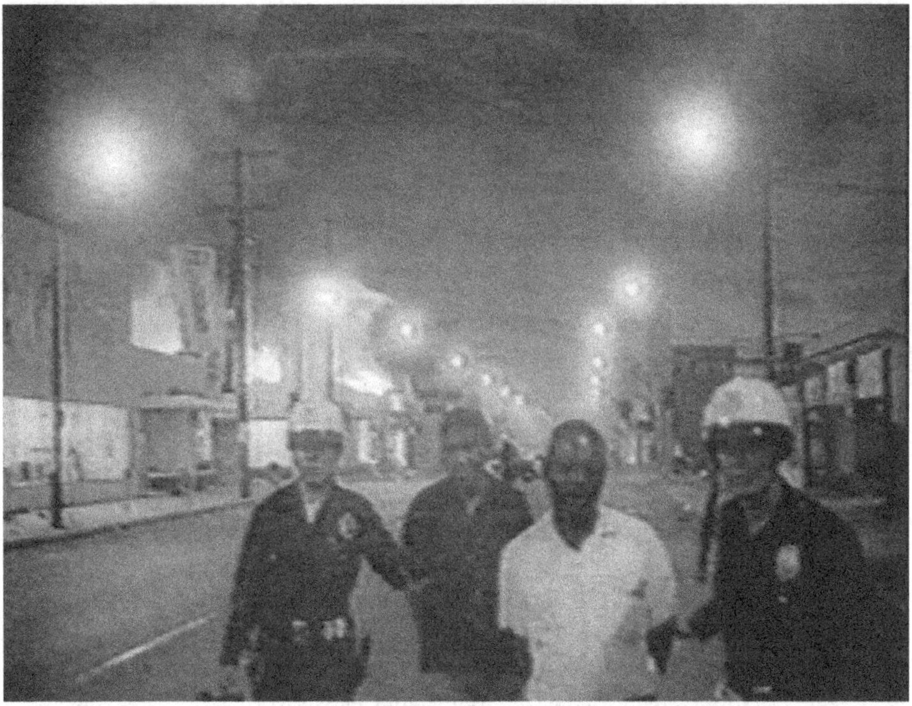

FIGURE 4.13 Tony Cokes, *Black Celebration (A Rebellion Against the Commodity)*, 1988. Single-channel video, black-and-white, stereo, 00:17:11. Courtesy the artist.

portrays in his video is not mere chaos; instead, unrest becomes a strategic act of liberation that rejects capitalistic oppression and objectification.

Cokes's use of archival footage in *Black Celebration* is like that of Latipa's three successive segments of archival film in that his viewers also become aware of their seeing. By slowing the speed of the footage and then repeating the scenes, Cokes provides viewers with the opportunity to focus on those caught on film—both the white law enforcement officers and the Black residents—including their specific movements and actions. To be clear, Cokes's use of slow motion and repetition is different from that employed by the defense team of the LAPD officers who beat King. While the defense team sought to limit both vision and understanding of what was seen on video to blame the victim and reify stereotypes, Cokes, as well as Latipa, instead strives to underscore such limits and disrupt the easy consumption of images encoded with xenophobia and prejudice. On the effect of Cokes's looping of scenes, including the incorporation of text and music, film historian Paul Arthur says:

FIGURE 4.14 Latipa, *Civil Society*, 2008. Three-channel video, 00:17:23. Courtesy the artist.

> It demands that we "look again," re-viewing the coded media spectacle of "rioters" and "peace-keepers." . . . In addition, the formal rigor of repetition is freighted with larger implications of historical redundancy, the accumulating onslaught of racially reductive images, as well as brutal physical acts, and the simmering resistance they provoke.[86]

Still, I understand a seemingly contrary notion: Repeated looking reveals our inability to see. This in itself is a revelation, and it undermines the notion that repetition leads to mastery. Indeed, the failure to "master" the three screens of delayed footage in *Civil Society* corroborates this insight.

Following the archival footage in *Civil Society*, at approximately the 00:17:17 mark, fragments of French words appear on each screen in various intervals as the music distorts with a screeching sound over a sustained note (Figure 4.14). Then a second narrator begins to speak and the music fades. The voice of French sociologist Nacira Guénif-Souilamas connects the 2005 French unrest to the 1965 Watts Rebellion, the 1992 Los Angeles Riots, unrest in Brixton, and the ongoing war in Palestine.[87] However, she points out that the perceived cultural and political distinctions of each event and locale often hinders others from making such global connections. As she makes these statements, the viewer's eyes dart across the three screens in an effort to make meaning out of the word fragments. The fragments for "FILLE" (girl or daughter) appear first, followed by "ELLE" (she), "FEU" (fire), and "FOU" (mad or crazy). After a few seeming nonsensical fragments, "SENS" (sense) appears and is held for a few seconds longer than the previous words, before briefly cutting to a black screen. The word fragments reappear with "DUR" (hard), "DURÉE" (duration), "ENDURE" (endure), "DEMAIN" (tomorrow), the English words "REMAIN" and "REMAINS," and "REVUE" (review), before a series of words appear with "TEMP" (time), including "VUE" (view), "EN" (in), and "ENTRE" (between). With the last word fragments spread across each screen as "EN," "TRE," "TEMP," Guénif-Souilamas links all the sites she speaks of as being "to a certain extent, in a permanent state of riot" (Figure 4.15). The three fragments hold as the music comes back in with the familiar solemn sustained notes.

There is a desire to read the fragments as a whole and make meaning out of them; yet the attempt to do so is a frustrating endeavor. The fragments, broken up across three screens, appear, disappear, and change, disrupting the flow of words and their legibility. If a viewer does not know French, the effort to make meaning becomes nearly impossible. For those with French-language skills, it may be difficult but not impossible to read the fragments as whole words, as I have done above. Still, I suggest that the language exercise Latipa has created is more than the possible understandings one might create with the word fragments; they also are a metaphor for the global disconnection Guénif-Souilamas speaks of in her voice-over. In addition, the seeming chaos of fragmentation could be viewed as "a state of riot"—the very phrase the French scholar uses to describe the different locales and the ongoing history of unrest. Ultimately, I argue that both Guénif-Souilamas and the word fragmentation describe the difficulty of fully comprehending what one sees, symbolizing a "vision in ruins" and expressing unrest in the effort to make connections. Furthermore, via the multichannel projection and disjunctive cycling of word fragments, Latipa disrupts the temporality and chronology that the act of reading typically requires. Thus the segment acts as a disjunctive montage of words and word fragments while distorting vision and taking the viewer out of time. The last fragments, "EN," "TRE," and "TEMP" (between time), then become a literal signpost of this effort, like the physical representation of "ET" in *Ici et ailleurs.*

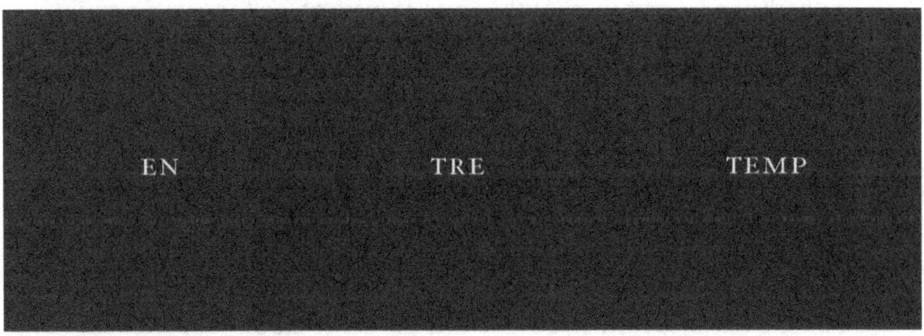

FIGURE 4.15 Latipa, *Civil Society*, 2008. Three-channel video, 00:18:23. Courtesy the artist.

Lexicon, Citizenship, and Unrest

After the word fragment section, the three channels project pixelated color footage of a car fire played at a reduced speed—a seeming reference to the slow-motion clip of the King video used during the trial.[88] In the background, a group of police or soldiers run, and, one at a time, each screen cuts to footage of smoke as the music begins to screech. The editing makes it appear as if the authorities are struck by an unseen explosive. Even though the cut is symbolic, the editing creates a violent act where there was not one originally, standing in stark contrast to the actual violence recorded in the videotaped police beating of King. If the technology of video could be used to deny an unjust act of violence, as with the handling of the King video in court by the defense, then it could also be used to fabricate one, as Latipa does in the segment.

After several other cuts, interspersed with black screens, the music fades and the video returns to fragmented words as Guénif-Souilamas discusses the car fires that characterized the 2005 French unrest. Word fragments, some in both French and English, appear together on the screen, forming words such as "POLITIQUE" (policy or political), "CRITIQUE," "LEXIQUE" (lexicon), and "CREATE." After Guénif-Souilamas discusses the car fires, she explains that those who participated in the unrest "were not going to internalize the suffering, internalize the despair and let it destroy themselves from the inside."[89] Instead, she says, "they were going to show it. And it was going to be a national show. Well, even an international show." As she speaks these last words, what remains on the screen are the fragments for the word "RUIN."[90]

In a 2009 public dialogue, Latipa states that the unrest in France presented a "fundamental crisis of representation," which is a politics of language.[91] Indeed, language is a powerful tool, one that can be used to assert authority and dominance. At the 00:25:32 mark of *Civil Society*, Guénif-Souilamas mentions the issues of language that arose during the 2005 French unrest, stating that language can act as "a barrier between me and the other." More than that, language also can be used to *other*, and the other's fluency in the official language of the nation-state can then affect perceptions of their belonging. In other words, language fluency is tied to who is and is not a "good citizen" in so-called civil society. Guénif-Souilamas goes on to state that the unrest could be read as an assertion of a new political lexicon that questions the legitimacy of official language. Pushing this idea further, I argue that the act of unrest supplants official language with the physical expression of rebellion and the rejection of dominant, normative ways of being and belonging. Language here is both literal, as in the French or English officially recognized and spoken in France and the United States, respectively, and symbolic of the greater logics that operate, control, and oppress peoples—citizens and noncitizens—in a capitalist and racist nation-state.

The solemn music returns, and color footage of the Clichy-sous-Bois neighborhood appears on the center screen and then the left and right ones. Latipa explains, "From the future, I see it," and proceeds to set the scene to describe why the anticipated threat of police harassment encouraged the boys to flee from authorities: "2005: an area known as the '9–3,' three boys fear they are being chased by the police. The police check them for their identification papers. Take them to the station and harass them. They don't want to be taken in. So they run." The center channel cuts to black-and-white archival footage of the Watts Rebellion, which portrays three Black boys as they scale a concrete fence. The helicopter reporter narrating the scene claims that the boys are running away from a fire, which he speculates they started. The footage of Clichy-sous-Bois on the left and right screens cuts away to black. Although the reporter admits that he is unsure of their involvement, he calls for a police unit and gives them the location of the three boys. Suddenly, the center channel cuts to a power substation in Clichy-sous-Bois. In a voice-over, Latipa sets the scene again: "From the future, I see it. They run into a power station, everywhere there are signs posted, 'Enter and risk death.' They hide. Soon, a blackout." The images cut to black screens. She continues, describing the situation as "the darkest silence" before the ambient music cuts out too. If the visual and aural silence is not clear to the viewer, Latipa explains, "Too close to an open circuit, and two boys are dead." The center channel then displays footage of an apartment building. The camera zooms closer to the wall and we see the spray-painted names of Benna and Traoré, the boys who died (see Figure 4.2). The phrase "From the future, I see it" also stands out. When paired with the cuts, it suggests that the future brings clarity, one of sight or vision, even when Latipa cuts to black. Together, her words and cuts enable us to look back in time, across space and geographic differences, and link the fragments of seemingly disparate pasts to create a fuller picture of how the experiences of discrimination, death, and unrest connect. Through her voice-over and editing process, Latipa again merges the French unrest with those of Los Angeles's past, creating inextricable connections between the two regarding race, citizenship, policing, news media, and memory. She also links the deaths of the two marginalized youth to the long history of violence that Black and Brown people have experienced at the hands of the state.

Once music and images return on all three screens, Latipa states how the civil unrest is known as "a riot of immigrants." She clarifies, "But they're not immigrants. They're citizens. Second, third generation citizens." She continues, "With this, I am thrown to the past." The images cut to blackness. Then, via the center channel, a time stamp appears near the bottom of the black screen. It is like the time stamp previously seen in the King clip, but it plays in real time. After a few moments, footage of the apartment building on fire appears on all screens with a time stamp appearing at the center (Figure 4.16). Latipa then begins to reflect intensely on her own experiences. She states:

> I am swimming in voices not all my own. I am the daughter of immigrants. I am no one's daughter. I am a citizen. I am not a citizen. I am one generation removed from a remote province in the third world. I don't even know its name. I am a good daughter. Like any good daughter, I have no needs. "We have healed," you say. "We have mourned," you say. "We have moved on." I am the daughter of immigrants. I am no one's daughter. "Back home things are bad," I am told. "Corruption, the heat, the desperation."

The three screens then cut to black, and Latipa states, "I am lucky to be born in America." In this passage, she expresses the precarious nature of citizenship and points to a generational forgetting prompted by her birth into a nation that is different from that of her parents. Yet, more than that, this segment expresses an internalized violence and points to the contradictions of citizenship or rather who is or is not considered a citizen, no matter their legal claims. In a 2013 lecture, Latipa explained how daughters particularly embody the potential for reproducing not only children but also the notion of the nation through those citizen children.[92] To be

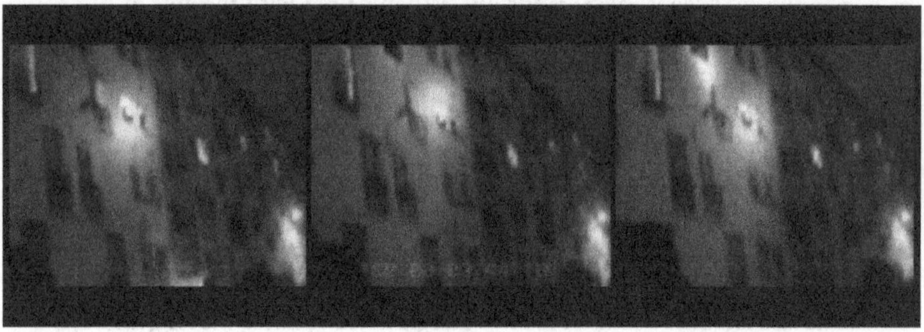

FIGURE 4.16 Latipa, *Civil Society*, 2008. Three-channel video, 00:22:38. Courtesy the artist.

a "good daughter," according to Latipa's voice-over in *Civil Society,* is not to make demands of one's parents *and* nation. Though the artist states she is "lucky to be born in America," the contradictory statements made moments earlier, of being and not being anyone's daughter and of being and not being a citizen, allow us to understand that this so-called luck comes with a sense of uncertainty and loss—a loss of familial ties, rights, and self-agency at home and in society.

Over a three-channel projection of repeated and delayed footage of apartment buildings, which look like the building on which the boys' names were spray-painted, Latipa expresses the pressures she feels to accomplish what previous generations in her family could not realize. Again, she repeats, "I am swimming in voices not all my own. I am the daughter of immigrants. I am no one's daughter." She continues:

> The nation is inscribed in my every day. It is something that I have to assimilate. Their vicarious life, they tell me. What they are unable to accomplish in their generation, I will realize. I, will realize. A good life will follow. The closer I come to the nation, the further I move from the past. I am the daughter of immigrants. I am no one's daughter. I have no needs. I see nothing. I will forget, and this makes it possible to continue. And this makes it possible to continue.

Her voice cracks slightly with emotion when she explains that she will forget. She repeats the last statement, that the forgetting will make it "possible to continue," as if she is trying to convince herself of its veracity. Nations often expect immigrants and their children to forget their pasts through processes of assimilation that are meant to make them proper citizens of "civil society."[93] Yet their perceived connections to those pasts by society continue to jeopardize their belonging and, at times, endanger their lives. The same is true for those who are generations removed from their family's ancestral pasts.

In 1994, scholar Elizabeth Alexander discussed citizenship in a critical analysis of the videotaped beating of King.

> African Americans have always existed in a counter-citizen relationship to the law; how else to contend with knowing oneself as a whole human being when the Constitution defined one as three-fifths? The American way with regard to the actual lived experience of African Americans has been to write a counter-narrative which erased bodily information as we knew it and substituted a counter-text which in many cases has become a version of national memory.[94]

Embedded in the idea of citizenship discussed by Alexander and in the notion of civil society is a profound question of democracy and representation. It necessarily includes and excludes certain people, and it extols rights—rights inextricably linked to the ability to live and survive in the United States. Questions surrounding democracy and representation only seem to rise to national attention during times of crisis, such as during unrest or a natural disaster; yet they are constant factors in the lives of marginalized peoples.

In a 2015 interview, Latipa discussed ruins and her understanding of what they encompass. Whereas one might understand ruins as traces of something that was once whole, she explains her understanding of the word as something that signifies absence. The artist explains that through absence, she tries to account for how few people truly recognize or see ruins. She emphasizes a clear distinction between "vision *in* ruins" and "vision *of* ruins."[95] Whereas "vision of ruins" suggests that the remains of that which has been destroyed can be seen, "vision in ruins" emphasizes the failures of seeing. It is the recognition that there are narratives and experiences that remain to be perceived by others. In *Civil Society*, Latipa creates space to make these modes or politics of seeing visible. She invites viewers to create links between episodes of unrest that have occurred in different nations and time periods. She also makes visible the painful experiences of assimilation and the dangers that lie in being marginalized and regarded as Other.

In a 2010 essay on *Civil Society*, Latipa discussed the French government's disregard for the motives that characterized the 2005 French unrest and the sorrow that many from the North African and Arab community experienced over the deaths of the two boys, Zyed Benna and Bouna Traoré. She wrote:

> The revolts were met with a de-politicization of the actions that were happening in the streets and an erasure that exists until this present day of not only the anger and frustration at the systematized violence of everyday life, but also, an erasure of the grief and loss that exists for these two young men. In Clichy Sous Bois [*sic*] there are many words that exist in the landscape. They are written on the walls where Bouna once lived, standing as a clear call to justice. It is the irrecoverable loss, the cry, in which the dead are summoned by name.

Revealing how this erasure and willful blindness had affected her, she continued, "Who hears this cry? This is the question and commitment that remains for me as I struggle to understand the way that 'life' is shaped in this world and to understand the forces that come to make some lives so much more vulnerable than others."[96]

At the 00:25:30 mark, after Latipa's struggle to convince herself that forgetting is a path forward, the music cuts and Guénif-Souilamas's voice returns, discussing the limits of language and the lexicon of the nation-state during the 2005 unrest in Paris. Like the earlier segment with her voice-over, French and English word fragments appear on the three screens, such as "PLI" (fold), "PLEA," "PLEUVOIR" (rain), "DEVOIR" (duty), "PASSÉ" (past), and "MESSAGE." She then suggests that the unrest "can be read as the invention of a new political lexicon," one that is "still to be learned by those" who believed "their grammar was the legitimate one." As she states this, fragments of the words "DETOUR," "RETOUR" (return), "REVOLT," "MANIÉ" (mania), and "REMNANT" appear on the screens, in addition to others that do not readily make sense. Finally, she asks, "How do we give a translation to that new grammar?" Then fragments across each screen form the word "IMMIGRÉ" (immigrant) (Figure 4.17).

In fact, this "new grammar," the "new political lexicon," Guénif-Souilamas speaks of, is not new at all, as the immigrant is not new or sometimes is a citizen who is misperceived as an immigrant. Still, unrest is a political lexicon, "the language of the unheard," a tool of the misperceived and ignored.[97] Like the word fragments and letters that seemingly appear at random in Latipa's film, unrest is a political lexicon and disorder. It refuses to abide by the logics of oppression—of the white supremacy, xenophobia, and state-sanctioned violence that brutalizes the lives of Black and other marginalized subjects, like the immigrant, the colonial subject, and her descendants. It is not new but generations old. One that is only perceived as new, one that always shocks but should not be a surprise, and, like the Black person, the immigrant, the colonial subject, and their

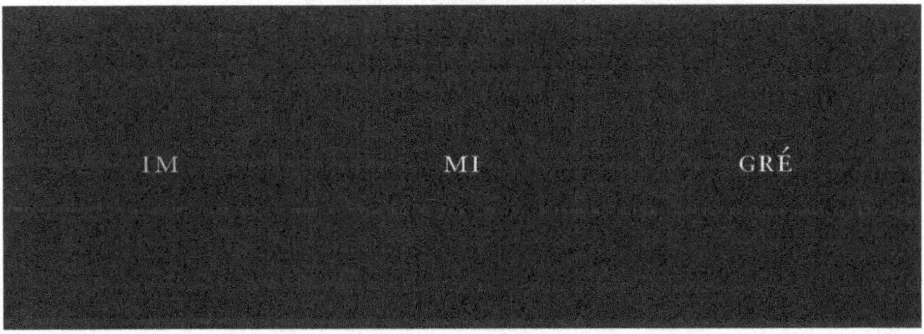

FIGURE 4.17 Latipa, *Civil Society*, 2008. Three-channel video, 00:26:55. Courtesy the artist.

descendants—those made marginal in the image of the nation—is hardly ever recognized, never truly seen, made the ultimate ruin of the (broken) vision of nation and white supremacy.

"From the Future, I See It"

Latipa sets the next scene in *Civil Society* with the familiar phrase, "From the future, I see it." At 00:27:07, over footage of an apartment complex where the 2005 unrest began, which moves across the three channels with a delay and sporadic cuts to black, Latipa cites her inability to explain why she is making the film and describes it as a "haunting." Touring the neighborhood with a university student who grew up in the Parisian outskirts, Latipa describes how they encounter children who scrutinize them, asking if they're from the "television." This, in addition to the student's desire not to be photographed, compels Latipa to self-reflection, wondering if she is being exploitative, perhaps like the media had been. She then wonders "where the desire to see comes from." She and the student continue their tour despite their conflicting feelings. Then, as explained by Latipa, "when the camera stops trying so hard to make sense of the situation, when there's no more recording being done," the student tells her, "At first, all anyone wanted is to see a policeman dead. But even in the logic of vengeance there are too many who have already died to account for—too many policemen to kill." Latipa says she responds to these statements by closing her eyes—"Not because of the violence, but because it is infinite." Then, with eyes closed, she realizes:

> All I wanted to see about this situation is most present in this state. Only off-frame, only off-frame might I understand the endlessness of this loss. Law is within the frame. It asserts the frame as fact. Justice lies outside the frame. We understand that we will never understand.

With the last statement, the three channels cut to black. The black screens, as they have throughout *Civil Society*, interrupt the normative flow of images, emphasize the editing process, and signal the gaps in the film's ability to fully capture an experience; yet here Latipa also seems to offer us the opportunity to see the infinite as she did when she closed her eyes. In the absence of footage and images, in the seemingly nothingness, is everything. As in the soundtrack's elongated and held notes of the harmonium, violin, and viola, the black screens signal the experiences of loss and what may be lost. Unrest may not make sense; however, for those who experience it, it instead is the bounds of laws, courts, video, and vengeance that

FIGURE 4.18 Latipa, *Civil Society*, 2008. Three-channel video, 00:29:40. Courtesy the artist.

is senseless. We understand that we will never understand the senselessness of injustice.

At 00:29:35, Latipa returns to the time stamp. This time, however, she portrays it over two of the three black screens, with the right screen's time stamp running in real time starting at a 3-minute mark and the left screen's time stamp running backward at a similar speed starting at a 5-minute mark (Figure 4.18). Over the quiet neighborhood sounds of youth talking and laughing, Latipa discusses film and representation.

> It's been said that in film there is no blood, only color. We see red. We don't see blood. In red, we move away from an image that represents and toward one that is aware of its inevitable failure. To embrace this failure is to say, "I see red and this does not mean blood," and to let the full weight bear upon you. Something so simple as a color might remove us from a demand for representation. What kind of history would we tell if we were freed from representation?

The time stamps, just 23 seconds away from reading the same time, suddenly cut away to black.[98] The statement is curious. At once, Latipa references Godard's *Weekend* (1967), film theory, and questions of representation, which seem out of place among the sensitive and emotional reflections on race, unrest, and the ruins of vision. Deleuze explains, "The formula in *Weekend*, 'it's not blood, it's red,' signifies that blood has ceased to be a harmonic of red, and that this red is the unique tone of blood. One must speak and show literally, or else not show and speak at all."[99] The statement seems to critique cinematic illusionism and representation as artifice.[100] This takes me to Adrian Piper's description of how understandings of others might be informed by minimalism as an "aesthetic strategy for drawing attention to the concrete, specific, unique qualities of individuals."[101] There seems to be potential freedom in such aesthetic strategies and interpretations of art or film; yet such modern art principles also compelled many to ignore sociopolitical issues when they were believed to be extraneous to art, even while artists used the same principles to reveal how oppression and racism exist and how the nature of violence and bigotry is inherently illogical. What Latipa's film segment exposes is not a theoretical inquiry or some sort of palate cleanser from the emotional gravity of the film but instead the real difficulties in being seen as more than a representation or fantasy in another's vision of art and the world. In this faulty vision, we are the ruins. We signify the demise of those in power, and we harbor the potential to undermine oppression and white supremacy.

In Walter Benjamin's discussion of allegory and the trauerspiel, or German mourning play, he writes, "The allegorical physiognomy of natural history [...] is actually present as ruin. In the ruin, history has passed perceptibly into the setting. And so configured, history finds expression not as process of an eternal life but as process of incessant decline."[102] Susan Buck-Morss, discussing Benjamin's concepts of allegory and ruin, states:

> The debris of industrial culture teaches us not the necessity of submitting to historical catastrophe, but the fragility of the social order that tells us this catastrophe is necessary. The crumbling of the monuments that were built to signify the immortality of civilization becomes proof rather of its transiency. And the fleetingness of temporal power does not cause sadness; it informs political practice.[103]

In unrest, we recognize not only disorder but also, using Latipa's phrase, vision in ruins. And we see ourselves. After Latipa's reflection on representation, the time stamps disappear, and each screen turns black. From the interstice, she proceeds, "I close my eyes. I wait for me. I see you." Then, a blur of buildings and other structures moves across the three screens in sequence, but each is slightly delayed (see Figure 4.1). Filmed from a fast-moving train, its quiet rumble acts as a soundscape while Latipa reflects on the unrest and its long-lasting impact on her: "You tell me, 'Fifteen years have passed. We have healed, we have mourned, we have moved on.' I have not."

At the conclusion of *Civil Society*, Latipa explains, "1992, Los Angeles. There is in fact nothing to see. To remain looking toward the past would mean to let this past die and—no, every part of me says, it must live on." Although this statement counters the earlier passage wherein the artist expresses notable distress as she contends with the pressure to forget the past, her position now has shifted toward resisting such pressure. She insists that the past must be remembered. Furthermore, she recognizes that it is the absence—those ruins not seen—that also shapes our present and future. She states, "You tell me, you understand. I've created a space to grieve." Indeed, through *Civil Society,* Latipa has created a space that recognizes the magnitude of loss in histories of unrest. She points to societal failures to recognize the enduring legacies of violence, and through her exploration of the Watts Rebellion, the police beating of King, and the deaths of Benna and Traoré, the artist connects them across time and national borders. As I have come to realize through the vision in and of ruins, unrest is a manifestation of sorrow, an act of the bereaved, and a gesture toward making loss visible when so many refuse to see. From the ruins, our unrest and grief can drive us toward justice. For those we lost, those who live, and those who will be born, we embrace our roles as the ruins of so-called civil society, undermining oppression and white supremacy and demanding and seeing to their end.

Epilogue

RECOLLECTING THE 1992 LOS ANGELES RIOTS TODAY

Unlike my father, I do not have a personal photo to mark the unrest in 1992. Still, I remember. My maternal grandmother rushed past me and my brothers to the front door, pushing the metal screen open with so much force that it swung back shut with a loud bang. We instinctively followed her outside, confused but alert. It was the early evening of April 29, but the springtime sun still lit up our neighborhood of mostly single-family homes with some garages that had been converted by *tíos* into modest abodes. For generations my family had lived in this part of unincorporated South Los Angeles, my grandfathers from both sides having grown up just a couple miles away in Watts and another section simply known as "Punkinville" by old-timers like them. When business was booming and the factory jobs along Alameda Avenue afforded a living, the area was racially and ethnically diverse, with white, Mexican, Black, and some Asian families. But by the time my brothers and I were born in the 1980s, it was predominantly Latino. The demographic shift was dramatic. When my grandparents attended the local elementary schools in the 1920s and 1930s, they had been punished, sometimes physically, by teachers for speaking Spanish; but by my generation it was commonplace to hear it in the classroom and on the playground—and if you were *pocho*, born in the United States and Americanized like us, you were ridiculed by peers for not knowing Spanish or not speaking it properly. Yet our neighborhood experienced more than demographic changes by the 1980s. The economy was terrible, and poverty had skyrocketed, as did policing.

The experience of policing surfaces in what may be my earliest childhood memory. I remember the sounds of a police helicopter as my mother opened my grandparents' door. With my youngest brother in her arms, she gently uses her hand to press his head back into her shoulder to lull him back to sleep. As we step outside to begin our walk home next door, the bright searchlights of the helicopter shine down harshly, illuminating the yard. Searching, the concentrated beam quickly finds us, illuminating our bodies with the spotlight like actors on a stage. Fixed on us, it lights our path as we walk down my grandparents' driveway and then up our own, not leaving until my mother opens our door, ushers us inside, and closes it. Being followed door to door by the searchlights would occur regularly throughout my childhood, but the presence of law enforcement also hit closer to home than the lights of their helicopters. In our neighborhood, it was not uncommon to have family members in prison or juvenile detention, like my own. The "War on Drugs" devastated many, and South Los Angeles, especially South Central, became infamous in the media and popular culture as crime ridden, gang infested, and violent. With family and neighbors incarcerated, it became my parents struggle to make sure my siblings and I stayed safe—safe from the streets and from the law. These experiences, part of our daily lives, was our "normal." Still, on the spring evening near the end of April 1992, something was uncharacteristically awry.

My grandmother stopped at the edge of the lawn in front of her pink stucco home and looked down the street. She placed her fists on her wide hips, and I held onto the side of her housecoat so she would not leave me behind again. I looked up at her powdered and wrinkled face to try to make sense of the situation and followed her gaze to the convenience store located at the center of our neighborhood, away from the major thoroughfares of Florence and Firestone Avenues. The small store, owned by a Japanese American family, had been a house once and still vaguely resembled the modest stucco dwellings around it. Open seven days a week, the store carried snacks, beverages, and shelf-stable foods, as well as some household and personal items. While the adults in my family only shopped there on occasion, my siblings and I frequented it as often as we could. Our routine was always the same: We would beg our grandfather for money, he would dispense a dollar or two from his leather wallet, and we would bolt from the house to the tiny store to buy treats. With a dollar, we could buy a handful of sugarcoated red licorice or Mexican candies, like gooey tamarind, crumbly de la Rosa marzipan, and spicy chili-covered watermelon lollipops. But as often as we frequented the store, we never exchanged more than a quick "Thanks!" with the owners at the counter, usually only the wife, before running back to eat our candies in our grandparents' yard.

With our gaze fixed on the convenience store, my brothers and I watched with my grandmother as a few neighbors entered it and then quickly left, carrying items in their arms without any bags. Soon other neighbors came out of their homes and our grandfather and parents joined us on the lawn too. For the first time anyone could recall, it appeared that the store was left unattended, the store owners gone. A woman emerged from the store with a few small items in her hands, and my grandmother openly ridiculed her: "Pssh! Can you believe what she's doing? What could she even take—stockings?!" Hearing her words, I realized we were watching our neighbors loot the store. From my grandmother, who was born during the Great Depression and came of age during World War II, I had learned that stockings were a rare commodity that she and other women across the country prized and some went to extreme lengths, like theft, to obtain. But the ridicule quickly morphed into anger. Neighbors were stealing from another working family—not just any family, but a family who had long been part of the neighborhood. As my mother later recalled, the store was owned by the parents of my father's high school friend—the one who took the photo of the birthday boys at Yosemite in August 1965, during "the First Los Angeles Riot."

Soon after my grandmother's comment, neighbors began yelling at the ones coming in and out of the store, exchanging expletives. The situation rapidly escalated. A middle-aged man who lived across the street from us went back inside his home and returned with a handgun. He brandished the weapon, holding it above his head while yelling at the looting neighbors before shooting into the air as an attempt to scare them away. My grandfather and other men followed suit, retrieving their guns from closets, drawers, and under beds. As the sun began to set, neighbors simultaneously raided the store while others tried in vain to protect it for a family that had already determined it best to vacate and flee.

Our grandmother and parents ushered my brothers and I back inside, and soon the convenience store became the least of their concerns. From phone calls and live television broadcasts, we learned that the jury's acquittal of the police who beat King incited protests and then unrest that was quickly spreading across South Los Angeles and the Southland. Two miles from our home, at Florence and Normandie Avenues, a helicopter news crew broadcast live footage of residents pulling drivers out of their vehicles and beating them. Replays of the earlier footage captured others looting the liquor store at the corner of the intersection. Perhaps it was that earlier footage that prompted my grandmother to go outside and check on our own neighborhood store.

Via television, we realized that the ubiquitous police cars that typically patrolled our streets were nowhere in sight, and we saw in real time—outside our home and on the television—how the violence was growing. With no safe way out of the neighborhood, our parents helped lock the doors of my grandparents' home and led us all to the back living room, away from the street and windows. Generations of my family lived through other episodes of unrest in Los Angeles, from the 1943 Zoot Suit Riots to the 1965 Watts Rebellion. Now my siblings and I were experiencing one too. Huddled around my grandparent's large television console, we watched live broadcasts and replays of looting, beatings, and destruction. After nightfall, we watched the city as it burned. The cityscape, usually illuminated by streetlights and helicopter searchlights, was now illuminated by fire.

For days, my brothers and I camped out on the floor of the living room and watched the unrest on television as we also heard it unfold outside with gunshots. Eventually, we caught footage of National Guardsmen and other troops as they descended across the city, echoing recollections of Watts in 1965. When the flames finally smoldered, the scars of unrest became even more evident throughout the cityscape, with blocks of destroyed buildings, some completely obliterated as if a bomb had been dropped on the neighborhood. It was during these days, during the other "Los Angeles Riot" and its immediate aftermath, when I began to understand my father's memories of the simultaneous awe and fear of it all.

In both 1965 and 1992, Los Angeles residents responded to racial and social injustice with protests, and some turned to looting, destruction, beatings, and arson. It was and still is too easy to sum up these acts as mere expressions of so-called Black rage, revenge, or retaliation against predominantly white law enforcement. As I have underscored in this book, the 1992 Los Angeles Riots involved Black, white, Latino, and Asian residents as both victims and participants. The expressionistic shorthand and limited racialized descriptions of the unrest gloss over the righteous grievances, daily brutality, and real death that marginalized populations far too often experienced at the hands of the law—not only by the overzealous or undertrained individual officer but by generations of agents representing the law.

In *Unrest*, we see how the work of artists reconceptualizes the political efficacy of visual art, broadening the discussion of racism and xenophobia and shedding light on the widespread nature of oppression. They challenge viewers to question their—our—complicity as passive, indifferent, and sometimes careless, urging us to recognize the complexities at hand as well as the bereavement and loss caused by the pain and injustice of discrimination, xenophobia, violence, and oppression.

Still, in today's context, what does the history of the King video and the 1992 Los Angeles Riots mean, especially when Black people continue to die unnecessary and highly visible deaths under the auspices of the law? What does this history mean in relation to recent unrest, such as that which occurred after the police killing of Michael Brown in 2014, Philando

Castile in 2016, George Floyd in 2020, and Tyre Nichols in 2023? In the aftermath of the 1992 Los Angeles Riots, unrest continues, and as an art historian, I continually find myself drawn to the work of artists who contend with the enduring legacy of state violence, asserting that Black lives matter and rejecting our collective dehumanization. From Jonathan Calm's series *Travel Is Fatal to Prejudice* (2017–18) and *Double Vision* (2018) to Vincent Valdez's *The Beginning Is Near, An American Trilogy* (2016–ongoing), and from Latipa's work at the Memory and Resistance Laboratory at the University of California, Riverside, to the abolitionist pods that Patrisse Cullors, alexandre ali reza dorriz, noé olivas, and collaborators of the Crenshaw Dairy Mart have created in community with others, I see the important work artists continue to do in times of unrest. You see, unrest does not end when the dead are buried, when the last arson fires are extinguished, or when rubble is cleared away. It is ever present, expressed in family oral histories, in intergenerational experience, living within our bodies and minds and those of our future kin. From the analyses of visual art in this book, we see how the work of artists broadens the discussion of racism and xenophobia and sheds light on the widespread nature of oppression. Most of all, we see with them how much we need each other as we see to the demise of these injustices.

Acknowledgments

This book was years in the making, as most books are, but one whose chapters began as experiences shared and remembered among family decades before I ever sought an academic career in art history. For this, I thank my family, especially my late father, George Salseda, for keeping our experiences, stories, and memories alive and passing them down for the next generations. I am also indebted to Cherise Smith at the University of Texas at Austin who recognized the 1992 Los Angeles Riots as my research topic with a certainty that took me some time to attain with equal confidence. While the history notably shaped my life and academic trajectory, my hesitation was marked by the closeness of the topic and the numerous complexities it encompassed, politically, socially, economically, and emotionally—not only for me, but for countless others. Such an endeavor can be intimidating, and I was certain to disappoint or offend, be misread, misunderstood, or projected upon, and characterized as too radical for some or not radical enough for others. But I had to move past these worries *for* the history that shaped me.

I could not have taken those first steps alone. So, many thanks are due to Cherise for mentoring me through an early version of this book. I also gained other incredible mentors at the University of Texas at Austin, including George Flaherty, Eddie Chambers (now at the School of the Art Institute of Chicago), and Frank Guridy (now at Columbia University). Yet, without Dr. Laura Augusta, who became my peer adviser and writing coach, I would not have finished my first draft—at least not on time. Her tough love and unwavering support were the steady pulse I needed to keep me focused.

My transition from a graduate student at UT Austin to an assistant professor at Stanford University correlated with an increasingly volatile political climate exacerbated by the COVID-19 pandemic. With almost two years away from the new workplace and colleagues, that transition took much longer than initially expected. Yet I experienced support from several key colleagues in the Department of Art & Art History: Alexander Nemerov, Johnathan Calm, and Marci Kwon. I am thankful for those Stanford colleagues who also became kind and dependable neighbors, writing partners, and good friends, including Usha Iyer, also my colleague in the department, and Elaine Ray, Colleen Hallagan Preuninger, and Gina Hernandez. Once in-person campus life resumed, my department colleagues Karla Oeler and Pavle Levi provided critical feedback on early drafts of my final chapter, which helped me write a narrative and analysis, for which I feel proud and am grateful. I also appreciate the support of Jennifer DeVere Brody from the Department of Theater & Performance Studies who moderated a conversation and gave me feedback on a presentation of the final chapter at the Center for Comparative Studies in Race & Ethnicity. She confirmed the political and emotional registers for me and pointed me to the work of other women who share an interest in the space of absence and the between. Likewise, I appreciate the Manuscript Review Workshop of the Stanford Humanities Center, especially Svetlana Turetskaya, who organized my review. With that, I am grateful to the scholars who participated in it by reading and providing feedback on my manuscript: Julia Bryan-Wilson (Columbia University), Jennifer González (University of California, Santa Cruz), and Roberto Tejada (University of Houston). I would be remiss not to recognize Susana Canales Barrón, who assisted me with image permissions for the book. A talented filmmaker, visual artist, and independent journalist, she went from being a Stanford graduate student to a research assistant and then a mural project collaborator before becoming a friend. Indeed, it is the friendship, generosity, and community of colleagues that make academia a worthwhile endeavor.

At the University of Chicago Press, I thank my editor, Dylan Montanari, who saw the potential of the manuscript as a book, and Fabiola Enríquez Flores, who helped Susana and me troubleshoot image permissions. I also thank the artists, Juan Capistrán, Seth Kaufman, Adrian Piper (and the Adrian Piper Research Archive team), and Latipa, for their generosity, time, and honesty. I first met most of them when I was a student, and over the years, with so much unrest still in the world, they continued to keep lines of communication open and read drafts of my writing about their art and practices. My hope is that this book inspires new interest, insights, and lines of research into their work, as I hope for the many other artists who have addressed the history surrounding the 1992 Los Angeles Riots. There is still much more to be written and remembered.

Finally, I thank my husband, Daniel Gomez, and our children. We began our family in my first year of graduate school, and, while I have always tried to keep us centered, I am grateful for their understanding and support when research, travel, studio visits, and writing inevitably encroached on our time together. Thank you for standing with me as I traversed the academic and first-book journeys and for continuing to be by my side for the second book and next chapters of our lives together.

Notes

Introduction

1. Before the assault, King had eluded officers in a car chase before exiting the freeway and being pulled over by the police.

2. Lou Cannon, "The King Incident: More Than Met the Eye on Videotape," *Washington Post*, January 25, 1998, https://www.washingtonpost.com/archive/politics/1998/01/25/the-king-incident-more-than-met-the-eye-on-videotape/2248e35e-178b-47e9-a8db-0734f88b46e0/?utm_term=.c51b5f1c6740; Andrew Blankstein, "Holliday's Videotape Sent L.A. Reeling," *Los Angeles Times*, July 5, 1997, http://articles.latimes.com/1997/jul/05/local/me-9885. Holliday recorded approximately 12 minutes, but only 9 minutes and 20 seconds included the beating and arrest of Rodney King. Only 81 seconds capture the actual beating, which was edited down to 68 seconds by KTLA staff before airing it. This edited version would be most widely used in the media. For more information about the KTLA editing, see Lou Cannon, *Official Negligence: How Rodney King and the Riots Changed Los Angeles and the LAPD* (Times Books, 1997).

3. Richard A. Serrano and Tracy Wilkinson, "All 4 in King Beating Acquitted," *Los Angeles Times*, April 30, 1992, http://www.latimes.com/local/california/la-me-all-4-in-king-beating-acquitted-19920430-story.html.

4. David Whitman, "The Untold Story of the L.A. Riots," *U.S. News & World Report*, May 31, 1993.

5. See Paul Ong and Suzanna Hee, *Losses in Los Angeles Unrest, April 29–May 1, 1992: Lists of the Damaged Properties* (UCLA Center for the Pacific Rim, 1993).

6. Ong and Hee, *Losses in Los Angeles Unrest*; Staff, "Deaths During the L.A. Riots," *Los Angeles Times*, April 25, 2012, http://spreadsheets.latimes.com/la-riots-deaths/.

7. See "Unrest, Noun: Meaning & Use," in *Oxford English Dictionary*, accessed March 26, 2024, https://www.oed.com/dictionary/unrest_n?tab=meaning_and_use#16443289.

8. "Unrest, Noun: Meaning & Use."

9. I am also thinking of President George H. W. Bush's televised address to the nation on May 1, 1992, during the LA unrest and his threat to "use whatever force is necessary to restore order" (see chapter 3), as well as the problems of the lexicon as expressed in Latipa's *Civil Society* (see chapter 4).

10. See "Un-, Prefix²: Meaning & Use," in *Oxford English Dictionary*, accessed March 26, 2024, https://www.oed.com/dictionary/un_prefix2?tab=meaning_and_use&hide-all-quotations=true#17138061.

11. See Hersey's *Rest Is Resistance: A Manifesto* (Hachette Book Group, 2022).

12. Hector Tobar, "Riot's Scars Include 200 Still-Vacant Lots," *Los Angeles Times*, April 21, 1997, https://www.latimes.com/archives/la-xpm-1997-04-21-mn-51014-story.html.

13. Tobar, "Riot's Scars Include 200 Still-Vacant Lots."

14. See Rose Salseda, "Creating Equity in Academia for Latinx Art History," *Latin American and Latinx Visual Culture* 1.3 (July 2019): 87–91, https://doi.org/10.1525/lavc.2019.130006d.

15. Rose Salseda, "Shared Struggles: African American and Latinx Art," *Lightning Round Panel on Latin X American Art*, Sixth Latino Art Now! Conference, Houston, TX, April 4–6, 2019; Rose Salseda, "Shared Struggles," in *Estamos Bien*, ed. Rodrigo Moura, Susana V. Temkin, and Elia Alba (Museo del Barrio, 2021), 309–14.

16. Latina Feminist Group, *Telling to Live: Latina Feminist Testimonios* (Duke University Press, 2001), 20.

17. Latina Feminist Group, *Telling to Live*, 2.

18. The Los Angeles institution is now referred to as the California African American Museum (CAAM). The exhibition was held from October 3, 1992, to July 5, 1993, and showed artwork by Nathaniel Bustion, Portia Cobb, Robert Colescott, Dewey Crumpler, Darryl Evers, Charles Gaines, Masud Kordofan, Joe Lewis, O. Funmilayo Makarah, Willie Middlebrook, Peter Miro, Alfonso Moret, Mary Lovelace O'Neal, Sandra Rowe, Matthew Thomas, Carrie Mae Weems, Rene Westbrook, Pat Ward Williams, and Richard Wyatt. This exhibition is not to be confused with *No Justice, No Peace: LA 1992* (2017), an exhibition of archival photographs, footage, and other types of documents, also curated for CAAM. This later exhibition, curated by Tyree Boyd-Pates, contained no visual artwork besides documentary photographs. However, public programming included a performance by multimedia artist and activist Patrisse Cullors.

19. Lizzetta LeFalle-Collins, "No Justice, No Peace: Resolutions . . . ," in *No Justice, No Peace? Resolutions . . .*, ed. Lizzetta Lefalle-Collins and Halford M. Fairchild (California Afro-American Museum Foundation, 1992), 21. The exhibition included a video work by Portia Cobb, which I explore in chapter 4.

20. Roland Charles and Toyomi Igus, Foreword to *Life in a Day of Black L.A.: The Way We See It: L.A.'s Black Photographers Present a New Perspective on Their City*, ed. Roland Charles and Toyomi Igus (Center for Afro-American Studies, University of California, Los Angeles, and Regents of the University of California, 1992), 9–10.

21. The photographers include Nathaniel Bellamy, Roland Charles, Don Cropper, Calvin Hicks, Jeffrey [*sic*], Mike Jones, Karen Kennedy, Rod Lyons, Willie Middlebrook, and Akili-Casundria Ramsess. The book was produced in collaboration with the UCLA Center for Afro-American Studies (renamed in 2003 the UCLA Ralph J. Bunche Center for African American Studies) and the Black Photographers of California (whose archives are now housed at the Tom & Ethel Bradley Center at California State University, Northridge).

22. See Noah Purifoy and Ted Michel, *Junk Art: 66 Signs of Neon* (n.p., 1966). Small press or self-published brochures on artists' works made in response to the 1992 Los Angeles Riots exist; however, their limited quantities, absence from major library and museum collections, and lack of digitization make them difficult to find and access. A few special issue magazines in 1992, such as *High Performance* and *Los Angeles Magazine*, also published artworks on the 1992 Los Angeles Riots.

23. Min Hyoung Song, *Strange Future: Pessimism and the 1992 Los Angeles Riots* (Duke University Press, 2005).

24. Song, *Strange Future*, 70. The author specifically expands on the concept of the black body in pain, as originated by scholar Elizabeth Alexander, in this discussion. See Elizabeth Alexander, "'Can you be BLACK and Look at This?': Reading the Rodney King Video(s)," *Public Culture* 7 (1994): 77–94. I return to Alexander's article in chapter 4.

25. See Victor M. Valle and Rodolfo D. Torres, *Latino Metropolis* (University of Minnesota Press, 2000), 47. One in three residents lived in households with incomes below the poverty line—a rate over twice that for the county in general—and only 59 percent of adults worked—a rate 16 percent lower than the rest of the county. This information is quoted in Song, *Strange Future*, 57. Song cites statistics by Valle and Torres that claim that 80 percent of those arrested during the 1992 Los Angeles Riots were mostly unemployed immigrants from Guatemala and El Salvador and that one-third of arrested immigrants were employed but mostly as "casual laborers" (Valle and Torres, *Latino Metropolis*, 47; quoted in Song, *Strange Future*, 5).

26. I discuss this coverage in chapter 1.

27. Song, *Strange Future*, 104–6. Song is quick to point out the differences in the Denny and King beatings, though, and outlines the attention, press, and privilege Denny experienced after his assault. Song also emphasizes the number of African American public figures and entertainers who came to Denny's hospital bedside and his financial aid. The racial dynamics of this situation are interesting, yet not fully fleshed out by the author. George J. Sánchez also delves into this incident, suggesting that its overemphasis in the media speaks to the ways in which the Black-white binary essentially dismissed the importance of anti-immigrant sentiment during the unrest. See George J. Sánchez, "Reading Reginald Denny: The Politics of Whiteness in the Late Twentieth Century," *American Quarterly* 47.3 (September 1995): 388–94.

28. Cherise Smith, *Enacting Others: Politics of Identity in Eleanor Antin, Nikki S. Lee, Adrian Piper, and Anna Deavere Smith* (Duke University Press, 2011). In the broader book, Smith discusses the performances of artists whose characters are identified by racial, ethnic, or gender categories different from their own.

29. Smith, *Enacting Others*, 137.

30. Smith, *Enacting Others*, 138.

31. Smith, *Enacting Others*, 188.

32. Smith, *Enacting Others*, 201. Also see Rose G. Salseda, "The New Wave of Identity Politics: Juan Capistrán's *White Minority*," *American Art* 26.1 (Spring 2014): 24–31.

33. Smith, *Enacting Others*, 7–8.

34. Ong and Hee, *Losses in Los Angeles Unrest.*

35. Erna Smith, "Transmitting Race: The Los Angeles Riot in Television News," *Joan Shorentein Center on the Press, Politics and Public Policy, Discussion Paper Series*, #R-11 (Harvard University, May 1994).

36. Sánchez, "Reading Reginald Denny"; George J. Sánchez, "Face the Nation: Race, Immigration, and the Rise of Nativism in Late Twentieth Century America," *International Migration Review* 31.4 (Winter 1997): 1009–30.

37. Nancy Abelmann and John Lie, *Blue Dreams: Korean Americans and the Los Angeles Riots* (Harvard University Press, 1995), 153, 159.

38. Smith states that only a quarter of news coverage highlighted the Latino experience—and most of this coverage occurred on foreign-language news

programs—even though more than half of those arrested during the 1992 unrest were Latino, a third of the stores destroyed were Latino owned, and the areas hardest hit in Los Angeles were mostly populated by Latino residents. See Erna Smith, "Transmitting Race," 2, 7.

39. See Gerald Horne, *Fire This Time: The Watts Uprising and the 1960s* (Da Capo Press, 1997). The book was first published in Charlottesville by the University Press of Virginia in 1995.

40. Horne, *Fire This Time*, 25.

41. Horne, *Fire This Time*, 25.

42. See Kellie Jones, *South of Pico: African American Artists in Los Angeles in the 1960s and 1970s* (Duke University Press, 2017); Daniel Widener, *Black Arts West: Culture and Struggle in Postwar Los Angeles* (Duke University Press, 2010).

43. Jones, *South of Pico*, 3; Widener, *Black Arts West*, 3–6, 287.

44. Widener's book includes an epilogue that touches on the 1992 Los Angeles Riots, see *Black Arts West*, 283–89.

Chapter One

1. My meeting with Capistrán occurred on November 12, 2015. Numero Uno Store #103 is located at 9127 S. Figueroa St., Los Angeles, CA 90003.

2. For eyewitness testimony and a breakdown of the events leading to Harlins's death, see Brenda Stevenson, "People v. Du: The Trial," in *The Contested Murder of Latasha Harlins: Justice, Gender, and the Origins of the LA Riots* (Oxford University Press, 2013): 133–67.

3. *The People of the State of California v. Soon Ja Du*, Cal. Super. Ct. L.A. County, Dept. 111, 1991, no. BA037738, vol. 1, Sept. 30, 1991, 94–55; also cited in Stevenson, *The Contested Murder of Latasha Harlins*, 142, 144.

4. Stevenson, *The Contested Murder of Latasha Harlins*, 140–41, 146, 270.

5. Brenda Stevenson pushes the comparison/contrast with the King incident further to emphasize the gendered and racial differences. See Stevenson, *The Contested Murder of Latasha Harlins*, xvi. I would like to note that in a March 8, 2015, interview I conducted with Capistrán he stated that he sees Du as an oppressor—as a symbol of the police.

6. Stevenson, *The Contested Murder of Latasha Harlins*, 236.

7. The conviction for voluntary manslaughter implies that the jury considered Du to have intent to kill and that the killing was unlawful.

8. *The People of the State of California v. Soon Ja Du*, Cal. Super. Ct. L.A. County, Dept. 111, 1991, no. BA 037738, vol. 3, October 2, 1991, 624; Stevenson, *The Contested Murder of Latasha Harlins*, 236.

9. *The People of the State of California v. Soon Ja Du*, Cal. Super. Ct. L.A. County, Dept. 111, 1991, no. BA 037738, vol. 3, October 2, 1991, 624; Stevenson, *The Contested Murder of Latasha Harlins*, 236.

10. Stevenson, *The Contested Murder of Latasha Harlins*, 237–39.

11. For more details on these incidents, including the shooting of the nine-year-old Korean girl Yuri Kang, see Stevenson, *The Contested Murder of Latasha Harlins*, 239–41. Stevenson also documents a contemporaneous trial in which a Korean immigrant, Brendan Sheen, was charged for abusing his cocker spaniel, Baby, and sentenced to thirty days in prison. Herschel Hunt of Placentia, CA, wrote a letter to the editor of

the *Los Angeles Sentinel* about the Du sentencing and the Baby case. Hunt wrote, "A Korean was sentenced to 30 days in prison for kicking his dog. Suddenly everything was clear to me. In my mind at this moment, a Black person's life is not worth as much as a dog." Stevenson documents that the dog received over $10,000 in donations from the public. Stevenson also cites another letter written by a Black woman to the *Los Angeles Times* about the Du sentencing. The woman states, "A woman who was convicted of voluntary manslaughter was given probation, community service and a $500 fine! This is a slap in the face of every African-American citizen . . . Judge Joyce A. Karlin has just told us that it is open season on our children" (242–43).

12. This date painting is not the only artwork in *From a Whisper to a Scream* that references Harlins's death. There are two other works. Sharing the name of the series, *From a Whisper to a Scream* (2012) includes ten black-and-white photographs, arranged evenly in a two-by-five grid, of two $1 bills. Through each of the ten photos, the two $1 bills are depicted slowly folding into the shape of an origami gun. *We all carry within us our places of exile, our crimes, and our ravages. But our task is not to unleash them on the world; it is to fight them in our selves and in others* (2012) references Harlins as well as police brutality and the idea of rebellion. It comprises an installation of two sets of offset gray-scale prints—one of a billy club and the other of a brick. Capistrán took some of the prints, set on a table, and folded them into the shape of a gun. Viewers were encouraged to pick their "weapon" of choice: the billy club, representing authority, or a brick, representing rebellion. They could then fold the item into a gun, should they choose to do so.

13. Stevenson's 2013 publication is a recent exception.

14. Juan Capistrán, email correspondence with the author, February 4, 2015; Juan Capistrán, interview with the author, Los Angeles, CA, March 8, 2015. Capistrán claims that he and Harlins "were in all the same classes in junior high."

15. Juan Capistrán, phone interview by the author, October 20, 2021.

16. Juan Capistrán, phone interview by the author, October 20, 2021.

17. Juan Capistrán, interview by the author, digital recording, Los Angeles, CA, March 8, 2015.

18. From Toni Morrison's *Beloved* (Plume, 1988): "Places, places are still there. If a house burns down, it's gone, but the place—the picture of it—stays, and not just in my rememory, but out there, in the world" (36).

19. The message of a paper banner hung up on the store read: "Closed for Murder and the General Disrespect of Black People." See Patt Morrison, "After the Riots: The Search for Answers: Symbol of Pain Survives Flames: Neighbors Rescue Market Where Latasha Harlins was Killed," May 7, 1992, https://www.latimes.com/archives/la-xpm-1992-05-07-me-2498-story.html; Stevenson, *The Contested Murder of Latasha Harlins*, 120.

20. Morrison, "After the Riots."

21. Elston Carr, "'Chaos' at Shuttered Store, Residents Say," *Los Angeles Times*, May 23, 1993, https:// latimes.com/archives/la-xpm-1993-05-23-ci-39030-story.html; Stevenson, *The Contested Murder of Latasha Harlins*, 311.

22. Juan Capistrán, conversation with the author, Los Angeles, CA, February 21, 2012. Pat Morrison's *Los Angeles Times* article confirms that Capistrán's memory of this tagging is correct. See Morrison, "After the Riots." Historian Brenda Stevenson mentions the banner in her book but does not mention the additional messages that residents added. See Stevenson, *The Contested Murder of Latasha Harlins*, 120.

23. Thank you to Javier Arellano Vences for his presentation on Capistrán's artwork in my 2021 seminar, "Riot: Visualizing Civil Unrest in the 20th and 21st Centuries." It was in Arellano Vences's presentation that I was introduced to the connection between the spray-painted message on Empire Liquor and the Trammps' lyrics. The Trammps' chorus recalls that of the Los Angeles deejay Nathaniel "Magnificent" Montague's catchphrase, "Burn, baby, burn!," which became infamous when protesters shouted it as Los Angeles erupted in flames during the 1965 Watts Rebellion. Demonstrators would use the phrase "Burn, baby, burn" again, during the 1992 Los Angeles Riots.

24. The August 1991 firebombing was the second to occur in South Central in less than a two-week period. Stevenson cites a 2012 *Los Angeles Times* article by Robert Greene ("Forgotten Flashpoint: A Week After Rodney King," *Los Angeles Times*, April 27, 2012, http://articles.latimes.com/2012/apr/27/news/la-ol-riot-latasha-harlins-20120426) that claims Empire Liquor was burned down during the 1992 Los Angeles Riots. However, this contradicts Pat Morrison's article, and Capistrán is adamant that the liquor store was not burned down. See Morrison, *The Contested Murder of Latasha Harlins*.

25. Penelope McMillan, "End to Market Violence Urged," *Los Angeles Times*, August, 19, 1991, https://www.latimes.com/archives/la-xpm-1991-08-19-me-735-story.html.

26. Ong and Hee provide data that list 2,073 Korean/Korean American businesses incurred damages, whereas Stevenson lists 2,300. It is unclear where Stevenson got her data since her footnote is unrelated to the statistic. See Ong and Hee, *Losses in Los Angeles Unrest*, 12; Stevenson, *The Contested Murder of Latasha Harlins*, 280, 379.

27. Carr, "'Chaos' at Shuttered Store, Residents Say"; Stevenson, *The Contested Murder of Latasha Harlins*, 311. Ron-Gong Lin II, "Request Stirs Memories of Time of Rage," *Los Angeles Times*, January 28, 2005, http://articles.latimes.com/2005/jan/28/local/me-liquor28. I have reviewed photographs of both Empire Liquor and Numero Uno. It does not appear that the original store was demolished completely, though this is how its renovation was described. It appears that it may have been remodeled and expanded to become a larger building for the grocery store. It is unclear, but because the Webb Motel shared a wall with Empire Liquor, the residence may have been purchased as well and part of the expansion for the grocery store. If this is true, were residents displaced? How does this factor into the history of Du's murder of Harlins and the 1992 Los Angeles Riots?

28. Morrison, *Beloved*, 35-36.

29. Christina Sharpe, *In the Wake* (Duke University Press, 2017), 105.

30. Sharpe, *In the Wake*, 9. Sharpe's expansive understanding of the wake includes the experience of keeping watch over and remembering the dead and the arrival at political consciousness.

31. Saidiya Hartman has developed similar ideas on trauma and Blackness and the legacies of colonialism and slavery, which also influenced Sharpe. See Saidiya Hartman, "Venus in Two Acts," *Small Axe* 26, 12.2 (June 2008): 1–14.

32. Juan Capistrán, interview with the author, Los Angeles, CA, March 8, 2015.

33. The whole passage from the letter reads: "Rather than running the risk of injustice we preferred disorder. But at the same time, that very detour constitutes our strength today, and as a result we are within sight of victory." Albert Camus, "Letters to a German Friend: Second Letter," in *Resistance, Rebellion, and Death* (Alfred A. Knopf, [1960] 1988), 12. A similar passage in the letter reads: "But, as I have already

told you, if at times we seemed to prefer justice to our country, this is because we simply wanted to love our country in justice, as we wanted to love her in truth and in hope" (13).

34. "You no longer distinguish anything; you are nothing but a single impulse. And now you are fighting with the resources of blind anger, with your mind on weapons and feats of arms rather than on ideas, stubbornly confusing every issue and following your obsession. We, on the other hand, started from the intelligence and its hesitations. We were powerless against wrath. But now our detour is finished. It took only a dead child for us to add wrath to intelligence, and now we are two against one." Camus, "Second Letter," 18.

35. Camus, "Second Letter," 15.

36. Camus, "Second Letter," 18.

37. Juan Capistrán, conversation with the author, Los Angeles, CA, February 21, 2012.

38. Martin Luther King, "The Other America," lecture, Stanford University, Stanford, CA. April 14, 1967, 17:24 min.

39. King, "The Other America," 24:37 min.

40. The Los Angeles News Service distributed local news footage and coverage to various stations. Also, Tur and Gerrard had spoken to residents in South Central Los Angeles before the verdict and claim to have been tipped off that violence would ensue if the LAPD officers were acquitted of charges for the beating of King. When Gerrard heard the verdict, she and Tur immediately set out to South Central to capture how the unrest would develop. See Bob Tur, "The L.A. Riots: 15 Years After Rodney King: Interviews: Bob Tur," *Time*, April 2007, http://content.time.com/time/specials/2007/la_riot/article/0,28804,1614117_1615206_1614874,00.html; Sasha Bronner, "Bob Tur and Marika Gerrard: LA Riots Reporters on Capturing the Reginald Denny Beating, Saving Lives & the Horror of 1992," *Huffington Post*, April 30, 2012, https://www.huffingtonpost.com/2012/04/30/bob-tur-marika-gerrard-la-riots_n_1459625.html. Tur has discussed the costly years of litigation he went through to protect the copyright of the Los Angeles News Service coverage of the riots, particularly the beating of Reginald Denny, which was used without permission across the nation and in other countries. Tur, "The L.A. Riots"; see also Bronner, "Bob Tur and Marika Gerrard."

41. During his narration, Tur cites the gunshots they received. In one interview, he claims that their helicopter incurred $137,000 in damage; in another, he claims the damage totaled $154,000. Tur, "The L.A. Riots"; see also Bronner, "Bob Tur and Marika Gerrard."

42. Tur, "The L.A. Riots"; Bronner, "Bob Tur and Marika Gerrard."

43. Sánchez, "Face the Nation," 1009.

44. Sánchez, "Face the Nation," 1010.

45. Sánchez, "Reading Reginald Denny," 388. Victims were immigrants from Mexico, Korea, Vietnam, and Guatemala and citizens who were Japanese American, Mexican American, and Latino. See Whitman, "The Untold Story of the L.A. Riots." Also cited in Sánchez, "Face the Nation," 1010. In both publications, one can also find the names of many of the victims and the injuries they received from the assaults.

46. Sánchez, "Reading Reginald Denny," 388.

47. Sánchez, "Face the Nation," 393.

48. Anna Deveare Smith, *Twilight: Los Angeles, 1992* (Anchor Books, Doubleday, 1994), xxi; also quoted in Sánchez, "Face the Nation," 1009.

49. Capistrán has one other similar painting dedicated to Rodney King, which incorporates the date of his beating.

50. Only a handful of reports address Lopez's attack. Los Angeles's Channel 2 News featured an exclusive televised interview with Lopez shortly after the incident, on April 29, 1992, which featured him at home recovering from his injuries. The interview was brief and required a family member to translate for Lopez who spoke Spanish and was visibly experiencing physical pain from his injuries. See Box 11, Los Angeles Webster Commission Records, Collection no. 0244, Regional History Collections, Special Collections, USC Libraries, University of Southern California. A few *Los Angeles Times* articles from 1992 and 1993 focus on Lopez's attack or Newton's rescue. For the twentieth anniversary of the riots, the *Los Angeles Times* featured a more thorough article about the attack that included a follow-up interview with Lopez and his wife on how it affected their lives. See Steve Lopez, "The Forgotten Victim from Florence and Normandie," *Los Angeles Times*, May 6, 2012, http://articles.latimes.com/2012/may/06/local/la-me-0506-lopez-riot-20120506.

51. Aside from a few news articles, there is no in-depth, scholarly investigation of Lopez's beating.

52. Juan Capistrán, phone interview with the author, October 20, 2021.

53. Juan Capistrán, interview with the author, Los Angeles, CA, March 8, 2015; Juan Capistrán, phone interview with the author, October 20, 2021.

54. For instance, even the mixed-race Latino background of one of the policemen who beat King has been largely disregarded or entirely unrecognized in major narratives. To this day, it is still most common to find the LAPD officers homogeneously racialized as white in histories of the riots.

55. The exhibition was held on April 18–22, 2012.

56. To be clear, this loss is only explained by the descriptor "Latino" and "Chicano." It is unclear how statisticians who came up with these numbers define "Latino." However, from my analysis, it seems that this term is often used to simultaneously describe US-born Latinos, those who have been naturalized, and those who are Latin American immigrants—both legal and undocumented residents. Statistic cited in Sánchez, "Face the Nation," 1018.

57. Latinos were arrested for curfew violations, undocumented status, and looting businesses, among other things. ACLU Foundation of Southern California, "Civil Liberties in Crisis: Los Angeles During the Emergency, Executive Summary," June 23, 1992; Box 151, Folder 3, Papers of Edmund D. Edelman, 1953–94, Huntington Library, Manuscripts Department.

58. Box 9, Folder 18, Los Angeles Webster Commission Records, Collection no. 0244, Regional History Collections, Special Collections, USC Libraries, University of Southern California. Sánchez claims that the INS deported far more Latinos, 2,000, who he claims were mostly arrested for city curfew violations. He does not provide a citation or footnote for these statistics. See Sánchez, "Face the Nation," 1018.

59. Specifically, this was Gates's response to a question asked by the Webster Commission about the 51 percent arrest rate of Hispanics. "Interview of Police Chief Daryl Gates by Richard J. Stone, General Counsel and Staff Director, Terry W. Bird, Deputy General Counsel, and Elizabeth D. Lear, Deputy General Counsel for Webster Commission (June 25, 1992; Summary published on July 1, 1992)," Series 16: Interviews 1992, Box 19, Los Angeles Webster Commission records, Collection no.

0244, Regional History Collections, Special Collections, USC Libraries, University of Southern California.

60. The RAND Corporation, a nonprofit research organization, reported the statistic in a news release on arrest and crime patterns during the 1992 Los Angeles Riots. See Box 2, Folder 11, Los Angeles Webster Commission Records, Collection no. 0244, Regional History Collections, Special Collections, USC Libraries, University of Southern California.

61. Capistrán and Mandujano have collaborated on other art projects as well and together ran the bookstore and exhibition space Mandujano/Cell in Inglewood, CA.

62. The print and booklet were made for the Mexican exhibition and its audience.

63. Steve Lopez, "The Forgotten Victim from Florence and Normandie," *Los Angeles Times*, May 6, 2012, http://articles.latimes.com/2012/may/06/local/la-me-0506-lopez-riot-20120506.

64. Lopez, "The Forgotten Victim from Florence and Normandie."

65. Clips of the amateur videotape of the Lopez beating can now be found on YouTube.

66. Sánchez, "Reading Reginald Denny," 392; Sánchez, "Face the Nation," 1024.

67. Sánchez, "Face the Nation," 1022.

68. Sánchez notes that each of these jobs were estimated to take another three associated jobs with them. "Face the Nation," 1022.

69. Sánchez states, "The average earnings of employed black men fell 24 percent from 1973 to 1989, and unemployment swelled to record levels in the inner city." "Face the Nation," 1022.

70. Sánchez, "Face the Nation," 1018.

71. Sánchez, "Face the Nation," 1011.

72. Sánchez, "Face the Nation," 1010.

73. Sánchez, "Face the Nation," 1011. In other instances, as heard on amateur video recordings taken at the intersection, Blacks are heard saying, "Let the Mexicans go," but "show the Koreans who rules." See Whitman, "The Untold Story of the L.A. Riots." Also cited in Sánchez, "Face the Nation," 1011.

74. Sánchez explains, "Although the violence began as a response to the verdict passed by an almost all-white jury against an almost all-white set of police officers, quickly other people of color—those deemed foreign or foreign looking—were engaged in the deadly exchange. The meaning of racial and national identities were consistently at issue at the corner of Florence and Normandie, with serious and sometimes bloody outcomes for all participants." "Face the Nation," 1011.

75. Sánchez states, "As the participants in the violence at Florence and Normandie indicate, interracial understanding and an inclusive sense of 'community' is not simply formed by living in close proximity to those from other racial/ethnic groups. Rather, what is disturbing about the Los Angeles riots is the insistence that 'community' reflects a single racial group." "Face the Nation," 1025.

76. Gerald Horne, *Fire This Time: The Watts Uprising and the 1960s* (Da Capo Press, 1997), 31.

77. See "Historical Census Racial/Ethnic Numbers in Los Angeles County 1850–1980," *Los Angeles Almanac*, https://www.laalmanac.com/population/po20.php.

78. Toni Morrison, "On the Backs of Blacks," *Time* 142 (Fall 1993): 57; Sánchez, "Reading Reginald Denny," 393.

79. Sánchez, "Face the Nation," 1015. An almost identical quote is found in Sánchez, "Reading Reginald Denny," 393.

80. Sánchez further warns after his discussion of Morrison's essay that those immigrants who are racially identifiable and fit established racial categories may very likely endure continued discrimination in the United States. He states, "With the increase of immigration from Asia and Latin American, a new American racism has emerged which has no political boundaries or ethnic categorizations. From the left and right of the political spectrum, and from both white and black individuals, this new racism [nativism] continually threatens to explode in contemporary American society." Sánchez, "Face the Nation," 1013.

81. Whitman, "The Untold Story of the L.A. Riots." Lopez incurred 29 stitches on his forehead, 12 stitches on his chin, and 17 stitches to his ear. Other accounts note that Lopez had a car stereo thrown at his head and motor oil poured down his throat and that he was spray-painted blue, not black.

82. Reverend Newton's act to save Lopez recalls the phrase "Love your neighbor as yourself," found in Leviticus and the New Testament, described as part of the "greatest commandment" in the latter. The reverend's actions could be analyzed as enacting this belief.

83. Sánchez, "Face the Nation," 1011; *Los Angeles Times*, May 8, 1992, B1–4; Whitman, "The Untold Story of the L.A. Riots."

84. Capistrán also references Camus in the title of his three-panel painting, *Rather than running the risk of injustice we preferred disorder . . .* (2012), and has referenced Camus's writing in other series of work, such as *What We Want, What We Believe, Towards a Higher Fidelity* (2014).

85. Capistrán calls his strategy of appropriation "bootlegging." For more about his method, see Salseda, "The New Wave of Identity Politics."

86. Caitlin Dover, "How On Kawara Made His Date Paintings," *Guggenheim: Checklist*, March 9, 2015, https://www.guggenheim.org/blogs/checklist/how-on-kawara-made-his-date-paintings.

87. Artist Byron Kim practices a form of process art for the series *Sunday Paintings*, which evokes Kawara's practice for the *Today* series.

88. Warhol's exhibition was held at the Sonnabend Gallery in Paris, France. Originally, Warhol referred to the artworks as his *Death in America* series. As an aside: The use of found magazine photographs can be tied to Seth Kaufman's *That Was Then, This Is Then* (1992).

89. For another visual analysis of Capistrán's work that discusses a similar effort to reconceptualize Minimalism via the appropriation of Frank Stella's *Zambezi*, see Salseda, "The New Wave of Identity Politics."

90. Andy Warhol, "Interview with Gene Swenson" (November 1963), in *Art in Theory 1900–1990* (Wiley-Blackwell, 1992), 732. When discussing Moore's photographs in an interview, he responds that the images merely "caught my eye." Andy Warhol, quoted in David Bourdon, *Andy Warhol* (Harry N. Abrams, 1989), 154.

91. This idea draws from Kang Seung Lee's understanding of the images he uses for his erasure series on the 1992 Los Angeles Riots. He explains, "I am also interested in taking out these bodies from photojournalistic popular images that continue to create racialized figures and perpetuate the stereotypes through graphic depictions of violence as the images circulate repeatedly though the media." See Kang Seung Lee,

"Conversation with Yoshua Okón," interview by Yoshua Okón, n.d., http://kanglee.net/section/457383-untitled-la-revoluci-n-es-la-soluci-n.html.

92. Kang Seung Lee, conversation with the author, September 18, 2017. Elsewhere, Lee states, "Ironically in my exhibition we still see 'race' in spite that all the human figures have been blurred and drawn only in graphite because our perception of race is so deeply registered with certain representations." See Lee, "Conversation with Yoshua Okón."

93. I have often been asked to address the possibility that artistic intentions may go unrecognized by viewers. I increasingly wonder if this is a problem other art historians face or if it is just a question asked of those who focus on artworks made by people of color.

94. See Salseda, "The New Wave of Identity Politics."

95. José Esteban Muñoz, *The Sense of Brown* (Duke University Press, 2020), 2–3, 138.

96. Juan Capistrán, email correspondence with the author, February 4, 2015.

97. A total of 63 people were killed during the 1992 Los Angeles Riots. Gallery 169 in Santa Monica, CA, featured a solo exhibition of the artist's series called *Unsolved: 1992 LA Uprising @ 25 Years*, which was held from April 29 to May 4, 2017. The short showing intentionally represented the 6-day duration of the 1992 unrest, from the first day of rioting to the day the mayor lifted the citywide curfew. Staff, "Deaths During the L.A. Riots," April 25, 2012, http://spreadsheets.latimes.com/la-riots-deaths/.

98. Carolina A. Miranda, "Of the 63 People Killed During the '92 Riots, 23 Deaths Remain Unsolved—Artist Jeff Beall Is Mapping Where They Fell," *Los Angeles Times*, April 28, 2017, http://www.latimes.com/entertainment/arts/miranda/la-et-cam-la-riots-jeff-beall-los-angeles-uprising-20170427-htmlstory.html.

99. Miranda, "Of the 63 People Killed During the '92 Riots."

100. Miranda, "Of the 63 People Killed During the '92 Riots."

101. Staff, "Deaths During the L.A. Riots." See also Miranda, "Of the 63 People Killed During the '92 Riots."

102. The former exhibition is the second iteration of a two-part exhibition at Commonwealth and Council from March 17 to April 29, 2017 (the first was titled *Absence Without Leave*). The latter series was curated by Yoshua Okón for Artpace in San Antonio, TX, from July 13 to September 2, 2017.

103. The artist's series included drawings as well as large-scale wall installations of the digitally manipulated images, tapestries, and text rendered as neon lights. He has noted in interviews that his intention is to reference commercial means of display, such as billboards and advertisements, and to embed them with political statements. Kang Seung Lee, "Conversation with Yoshua Okón."

104. Lee, "Conversation with Yoshua Okón."

105. Juan Capistrán, phone interview with the author, October 20, 2021.

106. See Anna C. Chave, "Minimalism and the Rhetoric of Power," *Arts Magazine* 64.5 (January 1990): 44–63. For discussion of Minimalism and Capistrán's reimagination of its politics, see Salseda, "The New Wave of Identity Politics."

107. Juan Capistrán, interview with the author, Los Angeles, CA, August 7, 2012.

108. Capistrán, interview with the author, Los Angeles, CA, August 7, 2012. Also cited in Salseda, "The New Wave of Identity Politics," 27.

109. Salseda, "The New Wave of Identity Politics," 27. For a deeper understanding

of how such seeming contradiction is a product of post-identity politics, see 24–31. I realize that this aspect of Capistrán's artistic practice is similar to that of Adrian Piper.

110. Pan Andreas West Theatre was formerly known as the Balboa Theatre. For more information about the history of this building and its uses, see Bill Counter's blog post "Los Angeles Theatres: Balboa," https://losangelestheatres.blogspot.com/2020/07/balboa-theatre.html.

111. The NOI is a Black Muslim separatist group founded in the 1930s. Perhaps of note is that Capistrán's first art teacher was a member of the NOI. The art teacher significantly influenced his political consciousness as a young person of color and an immigrant. However, the artist does not follow and does not agree with NOI's philosophy of racial separatism and history of antisemitism.

112. Capistrán, interview with the author, Los Angeles, CA, November 12, 2015.

113. As previously noted, the unrest caused $1 billion in damages and thousands of buildings were looted and burned. See Ong and Hee, *Losses in Los Angeles Unrest*.

114. Baca was also supported by Social and Public Art Resource Center (SPARC), a community art and cultural center cofounded by Baca, Donna Deitch, and Christina Schlesinger; and Adobe LA, an arts collective of architects and designers that included Ulises Diaz, Gustavo Leclerc, Laura Alvarez and Barbara Jones. From my research, it appears that the project officially began in 1993 under the coordination of Franklin U. D. Westbrook, a designer for SPARC, and with $50,000 in funding from the Hitachi Foundation and the National Endowment for the Arts. It is unclear what if any objects were created that year. The original artists commissioned to make monuments for the African American, Korean America, and Latino communities were, respectively, Pat Ward, Yong Soon Min, and David Avalos. See Lee Harris, "South Central: Artwork to Promote Ethnic Harmony," *Los Angeles Times*, July 18, 1993, http://articles.latimes.com/1993-07-18/news/ci-14471_1_ethnic-group.

115. The Koreatown monument was designed by artist David Chung; the Pico-Union structure was supposed to be a collaboration between Baca and artist Juan Edgar Aparicio, and the Leimert Park monument was to be made under the direction of artist Pat Ward Williams. See Maki Becker, "Monuments Aim to Mend Riot-Torn Areas," *Los Angeles Times*, May 11, 1996, http://articles.latimes.com/1996-05-11/local/me-2828_1_african-american-monument.

116. I have verbally confirmed with Baca that the project was never completed. A related exhibition of architectural models, photographs, and text of the project took place at SPARC in December 1994.

117. In 2016, Baca began developing a mural project to commemorate the 1965 Watts Rebellion. It is unclear if the project was completed. See https://sparcinla.org/projects/watts-riots-rebellion-50th-anniversary-commemorative-mural-project/.

118. Ybarra was a fellow classmate at Otis, and both graduated with BFAs in 1999. Both artists would go on to attend the MFA program at the University of California, Irvine. Ybarra graduated in 2001, and Capistrán graduated in 2002.

119. Rita Gonzalez, "Phantom Sites: The Official, the Unofficial, and the Orificial," in *Phantom Sightings: Art After the Chicano Movement* (Los Angeles County Museum of Art, 2007), 50. Gonzalez notes another project they did around the empty lots, titled *Poor Paintings*.

120. Juan Capistrán, conversation with the author, Los Angeles, CA, November 12, 2015.

121. It is significant to note that Long Beach has a large, racially diverse population of working-class and poor residents.

122. Section 187 of the California Penal Code includes the definition for murder. "April 29, 1992 (Miami)" was released on the self-titled album *Sublime* (1996). An alternate version, "April 29, 1992 (Leary)," was released a year later on the album *Second-Hand Smoke* (1997).

123. The inclusion of this piece of information calls for further analysis of class during the 1992 Los Angeles Riots and in Capistrán's artworks.

124. See Ong and Hee, *Losses in Los Angeles Unrest.*

125. The rave was at a lot near the intersection at 87th Place. Rose G. Salseda, "Black and Blue and Brown," KCET *ArtBound*, January 25, 2017, https://www.pbssocal.org/shows/artbound/black-and-blue-and-brown-artists-depict-police-brutality.

126. Salseda, "Black and Blue and Brown."

127. Makeda Easter, "How Guerrilla Art on the Streets of South L.A. Confronts Scars from the 1992 Riots," June 18, 2019, https://www.latimes.com/entertainment/arts/la-et-cm-juan-capistran-cola-awards-20190518-story.html.

128. Easter, "How Guerrilla Art on the Streets of South L.A. Confronts Scars from the 1992 Riots."

129. Easter, "How Guerrilla Art on the Streets of South L.A. Confronts Scars from the 1992 Riots."

130. Capistrán noted that the audio mostly comes from the looting of a major supermarket in Los Angeles. Juan Capistrán, phone interview with the author, October 13, 2022.

131. In addition to the shared title, each of the works included in the series is titled with the unique location where it was installed and documented (e.g., "Vermont Ave.," "Broadway"). I shared the book with Capistrán through a bibliography I had made when I began preliminary research on the history of the 1992 Los Angeles Riots. This was after conducting my first studio visit with Capistrán where I saw his date paintings.

132. Originally published in the *LA Weekly*, May 8–14, 1992, issue, George went on to republish her essay in other journals as well as in her collected book of essays, *No Crystal Stair: African-Americans in the City of Angels* (Verso, 1992).

133. Juan Capistrán, phone interview with the author, October 13, 2022.

134. Sánchez argues that diverse experiences and the emphasis on white on Black racial violence was due to the ways complex narratives disrupt understandings of community, immigration, and race. See Sánchez, "Face the Nation," 1018. Sánchez further explains, "The history of white on black racism blinds Americans from recognizing any forms of interracial tensions. Racism against Asians and Latin Americans is dismissed as either 'natural byproducts' of immigrant assimilation or as extensions of the white-black dichotomy. Moreover, when African Americans perform acts of racism, they are quickly ignored or recast except as a threat to a white-dominated society" (1025).

Chapter Two

1. Mindy Daluiso, "This is Then: Interview with Seth Kaufman," *Picturebook* 3 (1993): 2; Seth Kaufman, "Statement of Intent," in *LA Rebellion Series, '92* (unpublished artist's statement, 1993), n.p.; Seth Kaufman, "The Antiphony of Anarchy: Three Views After Curfew" (press release, 1993). To be clear, these sources confirm

where Kaufman culled items and does not compare his work to that of Purifoy or other artists. Also, I gathered the number of objects from an original itemized price list for Kaufman's 1993 exhibition, *Dwelling in Rebellion: A Year to the Day*, at Zero One Gallery. He also wrote and performed a spoken word piece, *Behind My Window Pain*, in the shell of a burned-out property. This performance was filmed live and then screened at this exhibition as well as a solo show at Zero One Gallery.

2. Kaufman titled the two-part billboard series *Absolut Hope*.

3. Various contradicting accounts exist as to how the assaults between officers and residents began and who they involved. Most agree that Minikus ordered Frye's vehicle to be impounded and Frye's brother Ronald, who was a passenger in the vehicle, walked home to inform their mother, Rena Price, of the situation. The arrest quickly escalated to unrest after Price arrived at the scene and assaults occurred among Price, the arresting officer, and other bystanders. Locals of the predominantly Black community began to flock to the streets in protest of the police violence—injustices that they were all too familiar with as Black residents in a time of deep racial discrimination in Los Angeles.

4. Ted Michel, as told by Noah Purifoy, "The Art of Communication as a Creative Act," in *Junk Art: 66 Neon Signs*, n.p.

5. The exhibition involved eight artists and sixty-six works made from the materials Purifoy and Powell sourced. See Ted Michel as told by Noah Purifoy, "The Art of Communication as a Creative Act."

6. Daluiso, "This is Then: Interview with Seth Kaufman," 2.

7. Seth Kaufman, interview by the author, digital recording, Torrance, CA, July 23, 2015.

8. Seth Kaufman, interview by the author, digital recording, Torrance, CA, July 23, 2015.

9. Seth Kaufman, interview by the author, digital recording, Torrance, CA, July 23, 2015.

10. On this date, Mayor Tom Bradley lifted the dusk-to-dawn citywide curfew.

11. Seth Kaufman, "Origin of the LA Rebellion Series," in *LA Rebellion Series, '92*. In this statement, Kaufman writes that May 4, 1992, fell on a Sunday, but the date actually fell on a Monday. Given that police, soldiers, Marines, and National Guardsmen still patrolled the streets of Los Angeles on Sunday, May 3, 1992, and a dusk-to-dawn curfew was still in place for residents, I believe Kaufman most likely made his visit on Monday.

12. Seth Kaufman, interview by the author, digital recording, Torrance, CA, July 23, 2015.

13. Kaufman, "Origin of the LA Rebellion Series." The fires created unstable structures all across the Southland, and the police barricades and fire department warning signs marked such sites as dangerous.

14. Kaufman, "Origin of the LA Rebellion Series"; Daluiso, "This is Then: Interview with Seth Kaufman," 2; Seth Kaufman, interview by the author, digital recording, Torrance, CA, July 23, 2015.

15. Kaufman, "Origin of the LA Rebellion Series."

16. Kaufman, "Origin of the LA Rebellion Series." Kaufman recalled a similar sentiment during our July 23, 2015, interview.

17. Kaufman, "Origin of the LA Rebellion Series." Kaufman further explained, "Nothing came to me, not an image, not a phrase, nothing." Kaufman is quoted as

similarly stating, "I was looking for a visual image to express what I was feeling. Nothing came. Nothing visual." See Eric La Brecque, "LA Aftermath," *Print* (September–October 1993), 18.

18. Daluiso, "This is Then: Interview with Seth Kaufman," 1.

19. Daluiso, "This is Then: Interview with Seth Kaufman," 1, 2; La Brecque, "LA Aftermath," 18.

20. Daluiso, "This is Then: Interview with Seth Kaufman," 1, 2; , 18.

21. Daluiso, "This is Then: Interview with Seth Kaufman," 1, 2; La Brecque, "LA Aftermath," 18; Kaufman, interview by the author, digital recording, Torrance, CA, July 23, 2015, and October 8, 2015.

22. Discovering the thousands of screws, Kaufman states that tears flowed as he thought, "The Muse has struck!" Kaufman, "Origin of the LA Rebellion Series"; Daluiso, "This is Then: Interview with Seth Kaufman," 2; Kaufman, interview by the author, digital recording, Torrance, CA, July 23, 2015, and October 8, 2015.

23. Kaufman, "Origin of the LA Rebellion Series." Kaufman estimates that he was standing on 3,000 wood screws.

24. Kaufman, interview by the author, digital recording, Torrance, CA, July 23, 2015.

25. It is unclear if Kaufman went home and returned the same day for the other materials he had found. In an artist statement, it seems as if he made only one trip the first day he explored the site. However, in his recollection of the time in the July 23, 2015, interview and the 1993 Daluiso interview, he states that he left and returned to the site the same day.

26. Kaufman, interview by the author, digital recording, Torrance, CA, July 23, 2015. La Brecque quotes Kaufman as stating, "I knew my path was laid out for me," after citing the discovery of the wood screws. See La Brecque, "LA Aftermath," 18.

27. Kaufman, interview by the author, digital recording, Torrance, CA, July 23, 2015.

28. La Brecque, "LA Aftermath," 18; Kaufman, interview by the author, digital recording, Torrance, CA, July 23, 2015.

29. Kaufman, interview by the author, digital recording, Torrance, CA, July 23, 2015.

30. Kaufman, interview by the author, digital recording, Torrance, CA, July 23, 2015.

31. Daluiso, "This is Then: Interview with Seth Kaufman," 2; Kaufman, interview by the author, digital recording, Torrance, CA, October 8, 2015.

32. Daluiso, "This is Then: Interview with Seth Kaufman," 2; Kaufman, interview by the author, digital recording, Torrance, CA, July 23, 2015.

33. Daluiso, "This is Then: Interview with Seth Kaufman," 2; Kaufman, interview by the author, digital recording, Torrance, CA, July 23, 2015.

34. Daluiso, "This is Then: Interview with Seth Kaufman," 2; Kaufman, interview by the author, digital recording, Torrance, CA, July 23, 2015.

35. Kaufman, "Origin of the LA Rebellion Series." Kaufman listed the store name as "Rod Martins Custom Furniture Shop," without the possessive "s," in his artist's statement. Also, Kaufman could not remember and has no record of the owner's name or where the business was exactly located. However, through my research of properties that endured fire damage during the unrest, I found out that the business was located at 7970 Beverly Blvd. and owned by Rod and Elsa Martin. It is possible that their

last name was spelled Martín (with an accent). I suspect that the business may have been named "Martin's" instead of "Martins." I found their names listed in Ong and Hee's *Losses in Los Angeles Civil Unrest*, 22. The name of the listed owner, Rod Martin, matches the name of the business, "Rod Martins Custom Furniture Shop," that Kaufman cited in his artist statement and recalls in interviews. Kaufman recalled that the business was located down the street from another business named Samy's Camera. The address listed in Ong's and Hee's registry is a four-minute drive from Samy's Camera and is located on the same boulevard. Last, Ong and Hee list the business owned by Rod and Elsa Martin as 100 percent damaged, which matches Kaufman's recollection of the site.

36. Kaufman, interview by the author, digital recording, Torrance, CA, October 8, 2015. La Brecque writes that Kaufman did not find the photo album until after he returned home to search through the materials he had salvaged the previous day. This differs from the information Kaufman recalled during our interview.

37. Kaufman, interview by the author, digital recording, Torrance, CA, July 23, 2015.

38. Daluiso, "This is Then: Interview with Seth Kaufman," 2.

39. Seth Kaufman, interview by the author, digital recording, Torrance, CA, October 8, 2015.

40. La Brecque, "LA Aftermath," 18; Kaufman, interview by the author, digital recording, Torrance, CA, October 8, 2015. There are no names mentioned in the La Brecque article or the Daluiso interview. However, as I previously noted, I found the name of the owner and wife based on my research of the burned properties (see n. 35 in this chapter).

41. La Brecque, "LA Aftermath," 18; Daluiso, "This is Then: Interview with Seth Kaufman," 2; Kaufman, interview by the author, digital recording, Torrance, CA, July 23, 2015, and October 8, 2015. In the Daluiso interview, Kaufman states that the owner was a "political dissident" during the Castro regime and left Cuba as a political refugee.

42. According to Ong and Hee, *Losses in Los Angeles Civil Unrest*, 22, the Martin's property is listed as 100 percent damaged and was estimated at a value of $400,000.

43. La Brecque, "LA Aftermath," 18.

44. Kaufman, interview by the author, Torrance, CA, October 8, 2015.

45. Seth Kaufman, conversation with the author, Torrance, CA, January 2, 2019.

46. Kaufman, conversation with the author, Torrance, CA, January 2, 2019. Kaufman did not discuss his Jewishness or Jewish history until I asked him about possible critiques of the notion of white privilege and exploitation.

47. Kaufman, interview by the author, Torrance, CA, October 8, 2015.

48. Kaufman, interview by the author, Torrance, CA, October 8, 2015. Samy's Camera was located at 7122 *Beverly Blvd*. Kaufman claims that Kamienowicz gave him temporary access to gather the unusable camera and film supplies. Indeed, much of Kaufman's assemblages contain camera parts and film canisters. To note, Hedy Kamienowicz is listed as the co-owner of Samy's Camera, and the business is listed as experiencing $960,000 in damage, or a 95 percent loss, in Ong and Hee, *Losses in Los Angeles Civil Unrest*, 21.

49. La Brecque, 18.

50. La Brecque, "LA Aftermath," 18. Seth Kaufman, "Modern Art Blitz, Episode #33, Part 2," Interview by Mat Gleason/Coagula Curatorial, May 1, 2017, https://youtu.be/nqXsbYwxCFg.

51. Kaufman, "Statement of Intent."

52. Kaufman, "Statement of Intent."

53. Kaufman, conversation with the author, Torrance, CA, January 2, 2019.

54. Vicky Osterweil, *In Defense of Looting: A Riotous History of Uncivil Action* (Bold Type Books, 2020), 3, 4. While I agree with some of Osterweil's compelling points about looting, she wrote several errors about the history of the 1992 Los Angeles Riots. For instance, she asserts that the four men who beat Denny were teenagers, when two were eighteen and nineteen and the others twenty-seven and thirty-three. She also states that those who rescued Denny were "rioters," when they were not (9, 229). She also states that the National Guard shot at residents and that they and police had "been violently battling a group of Black teenage boys" on the first day near the intersection where Denny was beaten, when guardsmen had not yet been deployed (9, 229).

55. Guy Debord, "The Decline and Fall of the Spectacle-Commodity Economy," *Internationale Situationniste* #10 (March 1966), tanslated by Ken Knabb. Accessed on *Situationist International Online*, August 30, 2024, https://www.sionline.researche-editions.cddc.vt.edu/si/decline.html.

56. Debord, "The Decline and Fall of the Spectacle-Commodity Economy."

57. Debord, "The Decline and Fall of the Spectacle-Commodity Economy."

58. It could be argued that the artist as "post-riot looter," in this sense, makes him akin to a sort of gleaner—someone outside the system of capitalism where the notion of private property and profit reigns, searching for the leftovers of a "harvest" (the "harvest" being the initial looting that took place during unrest and before policing, laws, and social norms were fully reconstituted). For a burgeoning assessment of the concept of gleaning after unrest, see Simon Valencia Bonilla's "Sandow Birk's Historical Painting: Transforming Nineteenth Century France into 1992 Los Angeles Riots" (unpublished), a short paper written for my winter 2025 seminar "Riot: 20th and 21st Century Episodes of Civil Unrest" at Stanford University. In it, Valencia Bonilla discusses the history of gleaning as a communal right in France and its upending by the development of private property and capitalism to provide a new reading of Birk's 1992 appropriation of Jean-François Millet's *The Gleaners* (1857). In Birk's rendition, *The Gleaners* are reimagined as people of color picking through the remains of a burned Los Angeles cityscape.

59. Daluiso, "This is Then: Interview with Seth Kaufman," 3. In this interview, he also described those who protested and looted as "the martyrs of our society, the victims of great pressure."

60. Osterweil, *In Defense of Looting*, 11. Debord states, "And all those who went so far as to recognize the 'apparent justifications' of the rage of the Los Angeles blacks (but never their real ones), all the ideologists and 'spokesmen' of the vacuous international Left, deplored the irresponsibility, the disorder, the looting (especially the fact that arms and alcohol were the first targets) and the 2000 fires with which the blacks lit up their battle and their ball. But who has defended the Los Angeles rioters in the terms they deserve? We will." "The Decline and Fall of the Spectacle-Commodity Economy."

61. Kaufman, conversation with the author, Torrance, CA,. January 2, 2019.

62. Kaufman, conversation with the author, Torrance, CA, January 2, 2019.

63. Kaufman, conversation with the author, Torrance, CA, January 2, 2019.

64. For some readers, this discussion may conjure the long history of looting in the art world and the many spoils that have decorated the walls of museums and pri-

vate collections across the world—including the ways in which these spoils have been reimagined as the property of the looter.

65. Kaufman's next series was commercially unsuccessful. Yet he continued to make art and took an interest in teaching, eventually becoming an adjunct art professor.

66. As an art historian trained in African American art and the history of unrest in Los Angeles, I was familiar with *66 Signs of Neon* and asked Kaufman if he knew the work of Purifoy or others when he was making his assemblages in 1992 and 1993. He responded that he was not. Seth Kaufman, interview by the author, digital recording, Torrance, CA, July 23, 2015. *Noah Purifoy: Junk Dada* was held at LACMA from June 7, 2015, to January 3, 2016, and was organized by Franklin Sirmans and Yael Lipschutz. For images and essays, see *Noah Purifoy: Junk Dada* (Los Angeles County Museum of Art and DelMonico Books/Prestel Publishing, 2015).

67. Purifoy, disillusioned with art-making, the art world, and the role of art in social change took a government appointed position at the California Arts Council where he built art education and artist residency programs. Lizzetta LeFalle-Collins, "Noah Purifoy: Outside and in the Open," in *Noah Purifoy: Outside and in the Open* (California Afro-American Museum Foundation, 1997), 23–24; Richard Cándida Smith, "Junk into Art: Noah Purifoy's Assemblage of Experience," in *Noah Purifoy: Outside and in the Open*, 77–78. Jones, *South of Pico*, 90.

68. Yael Lipschutz, "*66 Signs of Neon* and the Transformative Art of Noah Purifoy," in *L.A. Object & David Hammons Body Prints* (Tilton Gallery, 2011), 218.

69. Lipschutz, "*66 Signs of Neon* and the Transformative Art of Noah Purifoy," 218.

70. Lipschutz, "*66 Signs of Neon* and the Transformative Art of Noah Purifoy," 230.

71. Lipschutz, "*66 Signs of Neon* and the Transformative Art of Noah Purifoy," 221, 224. The use of italics in the quoted "work of *mourning*" is not original to Freud, and Lipschutz does not clarify if the emphasis is hers.

72. Lipschutz, "*66 Signs of Neon* and the Transformative Art of Noah Purifoy," 224.

73. Lipschutz, "*66 Signs of Neon* and the Transformative Art of Noah Purifoy," 225, 230. The quotes used by Lipschutz seem to have been edited to combine different parts of an interview to make a point. Upon examining the original interview, I found that Purifoy's statement arose when discussing graduate school and stating that he was embarrassed to get a PhD. He explained, "Well, I always associated Ph.D.'s with the elite, and I wanted to avoid these associations with the elite. . . . Because it was a white thing. I had experienced enough prejudice to not have an affinity for anything related to white society, and education of that ilk was related to white society." Then he went on to discuss his "self-imposed poverty in his art years" as an effort to relate to poor Black people and understand that condition to "report it as it was . . . To the world. To anyone who would listen . . . it was through art that I chose to express myself." So, while Lipschutz misquotes Purifoy, the rejection of elitism for the artist is indeed tied to class and art, in addition to an understanding of how higher education was framed by race and privileges that alienated him. See Noah Purifoy, *African-American Artists of Los Angeles: Noah Purifoy*, interviewed by Karen Anne Mason, Oral History Program, University of California, Los Angeles (Regents of the University of California, 1992), 15–16, 16–17. Available online at https://archive.org/details/africanamericana00puri/page/n7/mode/2up.

74. Daniel Widener, *Black Arts West: Culture and Struggle in Postwar Los Angeles* (Duke University Press, 2010), 10.

75. Cándida Smith, "Junk into Art," 77.

76. LeFalle-Collins, "Noah Purifoy: Outside and in the Open," 8–9.

77. See Purifoy, *African-American Artists of Los Angeles: Noah Purifoy*, 15–16, 16–17, https://archive.org/details/africanamericana00puri/page/n7/mode/2up. Also, Cándida Smith suggested that while Purifoy grew up working class and poor, "on its own terms" he did not experience it as a lack. "To experience this web of relationships as 'poor,' he had to reach a point where he could step outside it through education and advancement." Cándida Smith, "Junk into Art," 67.

78. Cándida Smith, "Junk into Art," 64.

79. Jones, *South of Pico*, 79.

80. Jones, *South of Pico*, 71–72.

81. Jones, *South of Pico*, 72.

82. Jones, *South of Pico*, 78.

83. LeFalle-Collins, "Noah Purifoy: Outside and in the Open," 17. LeFalle-Collins cites the following as her source: "Out of Ruins," *National Observer*, Monday, April 1966. Simon Rodia made the towers over a 34-year period between the 1920s and 1950s. For an overview of the history of the towers and the Watts Towers Arts Center, see Cécile Whiting, "The Watts Towers as Urban Landmark," in *Pop L.A.: Art and the City in the 1960s* (University of California Press, 2006), 139–65.

84. For brief mentions of the "junk hunts," see Jones, *South of Pico*, 78; Cándida Smith, "Junk into Art," 71.

85. Some of the pieces were also included in a German exhibition in 1972. Allison Glenn, "Chronology," in *Noah Purifoy: Junk Dada*, 80.

86. In a way, one might argue that this aligns Kaufman's practice closer to that of the museum and its history of looting, which created commodities out of others' objects, disregarding the intended meaning and original use of the object, for instance. However, this is not a like-for-like comparison. Looting in the realm of museum history is much deeper and exploitative, with direct links to histories of colonization, nation building, and wealth accumulation.

87. Ted Michel as told by Noah Purifoy, "The Art of Communication as a Creative Act."

88. Daluiso, "This is Then: Interview with Seth Kaufman," 4.

89. Suzanne Muchnic, "ART/LA92: Vote of Confidence: Art," *Los Angeles Times*, July 29, 1992, http://articles.latimes.com/1992-07-29/entertainment/ca-4625_1_art-fair. It is unclear if any of the listed programming actually occurred. The art fair has long been defunct. One future avenue of research might be through the Cultural Affairs Department, which is now known as the Los Angeles Department of Cultural Affairs.

90. The catalog for ART/LA92 included a full-page depiction of Sandow Birk's *George Bush Visiting the Riots in Los Angeles* (1992) and John Nava's *2nd of May, 1992 at Los Angeles* (1992), which referenced the unrest directly. However, from my research, it does not seem that these works were on display at the art fair. As a side note, these paintings were both inspired by Neoclassical art. They also both depict authority figures and people of color in an urban setting.

91. Daluiso, "This is Then: Interview with Seth Kaufman," 4.

92. Muchnic, "ART/LA92: Vote of Confidence: Art."

93. Seth Kaufman, interview by the author, unrecorded conversation, Torrance, CA, October 8, 2015; Seth Kaufman, "Modern Art Blitz, Episode #33, Part 2," Interview by Mat Gleason/Coagula Curatorial, May 1, 2017, https://youtu.be/nqXsbYwxCFg.

94. Muchnic, "ART/LA92: Vote of Confidence: Art"; Suzanne Muchnic, "News Analaysis: ART/LA92: Upbeat in a Down Year," *Los Angeles Times*, December 8, 1992, http://articles.latimes.com/1992-12-08/entertainment/ca-1935_1_art-fair. In this latter article, Muchnic states that exhibitors fell from a peak of 170 participants in 1987 to 100 in 1992. She also claims that no "big-name" New York dealers were present and "only a couple of heavy hitters from Europe."

95. Muchnic, "News Analaysis: ART/LA92."

96. Mat Gleason was also able to secure a free space at the fair for *Coagula*, an art magazine that had been in operation for less than a year at the time. Kaufman, "Modern Art Blitz, Episode #33, Part 2."

97. Kaufman, "The Antiphony of Anarchy." I believe Kaufman wrote this press release as the language is similar to his other writing. Found reviews for the art fair are very superficial and do not mention the unrest.

98. In 1992, the Santa Monica Museum of Art and the Los Angeles County Museum of art incurred fire-related damage. It is unclear if the Museum of Contemporary Art or other museums were affected.

99. Deliasofia Zacarias, "Ed Ruscha's Los Angeles County Museum of Art on Fire," *LACMA UnFramed*, October 4, 2024, https://unframed.lacma.org/2024/10/04/ed-ruscha-los-angeles-county-museum-art-fire.

100. To be clear, Ruscha's painting was begun before the Watts Rebellion in 1965 and was unrelated in concept.

101. Seth Kaufman, conversation with the author, Torrance, CA, January 2, 2019.

102. Two of the trucks seem to have a logo on the door, making me think that perhaps they are police vehicles.

103. The organization was called the Mandela Freedom Fund and was "dedicated to training and educating black South Africans." It was based in Washington, DC.

104. Daluiso, "This is Then: Interview with Seth Kaufman," 3.

105. Daluiso, "This is Then: Interview with Seth Kaufman," 3.

106. Seth Kaufman, interview by the author, digital recording, Torrance, CA, October 8, 2015.

107. Kaufman, "The Antiphony of Anarchy."

108. Kaufman, "The Antiphony of Anarchy." Kaufman does not have any close-up images of Norman's work. They are only captured partially in the background of one or two snapshots of *The Antiphony of Anarchy* that I found in Kaufman's personal archive. I have found an obituary for Norman, who died in 2009, but have yet to find contact information for his next of kin. So I have not seen any better images of his work. Furthermore, in the press release for *The Antiphony of Anarchy*, he is quoted as saying that he planned to return to the studio to paint what he had witnessed during and after the unrest. As an aside, in the July 23, 2015, interview I conducted with Kaufman, he claims that Norman had "no acceptance" as a Black man when he was a student at Chouinard and then Cal Arts. This influenced his change in careers to the film industry, according to Kaufman.

109. Kaufman, "The Antiphony of Anarchy."

110. Kaufman, "The Antiphony of Anarchy."

111. Gary Matteson, interview by the author, unrecorded conversation, Los Angeles, CA, June 7, 2016.

112. Matteson, interview by the author, unrecorded conversation, Los Angeles, CA, June 7, 2016.

113. Matteson, interview by the author, unrecorded conversation, Los Angeles, CA, June 7, 2016.

114. Matteson, interview by the author, unrecorded conversation, Los Angeles, CA, June 7, 2016.

115. Matteson, interview by the author, unrecorded conversation, Los Angeles, CA, June 7, 2016.

116. Kaufman, interview by the author, unrecorded conversation, Torrance, CA, July 23, 2015.

117. Matteson, interview by the author, unrecorded conversation, Los Angeles, CA, June 7, 2016.

118. Matteson, interview by the author, unrecorded conversation, Los Angeles, CA, June 7, 2016.

119. Matteson, interview by the author, unrecorded conversation, Los Angeles, CA, June 7, 2016.

120. Matteson, interview by the author, unrecorded conversation, Los Angeles, CA, June 7, 2016.

121. Matteson, interview by the author, unrecorded conversation, Los Angeles, CA, June 7, 2016.

122. Matteson, interview by the author, unrecorded conversation, Los Angeles, CA, June 7, 2016.

123. Seth Kaufman, interview by the author, digital recording, Torrance, CA, July, 23, 2015.

124. The billboard was located at the intersection of Sunset and Crescent Heights Boulevards.

125. La Brecque, "LA Aftermath," 18, 19. The Sunset Strip billboard purportedly garnered an audience of approximately 20,000 motorists each day. Carillon Imports also commissioned artists for Absolut Vodka advertisements that were distributed internationally in magazines and other types of publications.

126. Peter Trine, "Absolut Hope Artists Unveil New Work," *Venice: Los Angeles' Arts and Entertainment Magazine*, v.2 (June 1993), np. For the second billboard in the series, it seems that the artists had been given the option of either incorporating the Absolut Vodka name or the phrase "Absolut Hope," which was the title of the billboard series.

127. The billboard was very large, measuring 60 feet wide by 20 feet high. In total, it comprised 1,200 square feet.

128. Kaufman scoured local galleries to find the nine other artists for the two billboards in the series. The second in the series included artwork by Bernie Casey, Young Joo Choi, Patti Heid, Marc Katano, and Glugio Gronk Nicandro. The second billboard was unveiled on May 26, 1993. See Trine, "Absolut Hope Artists Unveil New Work."

129. Kaufman, interview by the author, digital recording, Torrance, CA, July 23, 2015. Each word of the slogan was stretched across the length of the billboard and each letter set between the "bottles." Kaufman would go on to collaborate on a work with Echo, a matchbook with the phrase "Response-Ability," which Kaufman remembered passing out at the art fair in Los Angeles in 1993. Echo notably worked on a billboard

with Absolut Vodka before Kaufman; it was called *Absolut Sunset* (1991) and included a tribute to and benefit for AIDS victims.

130. Koreans and Korean Americans experienced a devastating loss of property during the unrest. Other racial groups, including Latinos and African Americans, also experienced losses. See Ong and Hee, *Losses in Los Angeles Civil Unrest*.

131. Beasley's billboard contribution was technically three-dimensional; however, her work had very little depth and texture. Gronk's work for the second billboard rivals Kaufman's contribution for its seemingly gruesome content. I discuss it later in this chapter.

132. Kaufman stated in my interview that he salvaged all the materials (with the exception of the letters that comprise "Absolut Vodka") from properties that were burned during the unrest. Kaufman, interview by the author, digital recording, Torrance, CA, July 23, 2015.

133. Kaufman, "Biography."

134. Kaufman, interview by the author, digital recording, Torrance, CA, July 23, 2015.

135. Kaufman, interview by the author, digital recording, Torrance, CA, July 23, 2015; Kaufman, "Absolut Hope"; Kaufman, "The Antiphony of Anarchy"; Kaufman, "Biography"; Kaufman, "Dwelling in Rebellion."

136. The first billboard was unveiled on October 28, 1992. Hyesook Park's name was written "Hye Sook" in the documentation I found.

137. Trine, "Absolut Hope Artists Unveil New Work." This series was unveiled on May 26, 1993.

138. The women artists were Phoebe Beasley, Hyesook Park, Young Joo Choi, and Patti Heid.

139. There is no mention of women artists in any of the press releases or articles on the billboard series; however, including a range of artists based on race and ethnicity was an explicit intention according to the literature.

140. Trine, "Absolut Hope Artists Unveil New Work."

141. La Brecque, "LA Aftermath," 18. La Brecque also compared the billboard to the contemporaneous and racially controversial United Colors of Benetton advertisement campaign. Yet the author suspects that the message of *Absolut Hope* may have been completely lost to passersby. The billboard before the "Absolut Hope" campaign addressed AIDS, and Le Brecque claims that it went largely unnoticed by the public; however, the writer seems to suggest that for those who did pay attention to it, Kaufman's slogan "HAVE HOPE HELP HEAL" may have been confused as a message addressing the AIDS epidemic.

142. Rodney King, Televised public address, May 1, 1992; Rodney King, "Transcript of Rodney King's Statement," Associated Press, May 2, 1992. Note that the transcript was published the day after King's actual address.

143. The hamsa symbol is found in many religious practices, particularly those that originated in the Middle East.

144. In *Venice* magazine, Gronk's piece is simply described as representing the racial or cultural diversity of the city. See Trine, "Absolut Hope Artists Unveil New Work."

145. Gronk, conversation with the author, private message, September 21, 2015.

146. Daluiso, "This is Then: Interview with Seth Kaufman," 4.

147. Kaufman, interview by the author, digital recording, Torrance, CA, July, 23, 2015.

148. Kaufman, interview by the author, digital recording, Torrance, CA, July, 23, 2015. I could not find any published criticism for "Abolut Hope." In fact, I have found very little mention of the billboard campaign in major newspapers. Although Absolut Vodka came out with a book on their "Absolut Art" campaigns, it does not include any mention of "Absolut Hope." Artist Marc Katano emailed me the *Venice* magazine article mentioning the second billboard installation.

149. Catherine Wagley, "Mark Bradford's Art Doesn't Explain South L.A. and It Doesn't Need to," *LA Weekly*, July 1, 2015, http://www.laweekly.com/arts/mark-bradfords-art-doesnt-explain-south-la-and-it-doesnt-need-to-5749499.

150. Kaufman, interview by the author, digital recording, Torrance, CA, July, 23, 2015.

151. La Brecque, "LA Aftermath," 18; emphasis in original.

152. Kaufman, interview by the author, digital recording, Torrance, CA, October 8, 2015. There is also no mention of Kaufman in *Venice* magazine. See Trine, "Absolut Hope Artists Unveil New Work."

153. Seth Kaufman, "Seth Kaufman: Dwelling in Rebellion, A Year to the Day" (Exhibition press release, 1993), 1. The exhibition closed on May 29, 1993. I gathered the number of works presented from an original itemized price list for Kaufman's exhibition. The list clearly designated which artworks were on display and which were kept in inventory. Zero One Gallery, which was also known as the 0–1, closed down sometime in the late 1990s.

154. Apparently, the works sold from $200 to $3,000 each to mostly private collectors. Christopher Reynolds, "What the Riots Sparked," *Los Angeles Times*, April 28, 2002, G1, http://articles.latimes.com/2002/apr/28/entertainment/ca-reynolds28.

155. Kaufman, interview by the author, digital recording, Torrance, CA, October 8, 2015.

156. Kaufman, interview by the author, digital recording, Torrance, CA, October 8, 2015.

157. Reynolds, "What the Riots Sparked."

158. Reynolds, "What the Riots Sparked."

159. In 2015, I spearheaded a digitization project of Kaufman's work in partnership with Jeffrey Ryan of the Visual Resource Center at California State University, Long Beach. Ryan also helped digitize the artwork of Sandow Birk and Man One, who also made work about the 1992 Los Angeles Riots. All three artists received digital copies of their artworks, and the images are available to students and other researchers at the university. The University of Texas at Austin also included some of these images in their library's digital repository.

160. Man One, a Los Angeles graffiti artist, was one of the artists whose work was featured in this billboard, and he is seen in the photographs painting the figure he designed. Coincidentally, after Kaufman's career took off from his 1992 Los Angeles Riot series and before Man One began his successful graffiti art business, Kaufman hired him as his artist assistant.

161. Chon Noriega has told me that Elsa Flores Almaraz may have made a painting with wood salvaged from a destroyed property. After contacting her, I learned that it is titled *Stigmata over the City of Los Angeles* (1992).

162. I have viewed the pieces in Kaufman's collection, and many of them are well kept, though they need to be preserved in better conditions. Because the materials incurred fire and water damage, many of the works are very fragile. For instance, when I gently handled *That Was Then, This Is Then* it left charcoal residue on my hands.

Chapter Three

1. Sarah J. Rogers curated the group exhibition, which was held at the Wexner Center from September 26 to December 27, 1992. Ann Bremner, "Adrian Piper: Black Box/White Box," in *Will Power: New Works by Papo Colo, Jimmie Durham, David Hammons, Hachivi Edgar Heap of Birds, Adrian Piper, Aminah Brenda Lynn Robinson* (Wexner Center for the Arts, The Ohio State University, 1993), 56.

2. Bremner, "Adrian Piper: Black Box/White Box," 36.

3. Bremner, "Adrian Piper: Black Box/White Box," 36. Piper was at the Wexner Center for this visit from April 30 to May 1, 1992. Bremner rose within the Wexner to become its publications editor, a position from which she retired in 2013.

4. Bremner, "Adrian Piper: Black Box/White Box," 36.

5. Bremner, "Adrian Piper: Black Box/White Box," 36.

6. Bremner, "Adrian Piper: Black Box/White Box," 57, 61.

7. Bremner, "Adrian Piper: Black Box/White Box," 56.

8. Bremner, "Adrian Piper: Black Box/White Box," 57, 61.

9. For a concise discussion of the similarities between the artistic concerns of Judd, Morris, Smith, and Piper, see Cherise Smith, "The Politics of My Position: Adrian Piper and *Mythic Being*," in *Enacting Others*, 65.

10. Piper began making minimalist artworks in the mid-1960s. Cherise Smith notes that in the late 1960s Piper's work was shown at Dwan Gallery and Paula Cooper Gallery (two major conceptual art exhibition spaces in New York); Piper also had work included in major conceptual art exhibitions, such as *557,087* at the Seattle Art Museum (1969), *Plans and Projects as Art* at the Kunsthalle Bern (1969), and *Information* at the Museum of Modern Art in New York (1970). See Smith, "The Politics of My Position," 38–39.

11. In fact, LeWitt became a mentor to Piper. See John P. Bowles, "Contingent and Universal: Adrian Piper and the Minimalist Ideal," in *Adrian Piper: Race, Gender, and Embodiment* (Duke University Press, 2011), 34–68. Bowles's book provides a thorough examination of Piper's work in minimalism, conceptualism, and performance.

12. Bowles, "Contingent and Universal," 26–27, 35.

13. While Piper used "Minimalist," she prefers to describe her work as "abstraction." Adrian Piper, "Flying," in *Reflections, 1976–1987* (Alternative Museum, 1987), 27.

14. Bowles, "Contingent and Universal," 34.

15. Adrian M. S. Piper, "Chapter XI. Xenophobia and Moral Anomaly," in *Rationality and the Structure of the Self, vol. 2: A Kantian Conception*, 2nd ed. (APRA Foundation, 2013), 461.

16. Piper, "Chapter XI. Xenophobia and Moral Anomaly," 461–62.

17. See Anna C. Chave, "Minimalism and the Rhetoric of Power," *Arts Magazine* 64.5 (January 1990): 44–63; Salseda, "The New Wave of Identity Politics," 24–31.

18. In fact, based on her name, many had assumed Piper was a white male artist, which she realized gave her credibility as a minimalist. Bowles, "Contingent and Universal," 37–40; Smith, "The Politics of My Position," 39–40.

19. Adrian Piper, "My Slave Name," in *Decide Who You Are: Texts* (Paula Cooper Gallery, 1992), n.p. Also cited in Bowles, "Contingent and Universal," 38. During an interview with the art historian Cherise Smith, she claimed she was "dropped by the art world" after her identity as a black woman became well known. See Smith, "The Politics of My Position," 39.

20. For Piper's discussion of some of these experiences in US academic institutions, see Adrian Piper, *Escape to Berlin: A Travel Memoir* (Adrian Piper Research Archive Foundation, 2018).

21. Bowles, "Contingent and Universal," 33; Smith, "The Politics of My Position," 39. Smith states that the student deaths "made a particularly strong impact" on Piper. It is worth researching this impact further: How did she relate to the wars and the antiwar student movement before these events? What exactly about the invasion and the student deaths moved her? In what specific ways did this change her political consciousness—beyond the recognition that she could not escape her subjectivity?

22. Smith, "The Politics of My Position," 39.

23. Bowles, "Contingent and Universal," 34.

24. Bowles, "Contingent and Universal," 34.

25. Bremner, "Adrian Piper: Black Box/White Box," 57; Smith, "The Politics of My Position," 39. Original quote from Claudia Barrow, "Adrian Piper: Space, Time, and Reference, 1967—1970," in *Adrian Piper* (Ikon Gallery and Cornerhouse, 1991), 15. For a deeper look at Piper's politics of identity, see Smith's chapter.

26. See Robert Pincus-Witten, *Postminimalism to Maximalism: American Art, 1966–1986* (UMI Research Press, 1987).

27. Bowles, "Contingent and Universal," 34–68.

28. William J. Horrigan, "Columbus in 1992," in *Will/Power*, 72.

29. Sarah J. Rogers, "Introduction: Poetry and Politics," in *Will Power*, 8. For criticisms from William Box Cook, Rogers, and Horrigan, respectively, see *Will Power*, 4, 8, 72.

30. William Box Cook, Foreword to *Will/Power*, 4.

31. Rogers, "Introduction: Poetry and Politics," 9.

32. Adrian Piper, "News: September 2012," September 20, 2012, http://www.adrianpiper.com/berlin/news.shtml#September_2012. The news item on the artist's website explains, "In the future, for professional utility, you may wish to refer to her as The Artist Formerly Known as African-American," and in the signed announcement, typed over a portrait of the artist with her skin color changed to a dark-grayish hue, Piper explains that she "decided to change [her] racial and nationality designations" for her sixty-fourth birthday, declaring her new racial designation as "neither black nor white but rather 6.25% grey, honoring [her] 1/16th African heritage" and her nationality as "not African American but rather Anglo-German American, reflecting [her] predominantly English and German ancestry." She ends her statement by asking readers, "Please join me in celebrating this exciting new adventure in pointless administrative precision and futile institutional control!" For me, this statement makes clear not only Piper's sardonicism and humor, but a critical view of the Black-white racial binary—how it "boxes" in understandings of the self and others.

33. Rogers, "Introduction: Poetry and Politics," 12.; Bremner, "Adrian Piper: Black Box/White Box," 56.

34. Rogers, "Introduction: Poetry and Politics," 12.

35. Rogers, "Introduction: Poetry and Politics," 12.

36. The Wexner Center for the Arts opened on November 17, 1989.

37. The retrospective debuted at MoMA PS1 in Long Island City, New York, in 1991. It ended at LACMA, where it was on view from March 26 to May 31, 1992. Its happenstance exhibition at the Los Angeles institution during the 1992 Los Angeles Riots is interesting.

38. Cathy Curtis, "The Wasteland: The World of Photographer Lewis Baltz Lies Just Beyond the City, Where He Records Bleak Images of the American West," *Los Angeles Times*, March 29, 1992, http://articles.latimes.com/1992-03-29/entertainment/ca-372_1_photographer-lewis-baltz.

39. Curtis, "The Wasteland."

40. The unrest in Ferguson, Missouri, in 2014, after the police shooting of Michael Brown, and the 2020 George Floyd Uprising in Minneapolis, Minnesota, further underscores the relevancy of the Midwest to histories of unrest in the United States.

41. Rogers also juxtaposes the two artists, claiming that Hammons's practice "had been to work outside the systems—of institutions, social politics, or conventions of western art." "Introduction: Poetry and Politics," 13.

42. Rogers, "Introduction: Poetry and Politics," 9.

43. Rogers, "Introduction: Poetry and Politics," 9.

44. Rogers, "Introduction: Poetry and Politics," 8.

45. Rogers, "Introduction: Poetry and Politics," 8.

46. The performances and film are specifically referred to by the artists as *The Year of the White Bear* and *Two Undiscovered Amerindians Visit the West* (1992–94) and, made in collaboration with the filmmaker Paula Heredia, *The Couple in the Cage: Guatinaui Odyssey* (1993).

47. Coco Fusco, "Stalking the White Bear," in *Will/Power*, 78.

48. Horrigan, "Columbus in 1992," 72.

49. Fusco, "Stalking the White Bear," 82.

50. Coincidentally, like Piper's *Black Box/White Box*, Hammons' *Black Star Line* was his second project idea for the group exhibition. See Rogers, "Introduction: Poetry and Politics," 12.

51. Indeed, the UNIA perceived this return as a human right of Black people in the United States.

52. Marcus Garvey, "Excerpts from a Speech," in *Will/Power*, 39–38; Also found in Marcus Garvey, "Speech Delivered at Madison Square Garden, New York City, N.Y., U.S.A., Sunday, March 16, 1924. In honor of the Return to America of the Delegation Sent to Europe and African by the Universal Negro Improvement Association to Negotiate for the Repatriation of Negroes to a Homeland of Their Own in Africa," in *The Philosophy and Opinions of Marcus Garvey: Africa for the Africans*, ed. Jacques Garvey (Routledge, 2006), 118.

53. Garvey, "Speech Delivered at Madison Square Garden," 120.

54. Garvey, "Speech Delivered at Madison Square Garden," 120.

55. Garvey, "Speech Delivered at Madison Square Garden," 120.

56. Rogers, "Introduction: Poetry and Politics," 12.

57. Rogers, "Introduction: Poetry and Politics," 8.

58. For a video of President Bush's address to the nation, see "Reaction to the Los Angeles Police Trial: May 1st, 1992," aired on C-Span: http://www.c-spanvideo.org/program/25847-1.

59. "Reaction to the Los Angeles Police Trial: May 1st, 1992."

60. That Bush's statement recalls the civil rights leader Malcolm X's famous speech on behalf of the Organization of Afro-American Unity (OAAU), known as "By Any Means Necessary" (1964), makes the promise even more ironic. For a transcript of the speech, see "Malcolm X's Speech at the Founding Rally of the Organization of Afro-American Unity," *BlackPast*, http://www.blackpast.org/1964-malcolm-x-s-speech-founding-rally-organization-afro-american-unity.

61. Gaye cowrote the song with Renaldo Benson of the Four Tops and Al Cleveland, a Motown Records lyricist. See "Obie Benson, Original Bass Singer of the Four Tops, Succumbs at 69," *Jet* (August 1, 2005), 46.

62. David Coffey, "African Americans in the U.S. Military," in *The Encyclopedia of the Vietnam War: A Political, Social and Military History, Second Edition, Volume II: H–P* (ABC-CLIO, 2011), 9.

63. Coffey, "African Americans in the U.S. Military," 9.

64. Coffey, "African Americans in the U.S. Military," 9.

65. See Francis Frascina, "Class, Conflict, Race and Remembrance: Adrian Piper's *Black Box/White Box*, Greensboro, NC, 1 November 2001," *Oxford Art Journal* 28.1 (2005): 3–24.

66. Bowles, 34.

67. A defining characteristic of post-traumatic stress disorder (PTSD), for example, is also the persistent reexperience of an event via "unwanted upsetting memories" or flashbacks. "PTSD and DSM-5," PTSD: National Center for PTSD, https://www.ptsd.va.gov/professional/ptsd-overview/dsm5_criteria_ptsd.asp.

68. Jill Bennett, *Empathic Vision: Affect, Trauma, and Contemporary Art* (Stanford University Press, 2005), 2.

69. Bennett, *Empathic Vision.*

70. Bremner, "Adrian Piper: Black Box/White Box," 60.

71. Suzanna Muchnic, "King Beating Footage Comes to the Art World: Art: George Holliday's tape represents 'a new way of seeing what is around us,' says the Whitney curator who chose it for the museum's Biennial," March 10, 1993, https://www.latimes.com/archives/la-xpm-1993-03-10-ca-1355-story.html.

72. Muchnic, "King Beating Footage Comes to the Art World."

73. Muchnic, "King Beating Footage Comes to the Art World."

74. John G. Hanhardt, "New Media Art Worlds: New Expressions in Film and Video, 1991–93," in *1993 Whitney Biennial*, ed. Elisabeth Sussman, Thelma Golden, John G. Hanhardt, and Lisa Phillips (Whitney Museum of American Art and Harry N. Abrams, 1993), 46.

75. Hanhardt, "New Media Art Worlds," 51.

76. See p. 170 of the *1993 Whitney Biennial* exhibition catalog. Note that Lee's short is in collaboration with Prince, who provided the song "Money Don't Matter 2 Night" from his album *Diamonds and Pearls* (1991). Piper made sure to acquire proper permission from Holliday for her use of his video for *Black Box/White Box* with support from the Wexner Center and the Ohio State University Office of Legal Affairs. See Sarah J. Rogers, "Acknowledgments," in *Will/Power*, 6.

77. Eddie Chambers, personal correspondence with the author, June 29, 2018.

78. Brian Wallis, "Columbus: 'Will/Power' at the Wexner Center," *Art in America* 81 (February 1993): 117.

79. The original quotation from a 1968 English translation reads, "Just understand one thing, and pass it along to anyone at the top who still doesn't know that you are

strong only as long as you don't deprive people of *everything*. For a person you've taken *everything* from is no longer in your power. He's free all over again" (emphasis in original). Alexander Solzhenitsyn, *The First Circle*, trans. Thomas P. Whitney (Bantam Books and Harper & Row, 1968), 96. In later English translations of the book, the title as well as the passage quoted here changed. For example, in the 2009 uncensored English edition, the text reads, "In fact, you should get it into your head, and pass it on to whoever needs to know up above, that your power depends on not taking absolutely everything away from people. The man from whom you've taken everything is no longer in your power; he is free again." Alexander Solzhenitsyn, *In the First Circle*, trans. Harry T. Willetts (HarperCollins, 2009), 95.

80. Adrian Piper, "New Objectivity," *Art Forum* 56.4 (December 2017).

81. In fact, the interior spaces of the cubes are smaller than those of cells in US correctional facilities. According to a 1986 publication on state prison statistics, the average single-person cell was 68 square feet. In 2010, the American Correctional Association published standards that stipulated single-person cells must provide 70 square feet of floor space "when a prisoner is confined for more than ten hours per day" and at least 35 square feet of "unencumbered" or usable space. See Christopher A. Innes, "Population Density in State Prisons," in *Bureau of Justice Statistics: Special Report* (US Department of Justice, 1987); American Correctional Association, "Core Jail Standards," http://correction.org/core-jail-standards/.

82. V. S. Pritchett, "Hell on Earth," *New York Review of Books*, December 19, 1968.

83. Martin Luther King Jr., "The Other America," April 14, 1967. A filmed recording of the speech is available: Stanford University Libraries' "Martin Luther King, Jr. Visits Stanford (1967)," https://youtu.be/cYK9xGALPrU.

84. For a transcript of the original address, see Rodney King, "Rodney King Appeals for Calm in Wake of L.A. Riots," *NBC Nightly News*, May 1, 1992, from *NBC Learn*: https://archives.nbclearn.com/portal/site/k-12/browse/?cuecard=776.

85. Jeffrey Syfu, "Black Box/White Box, 1992: 1997, Mixed Media Installation," *Ibrarian*, http://www.ibrarian.net/navon/paper/Black_Box_White_Box__1992_1997_.pdf?paperid=4594740.

86. The four policemen were tried for intentionally violating King's civil rights. Seth Mydans, "2 to Be Sentenced Today in Rodney King Beating," *The New York Times*, August 4, 1993. Two were charged with excessive force and failing to protect the welfare of King after they arrested him on March 3, 1991.

87. Mydans, "2 to Be Sentenced Today in Rodney King Beating." Mydans reports that in a departmental newsletter, *The Thin Blue Line*, Powell described himself and Koon as "sacrificial lambs."

88. King won $3.8 million as compensation for the beating, for which the city admitted liability. Seth Mydans, "Rodney King Is Awarded $3.8 Million," *The New York Times*, April 20, 1994.

89. For a brief overview, see Todd E. Bricker, "Rampart Scandal: United States History," *Encyclopedia Britannica*, https://www.britannica.com/topic/Rampart-scandal.

90. Bricker, "Rampart Scandal." The monologue as reported by Syfu in his review of Piper's work is different from the televised speech. It seems that Piper cut the monologue and rearranged certain blocks of statements. King's address, according to transcript, is as follows: "People, I just—I just want to say, you know, can we—can we all get along? Can we—can we get along? Can we stop making it—making it horrible for—for the—for the older people and the—and the kids? We'll get our justice;

they've won the battle, but they haven't won the war. We—we'll have our day in court, and that's all we want. And just—I—I lov—you know, I'm—I'm neutral. I lov—I love every—I love people of color, you know. I'm not a—I'm not like they're—picking me out—picking me out to be. We've gotta—we've got to quit. We've got to quit. After all, I mean, I can understand the—the—the first upset for the first two hours after the verdict. But to go on—to keep going on like—like this and to see the security guard shot on the—on the ground, it—it's—it's just not right. It's just not right. Because those people are—will never go home to—to their families again. And I mean—please, we can get along here. We—we all can get along. We just gotta—we just gotta, you know—I mean, we're all stuck here for a while. Let's, you know, let's—let's—let's try to work it out." Rodney King, "Rodney King Appeals for Calm in Wake of L.A. Riots," *NBC Nightly News*, May 1, 1992, from *NBC Learn*: https://archives.nbclearn.com/portal/site/k-12/browse/?cuecard=776.

91. Brian Wallis, "Columbus: 'Will/Power' at the Wexner Center," *Art in America* 81 (February 1993): 117.

92. Rogers, "Introduction: Poetry and Politics," 12.

93. Rogers, "Introduction: Poetry and Politics," 12–13.

94. Bremner, "Adrian Piper: Black Box/White Box," 61.

95. Rogers, "Introduction: Poetry and Politics," 13.

96. Bush lost to William "Bill" Clinton, who went on to serve two terms, from 1993 to 2001.

97. Katie Kitamura, "Adrian Piper: 'Past Time: Selected Works 1973–95' at Elizabeth Dee," *Frieze Art Magazine*, April 1, 2011, https://frieze.com/article/adrian-piper-0.

98. Ewan Morrison, "Vote/Emote: The Responsibility of the Viewer in the Work of Adrian Piper," *Variant* 10 (Winter 1991): 22–23.

99. Morrison, "Vote/Emote."

100. The Voting Rights Act of 1965 prohibits racial discrimination. It is important to note that President Lyndon B. Johnson felt pressure to address voting rights and that this legislation found widespread support only after police violently clashed with marchers in Alabama and footage of their excessive force circulated nationally.

101. Morrison, "Vote/Emote."

102. Franklin Sirmans, "Letter from Milan: An Interview with Adrian Piper," *ArtNet*, March 1998, http://www.artnet.com/magazine_pre2000/features/sirmans/sirmans3-3-98.asp.

103. Interestingly, Clive Phillpot racializes the monologues as "White responses" to the images in "Adrian Piper: Talking to Us," *Adrian Piper: Reflections, 1967–1987* (Alternative Museum, 1987), 11.

104. Adrian Piper, "Monologues from 'Four Intruders Plus Alarm Systems' and 'Safe,'" in *Feminism and Tradition in Aesthetics*, ed. Peggy Zeglin Brand and Carolyn Korsmeyer (Pennsylvania State University Press, 1995), 236–37; emphasis in original.

105. Piper, "Monologues from 'Four Intruders Plus Alarm Systems' and 'Safe,'" 241.

106. Piper, "Monologues from 'Four Intruders Plus Alarm Systems' and 'Safe,'" 241.

107. Piper, "Monologues from 'Four Intruders Plus Alarm Systems' and 'Safe,'" 241.

108. Piper, "Monologues from 'Four Intruders Plus Alarm Systems' and 'Safe,'" 241.

109. Piper, "Monologues from 'Four Intruders Plus Alarm Systems' and 'Safe,'" 241.

110. Morrison, 22.

111. *Dislocations* was curated by Robert Storr and on view from October 20, 1991 until January 7, 1992 at the Museum of Modern Art in New York.

112. Commodores, "Zoom," *Commodores* (Motown Records, 1977).

113. Piper, "Flying," 24–33.

114. Piper, "Flying," 25.

115. Piper, "Flying," 25.

116. Piper, "Flying," 25–26.

117. Piper, "Flying," 26.

118. Piper, "Flying," 26.

119. Piper, "Flying," 28.

120. Piper, "Flying," 28.

121. Piper, "Flying," 29.

122. Piper, "Flying," 30.

123. Piper, "Flying," 31.

124. Piper, "Flying," 32–33.

125. Piper, "Flying," 32–33.

126. Piper, "Flying," 33.

127. Piper, "Flying," 33.

128. Piper, "Flying," 33.

129. For video documentation of the installation, see Piper, "What It's Like, What It Is, #3."

130. Piper chose a meta-pattern for the installation: The man makes four quarter-turns; he speaks a total of sixteen statements, but he recites them in four groupings of four; and four monitors are embedded in each of the four sides of the box.

131. I view Piper's image screen of King and mirror device as an attempt to elicit viewer empathy for victims of racist-fueled violence. This seems related to Piper's *Imagine* (2013), which includes text on the bottom right of the work that reads, "Imagine what it was like to be me." I discuss *Imagine* later in the chapter.

132. David Deitcher, "Art on the Installation Plan: MoMA and the Carnegie," *Artforum International* 30.4 (January 1992): 82, 83.

133. Piper, "Xenophobia and the Indexical Present II: Lecture," 257. This lecture was also published as Adrian Piper, "Xenophobia and the Indexical Present," *Place Position Presentation Public*, ed. Ine Gevers (Jan van Eyck Akademie, 1991), 135–56.

134. Piper, "Xenophobia and the Indexical Present II: Lecture," 257.

135. In addition, at least one African American police officer was present during the beating of King, and he participated in the 1991–92 state trial as a defense witness. Furthermore, news outlets had described the jury as nearly all white and often dismissed the fact that one was Latina and another Filipino American. To make things more (racially) complicated, years later during a 2012 interview reflecting on the 1992 verdict, one of the white-identified jurors revealed that he is a racially mixed Black person.

136. Sánchez, "Face the Nation," 1018; ACLU Foundation of Southern California, "Civil Liberties in Crisis: Los Angeles During the Emergency, Executive Summary," June 23, 1992; Box 151, Folder 3, Papers of Edmund D. Edelman, 1953–1994, Huntington Library, Manuscripts Department; Ong and Hee, *Losses in Los Angeles Civil Unrest*, 12.

137. Abelmann and Lie, *Blue Dreams*, 153.

138. Abelmann and Lie, *Blue Dreams*, 159.

139. Roy L. Brooks and Kirsten Widner, "In Defense of the Black/White Binary:

Reclaiming a Tradition of Civil Rights Scholarship," in *Critical Race Theory: The Cutting Edge*, ed. Richard Delgado and Juan Stefancic (Temple University Press, 2013), 499.

140. Brooks and Widner, "In Defense of the Black/White Binary," 499.

141. See Juan F. Perea, "The Black-White Binary Paradigm of Race," in Delgado and Stefancic, *Critical Race Theory*, 457-465.

142. Perea, "The Black-White Binary Paradigm of Race," 463-464. For Toni Morrison's essay, see "*On the Backs of Blacks*."

143. Perea, "The Black-White Binary Paradigm of Race," 464.

144. Perea, "The Black-White Binary Paradigm of Race," 464.

145. In line with Perea's thinking, George J. Sánchez suggests, "Scholars studying both 'whiteness' and 'blackness' in modern U.S. society, therefore, have to account for the myriad ways that these two racial categories are projected onto the bodies of individuals who are neither 'white' nor 'black.'" See Sánchez, "Reading Reginald Denny," 392.

146. Sánchez, "Reading Reginald Denny," 392–93.

147. Sánchez, "Face the Nation," 1015. An almost identical quote is found in Sánchez, "Reading Reginald Denny," 393.

148. Brooks and Widner, "In Defense of the Black/White Binary," 504.

149. Brooks and Widner, "In Defense of the Black/White Binary,"504.

150. Brooks and Widner, "In Defense of the Black/White Binary," 510.

151. Brooks and Widner, "In Defense of the Black/White Binary," 510.

152. Adrian Piper, "Caste in Stone: Why Classifying Artists by Race Is Not Just a 'Social Construct," *The Burns Halperin Report*, December 16, 2022, https://news.artnet.com/art-world/caste-in-stone-why-classifying-artists-by-race-is-not-just-a-social-construct-2229595; emphasis in original.

153. Piper, "Caste in Stone."

154. As mentioned in note 32, above, Piper's retirement from being Black included what seems to be an embrace of gray, including an image of her with a gray skin color and a declaration that she is not white or Black but "6.25% grey." See Piper, "News: September 2012." My reframing of "the gray zone" and discussion of it for *Black Box/White Box* may also be generative in a focused examination of Piper's 2012 decision and related materials.

155. Lauren O'Neill-Butler, "Adrian Piper Speaks! (for Herself)," *The New York Times*, Opinion, The Stone, July 5, 2018, https://www.nytimes.com/2018/07/05/opinion/adrian-piper-speaks-for-herself.html; Piper's emphasis. In the same article, Piper provides a concise definition of transpersonal rationality as the "hardwired cognitive dispositions that define us as human beings: to consistency, coherence, impartiality, impersonality, intellectual discrimination, foresight, deliberation, self-reflection and self- control." She also states its opposite, egocentric rationality, as that which uses the above characteristics to serve personal desires and self-interest.

Chapter Four

1. Water Benjamin, "Allegory and Trauerspiel," in *Origin of the German Trauerspiel*, trans. Howard Eiland (Harvard University Press, 2019), 188; Susan Buck-Morss, "Historical Nature: Ruin," in *The Dialectics of Seeing: Walter Benjamin and the Arcades Project* (MIT Press, 1989), 170.

2. Michelle Yap Dizon, "Vision in Ruins" (PhD diss., University of California, Berkeley, 2011), vi. To watch the film, visit https://vimeo.com/22172925/5ca200e55a?share=copy.

3. Latipa, interview by the author, July 13, 2015.

4. When exhibited, the artist typically uses three projectors to play her video and the projected footage is displayed horizontally on a white wall. However, with the artist's permission, viewers can access a version of *Civil Society* online that simulates the three-channel installation.

5. Latipa earned an MFA in art with a specialization in interdisciplinary studies at UCLA in 2008 and an MA and PhD in rhetoric at UC Berkeley in 2011.

6. Latipa refers to this theoretical and conceptual understanding of ruins as both "ruins of vision" and "vision in ruins." See Dizon, "Vision in Ruins"; Michelle Dizon, "Untitled," in *Michelle Dizon* (Cue Art Foundation, 2010).

7. Dizon, "Vision in Ruins," viii; Latipa, interview by the author, July 13, 2015.

8. Latipa, correspondence with the author, December 19, 2018.

9. Carl Bialik, "We Still Don't Know How Many People Died Because of Katrina," *Five Thirty Eight*, August 26, 2016, http://fivethirtyeight.com/features/we-still-dont-know-how-many-people-died-because-of-katrina/.

10. Dave Martin took the photograph and wrote its caption, which read, "A young man walks through chest deep flood water after looting a grocery store in New Orleans on Aug. 30, 2005. Flood waters continue to rise in New Orleans after Hurricane Katrina did extensive damage when it made landfall on Monday." According to AP spokesman Jack Stokes, Martin followed AP guidelines regarding the use of the word "looting" versus "carrying," the former implying that a photographer witnessed a subject enter a property and take property. Tania Ralli, "Who's a Looter? In Storm's Aftermath, Pictures Kick Up a Different Kind of Tempest," *The New York Times*, September 5, 2005, http://www.nytimes.com/2005/09/05/business/whos-a-looter-in-storms-aftermath-pictures-kick-up-a-different.html.

11. Ralli, "Who's a Looter?"

12. West was referring to President George W. Bush. Mike Meyers and Kanye West, "A Concert for Hurricane Relief," *NBC*, September 2, 2005, https://youtu.be/9pVTrnxCZaQ. Chris Graythen took the photograph and wrote the caption for the AFP circulated image. He later said via email correspondence with *The New York Times* that taking supplies for survival should not be considered stealing. See Ralli, "Who's a Looter?"

13. The parents of Zyed and Bouna were from Tunisia and Mauritania, respectively. Muhittin Altun was a Turkish Kurd. It is unclear whether he was born in Turkey or if it was only his parents who were born there. The boys and the community in which they lived were Black, Brown, and Muslim.

14. Three hundred public buildings were burned or damaged. Thirty thousand trash bins were also set on fire. Laurent Mucchielli, "Autumn 2005: A Review of the Most Important Riot in the History of French Contemporary Society," *Journal of Ethnic and Migration Studies* 35.5 (May 2009): 733.

15. Peter Sahlins, "Civil Unrest in the French Suburbs, November 2005," *Riots in France*, October 24, 2006, http://riotsfrance.ssrc.org/. The website, which is run by the Social Science Research Council (SSRC), includes eleven essays written by social scientists and other scholars who address different issues surrounding the unrest in France.

16. The French unrest lasted nearly three weeks, from October 27 to November 16, 2005.

17. Michelle Dizon, "Untitled," 11; Latipa, in discussion with the author, July 13, 2015.

18. Conversation between Dalida Maria Benfield, Laura Fantone, and Michelle Dizon, moderated by Katherine Wallerstein, "The Politics of 'Third Space' in Global Videos and Installations," October 14, 2009, https://archive.org/details/ThePoliticsOfthirdSpaceInGlobalVideosAndInstallations.

19. Latipa, conversation with the author, November 12, 2024.

20. Latipa's parents continued to live in the same apartment complex for thirty years. Latipa, conversation with the author, November 12, 2024.

21. Latipa, conversation with the author, November 12, 2024.

22. Latipa, conversation with the author, November 12, 2024.

23. Latipa, conversation with the author, November 12, 2024.

24. Latipa, conversation with the author, November 12, 2024.

25. Latipa, conversation with the author, November 12, 2024.

26. Dizon, "Vision in Ruins," vi. Interestingly, Latipa began to work with video as a student at the Los Angeles County High School for the Arts around the time of the unrest. Latipa, in discussion with the author, July 13, 2015.

27. Dizon, "Untitled," 11; Dizon, "Vision in Ruins," vi.

28. Alexander, "'Can you be BLACK and Look at This?,'" 92; Patricia Greenfield and Paul Kibby, "Picture Imperfect," *The New York Times*, April 1, 1993, A19.

29. Their slow motion and freeze framing also apparently silenced the recorded exclamations of eyewitnesses. Alexander, "'Can you be BLACK and Look at This?,'" 83, 92; Greenfield and Kibby, "Picture Imperfect."

30. Seth Mydans, "The Police Verdict; Los Angeles Policemen Acquitted in Taped Beating," Special Issue of *The New York Times*, April 30, 1992, http://www.nytimes.com/books/98/02/08/home/rodney-verdict.html.

31. Lou Cannon, "The King Incident: More Than Met the Eye on Videotape," *Washington Post*, January 25, 1998, https://www.washingtonpost.com/archive/politics/1998/01/25/the-king-incident-more-than-met-the-eye-on-videotape/2248e35e-178b-47e9-a8db-0734f88b46e0/?utm_term=.246f6088a569.

32. Cannon, "The King Incident."

33. The police beating of Rodney King has been referenced in movies, documentaries, music, and even video games. For instance, as mentioned in chapter 3, *Malcolm X* includes an opening scene with footage of King's beating; and it is referenced to varying degrees in *Strange Days* (dir. Kathryn Bigelow, 1995), *American History X* (dir. Tim Kaye, 1998); and *National Security* (dir. Dennis Dugan, 2003), to name a few. Music with King references includes Ice Cube's albums *Death Certificate* (1991) and *The Predator* (1992) and the Offspring's "L.A.P.D." on *Ignition* (1992), among others. The video games *Earthbound* (1994) and *Grand Theft Auto: San Andreas* (2004) were also inspired by the police beating and acquittal, respectively.

34. Dizon, "Vision in Ruins," viii.

35. For a discussion about the issues that arise when asserting one visual analysis of the King beating over others or even asserting that it is possible to read the video, see Fred Moten, "Music Against the Law of Reading the Future and 'Rodney King,'" *Journal of the Midwest Modern Language Association* 27.1 (Spring 1994): 51–64.

36. See Alexander, "'Can you be BLACK and Look at This?'"; Patricia J. Williams, "The Rules of the Game," in *Reading Rodney King*, ed. Roberto Gooding-Williams (Routledge, 1993), 51–55.

37. Alexander, "'Can you be BLACK and Look at This?,'" 80, 91; Williams, "The Rules of the Game," 52–53.

38. The fact that the jury had no Black members is also significant. The jury was composed of ten whites, one Latina, and one Filipino American. This points to the possibility of a racially biased interpretation of the video. As an aside, years later, during a 2012 interview reflecting back on the 1992 verdict, one of the white-identified jurors revealed that he is a racially mixed Black person who has an African American father. He noted that during the time of the jury selection and trial, he would have identified himself as white, though. See Gretchen Wenner, "Rodney King Juror: 'My father was black,'" *Ventura County Star*, April 28, 2012, http://archive.vcstar.com/news/rodney-king-juror-my-father-was-black-ep-363661334-352091231.html/.

39. Huey P. Newton, "Black Capitalism Re-analyzed," in *The Black Panther: Intercommunal News Service*, vol. 6, no. 19 (June, 5, 1971), 14. While this was published in 1971, Newton had begun sharing versions of this statement earlier as the statement had been paraphrased by Bobby Seale, a cofounder with Newton of the Black Panther Party, who also cited it as belonging to Newton.

40. Newton, "Black Capitalism Re-analyzed," 14.

41. After my inquiry of her video, Cobb made it available online. To see the video in its entirety, visit https://vimeo.com/158298117.

42. This cut occurs precisely at the 56-second mark in Cobb's video, underscoring her repeated statement, "Fifty-six times in eighty-one seconds . . ."

43. Slightly different versions of this quote are often attributed to Wade W. Nobles, a psychology specialist and professor emeritus in the Department of Africana Studies at San Francisco State University, where Riley was an undergraduate student.

44. Gerrard recorded the scene and Tur narrated it for television viewers. Tur came out publicly as transgender in 2013. In 2014, after gender reassignment surgery, she legally changed her name to Zoey Tur. I use the name "Bob Tur" in my description of the Denny beating since this is the name she was known by at the time.

45. The term "high-tech lynching" originated from a statement Clarence Thomas made in 1992 during a Senate Judiciary Committee confirmation hearing for his nomination to the Supreme Court. He spoke the phrase when he testified about Anita Hill's allegations that he had sexually harassed her. Condemning the hearing altogether, he stated, "And, from my standpoint, as far as I'm concerned, it is a high-tech lynching for uppity blacks who in any way deign to think for themselves, to do for themselves, to have different ideas. And, it is a message that unless you kowtow to an old order, this is what will happen to you. You will be lynched, destroyed, caricatured by a committee of the U.S. Senate rather than hung from a tree." See "Flashback: Clarence Thomas Responds to Anita Hill," CNN, http://www.cnn.com/videos/politics/2016/04/13/flashback-clarence-thomas-denies-anita-hill-testimony-1991-cnn.cnn.

46. Frances Gateward, "Documenting the Struggle: African American Women as Media Artists, Media Activists," in *Still Lifting, Still Climbing: African American Women's Contemporary Activism*, ed. Kimberly Springer (New York University Press, 1999), 289. In her essay, Gateward analyzes Cobb's interviews of Black men visually, explaining the ways the artist manipulates the visual aspects of them via polarization and skipped-frame advance as "self-reflexive techniques."

47. This juxtaposition is similar to that which was done when online viewers compared the AP and AFP photographs that portrayed Black and white Hurricane Katrina victims.

48. Dizon, "Untitled," 11; Latipa writes a similar statement in her dissertation. See Dizon, "Vision in Ruins," vi.

49. Dizon, "Vision in Ruins," vi. Also see Dizon, "Untitled," 11.

50. In 2018, Latipa published *White Gaze*, a collaborative work with artist-writer Việt Lê that includes images from an archive of *National Geographic* to explore whiteness and racist visuality. Michelle Dizon and Việt Lê, *White Gaze* (Sming Sming Books, 2018).

51. There was a very important moment in the late 1980s and early 1990s with the advancement of film and video technology: Equipment became much more accessible to the public, cheaper and easier to use.

52. Latipa, in discussion with the author, December 14, 2015; King was beaten on Foothill Blvd. at Osborne St. in the San Fernando Valley in Los Angeles on March 3, 1991.

53. See chapter 1 for discussion of Capistrán's statement.

54. See chapter 3 for further discussion of the photograph.

55. Baltz also discusses his opinions regarding black-and-white and color photography. He states, "Black-and-white is two seconds ago and color is *now*. . . . You accept the black-and-white as reality and the color seems totally fake." He continues, "I hate color. I think it's really vulgar and awful. That's also what I like about it." See Curtis, "The Wasteland"; Baltz's emphasis.

56. This has become an increasing occurrence in the 2010s. Recent recordings of police killing Black people include Eric Garner, Philando Castile, and Tamir Rice, who was only a child, to name a few. In each of these incidents, the recordings were widely circulated in the media and via the internet. Also, like the police who beat King, many of the police in these incidents were not convicted of crimes.

57. Latipa named the footage "Air Shots of Los Angeles, California" (1960). Latipa, email correspondence with the author, November 22, 2015.

58. Latipa, correspondence with the author, December 19, 2018.

59. Throughout history, reporters and historians have described the 1965 Watts Rebellion as occurring on a hot summer day, which led many people to go outdoors, suggesting that this contributed to the unrest.

60. The clips include the National Guard, fires, and broken windows.

61. The footage is from a KTLA news segment on the Watts Rebellion. It is significant to note that twenty-seven years later, KTLA would be the first Los Angeles news station to air the 1991 Holliday videotape of the King beating. The artist acquired this footage, "Hell in the City of Angels" (1965), from the UCLA Film and Television Archive. Latipa, email correspondence with the author, November 22, 2015.

62. Pavle Levi, "The 'Between' of Cinema," in *Cinema by Other Means* (Oxford University Press, 2012), 144.

63. Levi, "The 'Between' of Cinema," 144.

64. Gilles Deleuze, *Cinema II: The Time-Image* (Bloomsbury [1989] 2013), 185.

65. Deleuze, *Cinema II*, 185. Also see Levi, "The 'Between' of Cinema," 144–45.

66. Deleuze, *Cinema II*, 185. Also see Levi, "The 'Between' of Cinema," 144–45.

67. Levi, "The 'Between' of Cinema," 147; emphasis in original.

68. Levi, "The 'Between' of Cinema," 147.

69. Levi, "The 'Between' of Cinema," 148.

70. Levi, "The 'Between' of Cinema," 148. About 25,000 Palestinians were killed in what became known as "Black September."

71. Levi, "The 'Between' of Cinema," 148.

72. After this section, returning to four monitors, a reporter shares information on the war's impact on Palestinians while a soccer game plays on one of the four monitors and an unseen audience cheers. The sound cuts when Godard asserts, "Little by little, we're replaced by chains of uninterrupted images. Enslaving one another." Then, as the French family watches TV, Godard explains, "Each image in its place, as are we, each in his place. In the chain of events over which we have lost all control."

73. In his discussion of *Ici et ailleurs*, Levi quotes Serge Daney as stating, "What Godard says, very uncomfortably and very honestly, is that the real place of the filmmaker is in the AND." Levi follows this by restating the English translation of the film's title to underscore the significance of the interstice: "Between 'here' and 'elsewhere,' *in* the interstice." Levi, "The 'Between' of Cinema," 148; emphasis in original. He states that the interstice "is a paroxysmal manifestation of the cut's ability to make two shots both attract and repel each other"—making it "a powerful instrument of political filmmaking" (145). Later, Levi underscores, "The 'and,' the interstice—the gutter!—is the engine of the cinematic imaginary. It is where the filmmaker *and* the spectator reside" (159; emphasis in original). This is true for Latipa's film too.

74. Latipa, correspondence with the author, December 19, 2018.

75. Latipa's rejection of the typical uses of montage and storytelling in video and film also seems to be a concerted effort to avoid the spectacle of the Black body in pain. Her particular use of the King video could be interpreted as such, as well as her general exclusion of images of the French boys who died via electrocution, Benna and Traoré, their surviving companion, Altun, or close-up or detailed images of King and those who participated or were victims of civil unrest. As a result, Latipa prevents her video from participating in a long troublesome visual history of lynching imagery and prevents her viewers from becoming members of a lynch mob viewership.

76. Latipa, conversation with the author, November 12, 2024.

77. Latipa, conversation with the author, November 12, 2024. It is noteworthy that Latipa uses a similar score for *Perpetual Peace* (2014), a film she made that explores the contemporary vestiges of colonialism and the US military occupation in the Philippines—one that she sees as directly connected to *Civil Society*.

78. Latipa, interview by the author, July 13, 2015.

79. Michelle Dixon [*sic*], Stockholm Assembly, InivaArts, October 2013, https://youtu.be/gT2ofy_z18E.

80. The video debuted in a 1988 group exhibition at the Hostos Community College in Bronx, New York, which had a satellite gallery of the Bronx Museum for the Arts. It was also screened at MoMA on November 18, 1991, in conjunction with his exhibition *Word 2 My Mother*. Since then, it has been screened across the nation. It stands as one of Cokes's most popular videos. With this said, it is worth digging deeper into video from the late 1980s and early 1990s and looking at those that might have informed not only Latipa but also Adrian Piper for *Black Box/White Box* (1992).

81. Skinny Puppy's "Antagonism," "200 Years," and "Dig It," all from the album *Mind: The Perpetual Intercourse* (1986), are the soundtrack for *Black Celebration*. The title of Cokes's video is a reference to the 1986 Depeche Mode song and album of the same name.

82. Cokes's use of music and lyrics as well as his use of artist manifestos and essays deserve a focused analysis. Not only are most of the bands English, but the artists are all white. How does race, nationality, avant-garde art, and alternative music factor into his video and its visual imagery of white law enforcement patrolling and arresting Black residents?

83. Debord's essay also provides Cokes with the subtitle for his video.

84. See Debord, "The Decline and Fall of the Spectacle-Commodity."

85. Tony Cokes, Statement quoted in the description for *Black Celebration* (1988), Electronic Arts Intermix, https://www.eai.org/titles/black-celebration.

86. Paul Arthur, "Springing Tired Chains: African American Experimental Film and Video," in *A Line of Sight: American Avant-Garde Film Since 1965* (University of Minnesota, 2005), 119. The "formal rigor of repetition" that Arthur mentions in his statement recalls the strategy of repetition in minimalism that Adrian Piper uses for *Black Box/White Box* (1992).

87. Guénif-Souilamas was an associate professor of sociology at the University of Paris Nord/13 (now Sorbonne Paris Nord University) in France and is currently a professor in the Education Sciences Department at the University of Paris 8 Vincennes-Saint-Denis. Unrest in Brixton occurred in 1981, 1985, and 1995. It is unclear if she is speaking about all the events, although each began with violent incidents between white police and Black citizens and residents of Caribbean communities.

88. Latipa has explained that this scene is an animation she made with still images she obtained free of charge form the Bibliothèque nationale de France in Paris. Latipa, correspondence with the author, December 19, 2018.

89. Latipa, *Civil Society*, 2008.

90. These other fragments are "CRÉE" (create), "CRI" (shout), "ATTEND" (waits), "EN" (in) and the English version "IN," and "FIN" (end).

91. Conversation between Dalida Maria Benfield, Laura Fantone, and Michelle Dizon, moderated by Katherine Wallerstein, "The Politics of 'Third Space' in Global Videos and Installations."

92. In this lecture, Latipa makes the provocative statement that the "process of decolonization is the radical refusal to reproduce nation." Michelle Dixon [*sic*], Stockholm Assembly, InivaArts, October 2013, https://youtu.be/gT2ofy_z18E.

93. See Laura Fantone, "Riots and Ruins of Citizenship," in *Michelle Dizon* (New York: Cue Art Foundation, 2010); also available online at https://www.academia.edu/11065397/The_Ruins_of_Citizenship.

94. Alexander, "'Can you be BLACK and Look at This?,'" 80. Cultural critic Mike Davis suggests that "the King case may be almost as much of a watershed in American history as Dred Scott, a test of the very meaning of the citizenship for which African Americans have struggled for 400 years." See Mike Davis, *L.A. Was Just the Beginning: Urban Revolt in the United States: A Thousand Points of Light*, Open Magazine Pamphlet Series #20 (Open Media, 1993), 5.

95. Latipa, interview by the author, July 13, 2015; emphasis mine.

96. Dizon, "Untitled," 18. For a similar passage, see Dizon, "Vision in Ruins," viii.

97. Martin Luther King Jr., "The Other America," lecture, Stanford University, Stanford, CA, April 14, 1967.

98. The left and right time stamps read as follows before the scene changes: 00:04:44:17 and 00:04:21:14, respectively.

99. Deleuze, *Cinema II*, 188.

100. I would like to recognize a conversation I had with Pavle Levi on this topic. I shared with Levi my understanding of Deleuze on Godard in relation to Latipa's film, which I go on to share here. Levi explained with further cinematic insight, "At that time, critique of cinematic illusionism (largely Brecht-inspired, in Godard's case, or articulated otherwise, in the case of other authors) was very much at the forefront of politically and formally/stylistically progressive filmmaking. Representation as (always) artifice, never identical with its referent. . . . Red color as both a representation of blood, and a structurally unavoidable failure of that representation to properly account for, to be, the real thing. . . . Deleuze, I think, is adding a twist to this by claiming that to be avoiding the above state of things (that is, cinema not bespeaking literally its artifices, not openly acknowledging the extent to which its representations can be illusionistic) is to be participating in this cinematic deception—and thus compromising one's entitlement to speak altogether." Pavle Levi, email correspondence with the author, February 8, 2024.

101. Piper, "Xenophobia and the Indexical Present II: Lecture," 257. This lecture was also published as Adrian Piper, "Xenophobia and the Indexical Present," in *Place Position Presentation Public*, ed. Ine Gevers (Jan van Eyck Akademie, 1991), 135–56.

102. Benjamin, "Allegory and Trauerspiel," 188.

103. Buck-Morss, "Historical Nature: Ruin," 170.

Index

Page numbers in italics indicate figures.

1992 Los Angeles Riots: anniversaries of, 6, 17, 42–45, 50, 83–85; arrests during, 2, 15, 30–31, 126, 187n25; art histories concerning, 9–12; art made in response to, 2–13, 17–24, 28–55, 57–59, 63–64, 67–87, 89–95, 97–100, 103, 105–9, 111–16, 125–27, 130, 134–35, 137–55, 158–73, 186n22; Asians and, 11, 28–30; author's personal experience of, 138–39, 175–78; Capistrán's experience of, 26; country- and worldwide responses to, 4, 57; deaths during, 2; Kaufman's experience of, 57, 85; land left undeveloped after, 6, 47–48, 50, 53; Latinos and, 11, 28–37, 53–54, 187n25, 187n38; Latipa's experience of, 137–40, 142; legacies of loss and sorrow from, 7, 17–20, 30, 53–54, 138–39, 141, 170, 172–73 (*see also* grief and bereavement); media coverage of, 1, 3, 9–11, 27–28, 58, 92, 98, 105–6, 177–78; police response to, 27, 50; post-riot community responses to, 77; precipitating factors for, 1–2, 6, 15, 17, 24, 26, 30, 48, 57, 63, 106–7, 150, 177–78, 198n3; property damage and loss during, 1–2, 11, 15, 19, 22, 30, 50, 57–61, 74, 78, 86, 126, 130, 176–78 (*see also* violence against people during); protecting of property during, 21, 177; related to other instances of injustice/unrest, 4, 8, 30, 53, 61, 74, 91, 98–100, 105, 111, 135, 139–40, 152, 159, 162–73, *173*; sites connected to, 15, 19–22, 26–27, 30, 42–43, 47–52, 73–74, 84, 151; socioeconomic factors underlying, 34, 74–75; terminology concerning, 4; violence against people during, 10, 15, 17, 27–36, 49, 52, 130, 191n45 (*see also* property damage and loss during)

2005 French unrest, 8, 139–41, 142, 162–65, 168–69

Abelmann, Nancy, 11, 126–27

Absolut Vodka, 7, 55, *56*, 76–83, 85–86; *Absolut Hope* billboards, 76–83, *77*, *79* (detail), *80*, 85, 207n148; *Absolut Hope* reception installation, *80*

abstraction, 41–42, 45, *46*, 122–24, 208n13

Ackerman, Ian, 159

Adrian Piper: A Synthesis of Intuitions, 1965–2016 (exhibition), 89, *90*

African Americans: anti-immigrant sentiment among, 33–35; Asians' relations with, 32; as casualties of the Vietnam War, 107; and citizenship, 167; hostility and violence directed at, 1, 16, 27–28, 38, 40, 97, 100, 107, 111, 137–38, 151–52, 178, 198n3; Hurricane Katrina's effect on, 141–42; Koreans' relations with, 11–12, 17, 22, 29, 126–27; Latinos' relations with, 24, 32; in

African Americans (*contiued*)
Los Angeles, 34–35; media portrayals of, 9, 40, 142, 146, 148; and Pan-Africanism/Black separatism, 102–5; poverty among, 25; sites connected to, 100; who saved people and property during LA Riots, 21, 31–32, 35–36. *See also* race and racism
Agence France-Presse, 142
Aguilar, Raul, 36
Alan-Williams, Gregory, 36
Alexander, Elizabeth, 167–68
allegory, 172
Altun, Muhittin, 142
Alvarado Park, 47
American Psychiatric Association, 108
AmeriFlora'92, 97–98
Angelou, Maya, "Still I Rise," 133
Antiphony of Anarchy, The: Three Views After Curfew (exhibition), 55, 68–76, *69*, 85
antiwar movement, 96, 107, 115, 119, 123, 209n21. *See also* Vietnam War
Ardmore Park, 47
art: made in response to the 1992 LA Riots, 2–13, 17–24, 28–55, 57–59, 63–64, 67–87, 89–95, 97–100, 103, 105–9, 111–16, 125–27, 130, 134–35, 137–55, 158–73, 186n22; made in response to the Watts Rebellion, 55–56, 64–67, 152, 153, 160; meanings and effects of, xvi; power of, in its critical engagement of viewers, 111, 119; viewers' missing the meaning of, 41, 119, 121–22
art history/historiography: and the 1992 LA Riots, 9–12; Capistrán's visual commentary on, 37–42, 46–47, 49; role of subjective experience in, 8–9
art world: artists' critiques of, 66, 67, 69–71; Kaufman's relationship to, 55, 63–64; looting in, 201n64, 203n86; Purifoy's relationship to, 66; racial politics of, 209n19
Arthur, Paul, 161–62
ART/LA92 (art fair), 7, 55, 56, 67–76, 86
Asians: and the 1992 LA Riots, 11, 28–30; African Americans' relations with, 32; anti-immigrant sentiment against, 33–34, 194n80; effects of Black-white binary on, 128. *See also* Koreans
assemblage, 6, 55, 56, 60, 62, 66
Associated Press, 142

Baca, Judith F., *Cultural Explainers: Portals, Bridges and Gateways*, 47
Baer, Jo, 131
Baltz, Lewis, *11777 Foothill Boulevard, Los Angeles, California*, 99–100, *99*, 151–52
Barr, John T., 94
Beall, Jeff, 42–44, 46; *Unsolved* series, 42–43, *43*; *Unsolved Site # 4 (Wilson Alvarez)*, *44*
Beasley, Phoebe, 76, 80, 81
Beat Generation, 66
Benjamin, Walter, 172
Benna, Zyed, 142, 168
Bennett, Jill, 108
bereavement. *See* grief and bereavement
Bigelow, Kathryn, *Strange Days*, 10
binary thinking, challenges to, 3, 5–6
Birk, Sandow, 12; *The Apprehension of Rodney King*, 12; *George Bush Visiting the Riots in L.A.*, 12
Black Arts Movement, 12
Black Flag, "Rise Above," 133
Black Lives Matter, 132–33, 179
Black Star Line (shipping line), 102–3
Black-white binary: Capistrán and, 6, 18, 37, 54; challenges to the simplistic and limiting character of, 3, 6, 11–12, 18, 29–30, 34–35, 37, 54, 91, 126–31, 187n27, 209n32, 215n145; in media coverage, 3, 11, 30, 40, 187n27; Piper and, 7, 90–91, 95, 98, 118, 126–27, 129–31, 209n32; predominance of, in American racial discourse, 7, 10, 30, 34–35, 54, 95, 126–30, 187n27, 215n145
Bowles, John, 95–97
Bradford, Mark: *Rebuild South Central*, 83; *Scorched Earth* series, 12
Bradley, Tom, 1, 22
Bremner, Ann, 92, 109

Brewer, Debby, 66
Briseno, Theodore, 1, 113, 126
Brooks, Roy L., 127–29
Brown, Michael, 133, 178
Brownness, 41–42
Buck-Morss, Susan, 172
Burden, Chris, *L.A.P.D. Uniform*, 12
Bush, George H. W., 93–94, 106–7, 114–16, 125, 134–35
Bush, George W., 142

California Afro-American Museum, 9, 186n18
California Highway Patrol, xiv
California Korean Bank, 21, 22
Calm, Jonathan: *Double Vision*, 179; *Travel Is Fatal to Prejudice*, 179
Camus, Albert, 46, 194n84; *The Rebel*, 36; "Second Letter," 23–24, 26, 115
Cándida Smith, Richard, 66
Capistrán, Juan, 2, 3; art made by, in response to 1992 LA Riots, 17–24, 28–54; education of, 20, 47; experience of the 1992 LA Riots, 26; and Harlins, 6, 17, 19–20, 42, 46, 54, 189n12; and the Latino experience of the 1992 LA Riots, 28–37; and Lopez, 6, 28–32, 54; personal experience of the 1992 LA Riots, 26; personal experience reflected in the art of, 17–20, 40–42, 46; and race, 6, 18–19, 24, 41–42, 46, 48, 53–54, 196n111; racial conflict and injustices experienced by, 24; and South Central sites, 6, 15, 19, 21–22, 26–27, 30, 47–52; uses of conceptualism by, 17–18, 37; uses of minimalism by, 17–18, 43, 45, 46
Capistrán, Juan, works: date paintings, 37, 40–42; *From a Whisper to a Scream* art work, 189n12; *From a Whisper to a Scream* exhibition booklet (with Hazel Mandumano), 31, 32, 33, 36–37; *From a Whisper to a Scream* series, 17, 20, 21, 23, 30–31, 42; *Sunday, March 3, 1991 (Rodney)*, 17, 38; *Psychogeography of Rage (sending up searchlights in the form of flames), Broadway*, 50, 51; *Psychogeography of Rage (sending up searchlights in the form of flames), Vermont Ave. 1992*, 51–52, *52*; *Psychogeography of Rage* series, 50–53; *Rather than running the risk of injustice we preferred disorder . . .*, 21–23, *21*, 26; *Saturday, March 16, 1991, (Latasha)*, 17–18, *18*, 20, 23; *Still I Rise Above*, 133–34, *134*; *We all carry within us our places of exile, our crimes, and our ravages. But our task is not to unleash them on the world; it is to fight them in our selves and in others*, 189n12; *Wednesday, April 29, 1992 (Fidel)*, 28–30, *29*
capitalism, critiques/disruptions of, 5, 62–65, 72, 75, 158, 160
Carillon Imports, 76, 80, 84
Casey, Bernie, 80, 82
Castile, Philando, 178–79
Cave, Nick, 12
Chambers, Eddie, 111
Charles, Roland, *Life in a Day of Black L.A.* (edited photographic collection, 9
Choi, Sai-Choi, 36
Choi, Sung Ho, *Choi's Market*, 12
Choi, Young Joo, 80, 82
citizenship, 8, 24, 34, 35, 116, 139–40, 142–44, 164–68. *See also* civil society
civil rights/civil rights movement, 11, 25, 38, 40, 66, 96, 97, 103, 106, 107, 111, 116, 119, 128–29
civil society, 8, 139, 164, 167–68, 173. *See also* citizenship; Latipa (née Michelle Dizon), works: *Civil Society*
Clinton, Bill, 86
CNN, 1, 146
Cobb, Portia, *No Justice, No Peace: Young, Black, ImMEDIAte*, 146–52, *147*, *149*, *150*, 160
Cokes, Tony, *Black Celebration (A Rebellion Against the Commodity)*, 160–62, *161*
Colo, Papo, 100
Columbus, Christopher, and the Columbus Quincentennial, 7, 90, 91, 97–98, 101, 135
Commodores, "Zoom," 122, 124

Conal, Robbie: *Disarm*, 13; *Taken Out and Shot* (with Patrick Crowley), 12
conceptualism, 160; Capistrán and, 17–18, 37; Piper and, 89, 91, 95–97, 118–19, 135, 208n10; viewers' missing the meaning of, 41
Cook, William Box, 98
Crenshaw Dairy Mart, 179
Crowley, Patrick, and Robbie Conal, *Taken Out and Shot*, 12
Cullors, Patrisse, 132, 179

Davis, Mike, 221n94
Debord, Guy, 53, 62–63, 65, 201n60; "The Decline and Fall of the Spectacle-Commodity," 160
Deitcher, David, 125
Deleuze, Gilles, 155, 171
Denny, Reginald, 10, 27–29, 32, 34, 36, 49, 52, 148–50, 187n27
Depeche Mode, 160
Diagnostic and Statistical Manual of Mental Disorders (DSM-5), 108
disadvantaged communities. *See* marginalized communities
Dislocations (exhibition), 122, 125
disorder, 5, 21, 23, 26, 30, 45–46, 54, 169
Dizon, Michelle. *See* Latipa
documentary filmmaking. *See* video
dorriz, alexandre ali reza, 179
Du, Soon Ja, 15–17, 20–22, 24, 29–30, 188n11
Durham, Jimmie, 100
Dwelling in Rebellion: A Year to the Day (exhibition), 55, 83–85, *84*
Dziga Vertov Group, 155–59

Easter, Makeda, 52
Echo, Alex, *Love Life Live Safe*, 77
Eisenstein, Sergei, 159
Elizabeth Dee Gallery, New York, 118
Ellis, Jimmy, 21
Empire Liquor Market Deli, 15–17, 19–23, 26, 47, 190n24, 190n27

film. *See* video/film
Flores, Elsa, *Stigmata over the City of Los Angeles*, 13
Floyd, George, 179
formalism, 41–42
French Resistance, 23–24
Freud, Sigmund, 65
Frye, Marquette, xiv, 56, 198n3
Frye, Ronald, 198n3
Fusco, Coco, and Guillermo Gómez-Peña, *The Couple in the Cage*, 101–2

Garvey, Marcus, 102–5
Garza, Alicia, 132
Gates, Daryl, 31
Gateward, Frances, 149
Gaye, Marvin, "What's Going On," 106–8, 125, 134
Generali Foundation, 89
Geography of Rage: Remembering the Los Angeles Riots of 1992 (anthology), 53
George, Lynell, 53
Gerrard, Marika, 27–28, 31, 49, 148, 191n40
Godard, Jean-Luc, 155–58; *Weekend*, 171
Gomez, Pat, *Stay Tuned*, 13
Gómez-Peña, Guillermo. *See* Fusco, Coco
Gorbachev, Mikhail, 72
Gorin, Jean-Pierre, 155
grief and bereavement, unrest as an outgrowth and manifestation of, 2, 5, 6, 8, 19, 46, 54, 138–39, 168, 173. *See also* 1992 Los Angeles Riots: legacies of loss and sorrow from; violence: legacies of loss and sorrow from
Grigg, Robert W., 110
Gronk. *See* Nicandro, Glugio Gronk
Guénif-Souilamas, Nacira, 162–64, 169
Guevara, Elmer, *Dried up on a Sunday*, 13
Gutierrez, Frank, 76, 80, 81

Hammons, David, 100–105; *African American Flag*, 103; *Black Star Line*, 102–5, *102*, *104*
Hanhardt, John G., 109–10
Harlem Renaissance, 66
Harlins, Latasha, 6, 15–17, 19–24, 29–31, 42, 44, 46, 54, 133, 189n12

Hart-Celler Immigration and Nationality Act (1965), 10
Hee, Suzanne, and Paul Ong, *Losses in Los Angeles Unrest*, 11
Heid, Patti, 80, 82
Hennessey + Ingalls, 143
Henry, James, 36
Herlihy, Ed, 160
Hersey, Tricia, 5
Hirata, Takao, 36
Holliday, George, 1, 105, 109–11, 152, 185n2
Hollywood Athletic Club, 86
Horne, Gerald, *Fire This Time*, 12
Horrigan, William J., 101
Huerta, Salomón, *Three Horsemen*, 13
human figure, obscuring/abstracting of, 17–18, 40–46
Hurricane Katrina, 8, 139, 141–42

Ici et ailleurs (*Here and Elsewhere*) (film), 155–58, *156*, *157*, *158*, 163
Igus, Toyomi, *Life in a Day of Black L.A.* (edited photographic collection), 9
Ikon Gallery, Birmingham, United Kingdom, 118
immigrants: and anti-immigrant sentiment, 33–35, 77, 194n80; in France, 142, 166; Latipa's experience in a family of, 137, 143, 166–67; ongoing injustices faced by, 46, 133; politics and legislation concerning, 10; white attitudes toward, 128
Immigration and Naturalization Service (INS), 31
injustice: 1992 LA Riots likened to other instances of, 4, 8, 30; failures to recognize, 8, 25–26, 36, 46, 168, 170, 173; marginalized communities' ongoing experiences of, 8, 46, 133–35, 169–70, 178; unknowability/unrepresentability of, 170–71; unrest as the making visible of, 2, 5, 6, 8, 19, 26, 54, 139, 164. *See also* violence
Isozaki, Arata, 69

Jews and Jewish Americans, 61, 72, 200n46
Jones, Donald, 36
Jones, Kellie, 66; *South of Pico*, 12
Judd, Donald, 95, 108
junk art: created by Purifoy and collaborators after the Watts Rebellion, 6, 56, 66-67; etymology of the term, 56; junk hunts at Watts Towers Arts Center as precursor to, 66; as philosophical and social tool, 67; post-riot looting compared to, 65–67; shift in Purifoy's conception of, 64

Kamienowicz, Samy, 61, 200n48
Karlin, Joyce, 16–17
Katano, Marc, 80, 82
Kaufman, Seth, 2, 3, 45–46; and Absolut Vodka, 7, 55, 56, 76–83, 86; and ART/LA92 art fair, 7, 55, 56, 67–76, 86; art made by, in response to 1992 LA Riots, 55, 57–59, 63–64, 67–87; commercial opportunities for the post-riot looting art of, 7, 55, 56, 67–83; Jewish heritage of, 61, 200n46; loss and negation captured in the work of, 7; opportunism of, 7, 56, 63–64, 82; personal experience of the 1992 LA Riots, 57, 85; and post-riot looting, 6–7, 55–64, 67, 84, 86–87, 201n58; relationship of, to the art world, 55, 63–64; and small business owners, 7, 56, 59–61; as a teacher, 202n65
Kaufman, Seth, works: *Absolut Triumph*, 77–79, *79*, 86; *Behind My Window Pain*, 84; *L.A. Rebellion* series, 55, 85; *State of the Art*, 69–70, *70*, 72; *That Was Then, This Is Then*, 69, *71*, 72–73
Kawara, On, 37; *Today* series, 37, 40, 42, 44
KCAL-TV, 1
Kim, Byron, *Synecdoche* series, 41
Kim-Gibson, Dai Sil, *Sa-I-Gu: From Korean Women's Perspective*, 10
King, Martin Luther, Jr., "The Other America," 24–26, 107, 113
King, Rodney: broadcast plea of, 80–81, 113–14, 134, 212n90; civil lawsuit brought by, 114; police beating of, 1,

King, Rodney (*contiued*)
6, 10, 27, 73, 105, 113–15, 134–35, 138, 144, 148, 151–52; post-beating photograph of, 94, 113–15, 125, 134, 144; racist/xenophobic framing of the beating of, 7, 16, 126–27, 145–46; trial and acquittal of officers in the beating of, 1, 7, 15–17, 21, 26–28, 46, 57, 77, 98, 106, 113, 138, 144–46, 150, 161, 177, 218n38. *See also* video of Rodney King's beating
Kitamura, Katie, 118
Koon, Stacey, 1, 113–14
Koppel, Ted, 144
Koreans: African Americans' relations with, 11–12, 17, 22, 29, 126–27; Latinos' relations with, 33; property damage and loss suffered by, 1, 11, 22, 126
Kruger, Barbara, 160
Kuta, Joseph, 159

La Brecque, Eric, 80, 83
LA Weekly (magazine), 53
language, politics of, 164–65, 169
Latasha Harlins Justice Committee, 22
Latina Feminist Group, 9
Latinos: and the 1992 LA Riots, 11, 28–37, 53–54, 126, 187n25, 187n38; African Americans' relations with, 24, 32; anti-immigrant sentiment against, 33–34, 194n80; deportation of, 31; effects of Black-white binary on, 127–29; poverty and unemployment among, 187n25; property damage and loss suffered by, 30, 126; significance of testimonios for, xvi, 9; in South Central LA, 32–33; uses of abstraction by, 122–24. *See also* marginalized communities; race and racism
Latipa (née Michelle Dizon), 2, 3; art made by, in response to 1992 LA Riots, 7–8, 137–45, 151–55, 158–73; as a child of immigrants, 137, 143, 166–67; education of, 143; engagement of viewers by, 140, 141, 152–55, 159, 168; personal experience of the 1992 LA Riots, 137–40, 142, 172; and the power and failures of vision, 8, 140–41, 144–45, 150–55, 159, 161–63, 168, 170, 172
Latipa (née Michelle Dizon), works: *Civil Society*, 7–8, 137–45, *138*, *140*, *145*, 151–55, *153*, *154*, 158–73, *162*, *163*, *166*, *169*, *171*; *My Child Anak*, 143; "Vision in Ruins," 145
law enforcement. *See* police/law enforcement
Lee, Chang-Rae, *Native Speaker*, 10
Lee, Kang Seung, 40, 44–46; *Leave of Absence* series, 44; *Untitled (Korean Merchants on the Rooftop)*, 45; *Untitled (la revolución es la solución)* series, 44
Lee, Spike, 110; *Malcolm X*, 109–11; *Money Don't Matter*, 110
Lee, Warren, 159
LeFalle-Collins, Lizzetta, 9
Leimert Park Village, 48
Leonardo, Shaun, *Rodney King, Before BLM*, 13
Levi, Pavle, 154–55, 222n100
LeWitt, Sol, 95, 108, 118, 208n11
Lie, John, 11, 126–27
Life (magazine), 37, 40
Lipschutz, Yael, 65, 67
liquor stores, prevalence of, in marginalized communities, 78, 83
looting, 62–64, 142, 176–77, 201n64, 203n86. *See also* post-riot looting
Lopez, Fidel, 6, 28–32, 35–36, 49, 54, 192n50
Los Angeles County High School for the Arts, 143
Los Angeles County Museum of Art, 64, 99
Los Angeles Cultural Affairs Department, Arts Recovery Program, 68
Los Angeles News Service, 27, 191n40
Los Angeles Police Department (LAPD), 1, 27, 50, 114
Los Angeles Times (newspaper), 6, 45, 52, 85, 99, 109

Mandela, Nelson, 73
Mandujano, Hazel, *From a Whisper to a Scream* exhibition booklet (with Juan Capistrán), 31, 32, 33, 36–37

marginalized communities: Black-white binary applied to, regardless of color/race, 128; hostility of 1990s political climate toward, 11; issues of democracy and political representation for, 168; ongoing injustices faced by, 8, 46, 133–35, 169–70, 178; in "The Other America," 25; prevalence of liquor stores in, 78, 83; recession's (1980s) effect on, 10; as ruins of "civil society," 8, 139, 170, 173; state violence and oppression directed at, 2. *See also* Asians; Koreans; Latinos; race and racism
Martin, Elsa, 60–61, 64, 84–87, 199n35
Martin, Rod, 59–61, 64, 67, 84–87, 199n35
Martin, Trayvon, 131–33
Martinez, Patrick: *Nine Deuce*, 13; *Vintage Throwback Po-lice*, 13
Matteson, Gary, 68, 74–76
media coverage: of 1992 LA Riots, 1, 3, 9–11, 27–28, 58, 92, 98, 105–6, 177–78; of 2005 French unrest, 142; Black-white binary as framing device in, 3, 11, 30, 40, 187n27; of Hurricane Katrina, 141–42; portrayals of Black men in, 142, 146, 148; racist coverage by, 141–42; video of Reginald Denny's beating used in, 10, 28, 187n27; video of Rodney King's beating used in, 28, 105–6, 109, 144, 146, 148, 185n2; viewer indifference to, 38, 40, 146; of the Watts Rebellion, 154
memorials/monuments, 6, 47–48, 50
Memory and Resistance Laboratory, University of California, Riverside, 179
Middlebrook, Willie, *In His Own Image*, 13
Miéville, Anne-Marie, 155–57
Min, Yong Soon, *Defining Moments*, 13
Minikus, Lee, 56, 198n3
minimalism: Capistrán and, 17–18, 43, 45, 46; Piper and, 7, 89, 91, 92, 95–97, 108–9, 116, 119, 122–26, 131, 135, 171, 208n11, 208n13; relationship of, to contemporaneous artwork, 95–96; repetition as a strategy of, 108–9; and social and political concerns, 96–97; viewers' missing the meaning of, 41
minorities. *See* African Americans; marginalized communities; race and racism
Miranda, Carolina A., 42–43
Mitchell, Lee Arthur, 22
modernism, 46
MoMA. *See* Museum of Modern Art
montage, 140, 154–60, 163, 220n75
Moore, Charles, 37–38, 40
Morris, Robert, 95, 108
Morrison, Ewan, 118–19, 122
Morrison, Toni: *Beloved*, 22–23; "On the Backs of Blacks," 35, 127
multiculturalism, 11, 80, 87, 101, 118
Muñox, José Esteban, *The Sense of Brown*, 41
Museum of Contemporary Art, 69
Museum of Modern Art (MoMA), New York, 89, 122, 125, 134

Nakamura, Joel, 76, 80, 82
National Guard, xv, 96, 106, 178
Nation of Islam (NOI), 47, 196n111
Neufeldt, Max, 66
New Negro Movement, 66
New York Review of Books (magazine), 112
Newton, Bennie, 31–32, 35–36
Newton, Huey P., 145–46, 148
Nicandro, Glugio Gronk (known as Gronk), 80, 82, 83
Nichols, Tyre, 179
Nighswander, Marcy, 93–94
Nightline (television show), 144
No Justice, No Peace: LA 1992 (exhibition), 186n18
No Justice, No Peace? Resolutions . . . (exhibition), 9, 186n18
Noah Purifoy: Junk Dada (exhibition), 64
Norman, Joseph E., Sr., 68, 73–74, 204n108
Nowell, Bradley, 48
Numero Uno Market, 15, 19–23, 26, 47, 190n27

olivas, noé, 179
Ong, Paul, and Suzanne Hee, *Losses in Los Angeles Unrest*, 11
opportunism, 7, 56, 63–64, 75–76
oppression: 1992 LA Riots rooted in a history of, 2, 7, 75; Camus on the dangers to society/humanity of, 24, 36; legacies of, 2, 4; "logic" of, 26, 165, 169; normalization of, 3; unrest in response to, 26; viewers' complicity with, 3, 91, 98, 112, 115, 178; visual culture's processing of, 13. *See also* race and racism; violence
Osterweil, Vicky, 62–63, 201n54
Otis College of Art and Design, 20, 47

Palestinian guerrillas, 155–56
Pan-Africanism, 102–3
Park, Hyesook, 77, 80, 81–82
Park, Tae Sam, 22
People (magazine), 94
Perea, Juan F., 127–28
Pereira, William, 70
Philippines, 143
Picturebook (magazine), 58
Piper, Adrian, 2, 3; art made by, in response to 1992 LA Riots, 7, 89–95, 97–100, 103, 105–9, 111–16, 125–27, 130, 134–35; engagement of viewers by, 7, 91, 95–98, 105–6, 108–9, 111–22, 125–26, 130, 132, 134–35; Hammons's work compared to that of, 100–105; and philosophy, 96, 124; and race, 7, 89–91, 96–98, 100, 117–22, 124–30, 208n18, 209n19, 209n32, 215n154; sexism and racism experienced by, 96; uses of abstraction by, 208n13; uses of conceptualism by, 89, 91, 95–97, 118–19, 135, 208n10; uses of minimalism by, 7, 89, 91, 92, 95–97, 108–9, 116, 119, 122–26, 131, 135, 171, 208n13; and xenophobia, 7, 89, 91, 98, 100
Piper, Adrian, works: *Black Box/White Box*, 7, 89–95, *90*, *92*, *93*, *94*, 97–100, 103, 105–9, 111–16, 125–27, 130, 134–35; *Catalysis*, 123; *Four Intruders Plus Alarm Systems*, 119–22, *120*, 124; *Imagine [Trayvon Martin]*, 131–33, *131*; *Vote/Emote*, 116–19, *117*, 122; *What It's Like, What It Is, #3*, 122, *123*, 124–26
police/law enforcement: author's personal experience of, 175–76; brutality of, xiv–xvi, 1–2, 38, 40, 72, 74, 82, 100, 110–11, 113–15, 133, 152, 198n3 (*see also* violence: state-sponsored)
post-identity, 11
post-minimalism, 97
postmodernism, 46
post-riot looting: critical inquiry stemming from Kaufman's, 6–7, 56, 59–61, 63, 69–70, 73, 78–79, 83, 87; junk art compared to, 64–67; Kaufman's practice of, 6–7, 55–64, 67, 84, 86–87, 201n58
poverty: African Americans in, 25; Latinos in, 187n25; in "The Other America," 25; unrest in response to, 25–26
Powell, Colin, 106
Powell, Judson, 10, 55–56, 65, 66
Powell, Laurence, 1, 113–14
Price, Rena (mother of Marquette Frye), xiv, 56, 198n3
Print (magazine), 60, 80
Pritchett, V. S., 112–13
Purifoy, Noah, 6, 10, 55–56, 64–67, 202n67, 202n73

race and racism: and Black-Korean relations, 11–12, 17, 22, 28–29, 126–27; and Black-Latino relations, 24, 32; Black-white binary in, 3, 6, 7, 10–12, 18, 29–30, 34–35, 37, 54, 90–91, 95, 98, 118, 126–31, 187n27; Capistrán and, 6, 18–19, 24, 41–42, 46, 48, 53–54, 196n111; challenges to simplistic narratives of, 7, 11–12, 18–19, 28, 30–31, 34–36, 90–91, 95, 109, 121, 126–33, 149–51, 178, 192n54, 197n134, 214n135; compounded/rainbow, 12; diverse victims of, 4; experience and solidarity shared across, 6, 11–12, 19, 35–37, 41–42, 54, 128–29; framing of Rodney King beating by, 7, 16, 126–27, 145–46; global instances of, 73; "logic" of, 37, 105, 126, 145–46; in Los

Angeles, 33–35; normalization of/indifference to, 36; persistence of, 2; Piper and, 89–91, 96–98, 100, 117–22, 124–30, 208n18, 209n19, 209n32, 215n154; pseudoscientific conceptions of, 129; stereotypes of, 40, 121–22, 124–25, 128, 142, 145; unrest in response to, 25–26; unrest linked to preconceptions about, 40; viewers' complicity with, 98, 109, 112, 115, 122, 130, 178; xenophobia in relation to, 3. *See also* African Americans; Asians; Koreans; Latinos; marginalized communities; white supremacy; xenophobia
Rampart Division Scandal (1997), 114
repetition, as an artistic strategy, 38, 40, 106, 108–9, 125, 146, 148, 152, 156, 160–63, 221n86
representation, and violence, 40, 45
Resnais, Alain, *Hiroshima mon amour*, 151
rest, concept of, 5
Reynolds, Christopher, 85
Rice, Tamir, 133
Richards, Michael, *A Loss of Faith Brings Vertigo*, 13
Richie, Lionel, 122
Riley, Boots, 148
"riot," use of term, 4–5
Rivera, Geraldo, 133
Rodia, Simon, Watts Towers, 66
Rogers, Sarah J., 98, 100
Roux, Michel, 80
ruins. *See* vision in/of ruins
Rule Without Exception (exhibition), 99
Ruscha, Ed, *The Los Angeles County Museum on Fire*, 70, 72, *72*

Sa-I-Gu: From Korean Women's Perspective (documentary), 10
Sánchez, George J., 11, 27–28, 32–35, 128, 193n74, 193n75, 194n80, 197n134, 215n145
Santa Maria (ship), 97
Santa Monica College, 143
Sarkozy, Nicolas, 142
Saturensky, Ruth, 66–67
Saulter, Leon, 67
Secunda, Arthur, 67
Serra, Richard, *Out-of-Round*, 42–43
Sharpe, Christina, 23
Shaw, Bernard, 146
Simon Rodia Commemorative Watts Renaissance of the Arts Festival, 67
Situationist International, 53, 160
66 Signs of Neon (exhibition), 10, 55–56, 64, 66–67
Skinny Puppy, 160
Smith, Anna Deavere: *Twilight: Los Angeles, 1992*, 10–11, 28
Smith, Cherise, 10–11
Smith, Erna, 11
Smith, Tony, 95
Smiths, The, 160
socioeconomic factors: disparities in American society, 25; junk art compared to post-riot looting art regarding, 67; underlying the 1992 LA Riots, 34, 74–75; underlying the Watts Rebellion, 12, 65, 74; underlying unrest, 6, 25–26, 62–63, 74
Solzhenitsyn, Alexander, *The First Circle*, 112–13
Song, Min Hyoung, 10
South Africa, 73
South Central Los Angeles: anti-immigrant sentiment in, 33–35; Capistrán and, 6, 15, 19, 21–22, 26–27, 30; economic and employment downturn in, 32, 34; effects of 1992 LA Riots on, 1, 4, 6, 15; effects of the "War on Drugs" in, 176; employment opportunities for, 32; recession's (1980s) effect on marginalized communities in, 10
Soviet Union, 72
Space Invaders 13, 48–49; *Sub/Lime*, 48–49, *49*
state-sanctioned violence, 2, 54, 91, 96–99, 106–8, 112, 115–16, 139, 141, 166, 169, 179
Stevenson, Brenda, 54, 188n11
Strange Days (film), 10
sublime, the, xiv, 48–50
Sublime, "April 29, 1992 (Miami)," 48

Tervalon, Jervey, *Geography of Rage: Remembering the Los Angeles Riots of 1992*, 53
testimonios, xvi, 5, 9
time: in Capistrán's work, 19, 42; in Latipa's work, 145, 153, 159, 163; in the Rodney King beating video, 144–45; in Toni Morrison's *Beloved*, 23
Time (magazine), 35
Tisdale, Danny, *Rodney King Police Beating*, 13
Tobar, Hector, 6
Tometi, Opal, 132
Trammps, "Disco Inferno," 21–22
Traoré, Bouna, 142, 168
trauma, 108–9
Tur, Bob, 27–28, 31, 49, 148, 191n40
Twilight (film), 10–11

United Negro Improvement Association (UNIA), 102–5
Universal Pictures Newsreel, 160
University of California, Berkeley, 140, 143
University of California, Irvine, 20
University of California, Los Angeles (UCLA), 140, 144
University of California, Riverside, 179
unrest: concept and characteristics of, 2, 5; the concept of rest and, 5; critical and creative inquiry driven by, 2, 3, 6, 19; disorder and, 5, 26, 45–46, 54, 169; making injustice visible through, 2, 5, 6, 8, 19, 26, 54, 139, 164, 173; motivations for, 4, 46, 113, 164, 168, 178; as an outgrowth and manifestation of grief and bereavement, 2, 5, 6, 8, 19, 46, 54, 138–39, 168, 173; racial preconceptions shaping attitudes about, 40; socioeconomic factors underlying, 6, 25–26, 62–63, 74; terminology concerning, 4, 46; unknowability/unrepresentability of, 45–46, 159, 164, 169; uses and value of, 5–6; violence linked to, 26. *See also* violence

Valdez, Vincent, *The Beginning Is Near, An American Trilogy*, 179
Valen, Mark, *No Justice, No Peace*, 13
Valencia Bonilla, Simon, 201n58
Venice (magazine), 80
victim blaming, 122, 133, 139, 146
video/film: critiques of conventional, 155–58, 161, 222n100; Latipa on the limitations and failures of, 8, 143–45, 150–55, 159, 161–62, 170, 172; role of, foregrounded by the Whitney Biennial's use of Rodney King beating video, 109–10. *See also* video of Rodney King's beating
video of Rodney King's beating: art made in response to, 10, 146–52, 217n33 (*see also* Latipa's use of; Piper's use of); author's personal experience of, 138; cultural role of, 2, 10, 144, 149–50, 221n94; Holliday's recording of, 1, 105, 109–11, 152, 185n2; Latipa's use of, 7–8, 142, 144–45, 149–51, 220n75; media's use of, 28, 105–6, 109, 144, 146, 148, 185n2; Piper's use of, 7, 89, 91, 94, 97, 105–11, 125, 134–35; scholarship on, 2; Spike Lee's use of, 110–11; use of, in the trial, 106, 111, 113, 144–46, 161, 164; viewer engagement elicited by, 91, 106, 109–10, 125, 134–35
Vietnam War, xv, 96, 107. *See also* antiwar movement
viewers: challenged to engage critically with issues of racism, violence, and oppression, 3, 7, 8, 13, 36–37, 40–41, 45, 72–73, 89, 91, 97–98, 108–22, 125–26, 130, 132–35, 141, 149, 154, 168, 178; Latipa's engagement of, 140, 141, 152–55, 159, 168; minimalism's and conceptualism's engagement of, 95–97, 171; Piper's engagement of, 7, 91, 95–98, 105–6, 108–9, 111–22, 125–26, 130, 132, 134–35; understanding of a work's meaning by, 41, 119, 121–22; of violent imagery, 3, 28, 38, 40, 111, 220n75
violence: author's personal experiences of, 137–38; imagery depicting, 3, 28, 38, 40, 111, 146, 148, 220n75; legacies of loss and sorrow from, 2, 5, 7, 8, 23, 36, 151, 173, 178 (*see also* grief

and bereavement); linked to unrest, 26; "logic" of, 37, 54, 126; normalization of/indifference to, 3, 31, 36–37; against people during the 1992 LA Riots, 10, 15, 17, 27–36; state-sanctioned, 2, 54, 91, 96–99, 106–8, 112, 115–16, 139, 141, 166, 169, 179; unrest as response to legacies of, 5; viewers' complicity with, 3, 109, 112, 115, 130, 134–35, 178; viewers' processing of, 3, 7, 13, 40, 146, 148; visual culture's processing of, 3–4, 13, 45. *See also* 1992 Los Angeles Riots; injustice; oppression; police/law enforcement: brutality of; unrest
vision in/of ruins, 8, 139–41, 155–56, 159, 163, 168, 172
voter registration, 115–16
Voting Rights Act (1965), 119
Vuillard, Jean-Édouard, 75

Wagner, Gorden, 67
Wallis, Brian, 111, 115
War, "Night People," 120
Warhol, Andy, 37, 40; *Death and Disaster* series, 38; *Red Race Riot*, 37–38, 39, 40
Washington, Denzel, 111
Watts Rebellion (1965): 1992 LA Riots and other unrest compared to, 8, 53, 74, 140, 159, 162, 165; art made in response to, 55–56, 64–67, 152, 153, 160; author's personal connection to, xiii–xv, 178; Black-white binary as framing device for, 11; Debord's response to, 62–63; land left undeveloped after, 6; legacies of loss and sorrow from, 65; media coverage of, 154; precipitating factors for, xiv, 25, 56, 178; Purifoy's experience of, 56; scholarship on, 12; socioeconomic factors underlying, 12, 65, 74
Watts Towers, 66
Watts Towers Arts Center, 55, 66
Webb Motel, 21
Weems, Carrie Mae, *Commemorating* series, 13
West, Kanye (now known as Ye), 142
West Hollywood, 6–7
Westcott, Gloria, *Adios Hollywood*, 13
Wexner Center for the Arts, Ohio State University, 7, 89, 91–95, 97–102, 105–6, 115–16, 118, 126, 130
white backlash, 25
white supremacy: Garvey's critique of, 104–5; legacies of, 2, 4; "logic" of, 54, 169; in Los Angeles, 24, 35; marginalized communities as the ruins of, 8, 170; oppressive goals and practices of, 24, 35, 122, 129, 131, 139, 146; unrest in response to, 25–26, 54; us-versus-them binary at the root of, 42; victim blaming practiced by, 122, 139; viewers challenged to confront, 135. *See also* race and racism; xenophobia
Whitney Biennial, 109–10
Widener, Daniel, 65–66; *Black Arts West*, 12
Widner, Kirsten, 127–29
Will, Gabriel, 159
Williams, Damian "Football," 52
Will/Power (exhibition), 91–92, 97, 100–105, 109, 115
Wind, Timothy, 1, 113

X, Malcolm, 111
xenophobia: 1992 Los Angeles Riots rooted in history of, 2, 7; artistic strategies for challenging, 125; framing of Rodney King beating by, 7, 145–46; "logic" of, 54, 145–46, 169; in Los Angeles, 35; Piper and, 7, 89, 91, 98, 100; racism in relation to, 3; unrest in response to, 54; us-versus-them binary at the root of, 42; viewers' complicity with, 130. *See also* race and racism; white supremacy

Ybarra, Mario, Jr., 48–49

Zero One Art Gallery, 55, 84
Zimmerman, George, 131–33
Zona Maco, art fair in Mexico City, 30–31
Zoot Suit Riots (1943), 178
Zuckerman, Margaret, 31